French literary theory today

This book is published as part of the joint publishing agreement established in 1977 between the Fondation de la Maison des Sciences de l'Homme and the Press Syndicate of the University of Cambridge. Titles published under this arrangement may appear in any European language or, in the case of volumes of collected essays, in several languages.

New books will appear either as individual titles or in one of the series which the Maison des Sciences de l'Homme and the Cambridge University Press have jointly agreed to publish. All books published jointly by the Maison des Sciences de l'Homme and the Cambridge University Press will be distributed by the Press throughout the world.

Cet ouvrage est publié dans le cadre de l'accord de co-édition passé en 1977 entre la Fondation de la Maison des Sciences de l'Homme et le Press Syndicate of the University of Cambridge. Toutes les langues européennes sont admises pour les titres couverts par cet accord, et les ouvrages collectifs peuvent paraître en plusieurs langues.

Les ouvrages paraissent soit isolément, soit dans l'une des séries que la Maison des Sciences de l'Homme et Cambridge University Press ont convenu de publier ensemble. La distribution dans le monde entier des titres ainsi publiés conjointement par les deux établissements est assurée par Cambridge University Press.

French literary theory today

A reader

edited by
TZVETAN TODOROV
Maître de Recherche, Centre National de la Recherche Scientifique, Paris

translated by R. Carter

CAMBRIDGE UNIVERSITY PRESS

Cambridge
London *New York* *New Rochelle* *Melbourne* *Sydney*

EDITIONS DE LA MAISON DES SCIENCES DE
L'HOMME

Paris

Published by the Press Syndicate of the University of Cambridge
The Pitt Building, Trumpington Street, Cambridge CB2 1RP
32 East 57th Street, New York, NY 10022, USA
296 Beaconsfield Parade, Middle Park, Melbourne 3206, Australia
and Editions de la Maison des Sciences de l'Homme
54 Boulevard Raspail, 75270 Paris Cedex 06

First published 1982

Printed in Great Britain at the Pitman Press, Bath

Library of Congress catalogue card number: 81–21656

British Library Cataloguing in Publication Data

Todorov, Tzvetan
  French literary theory today
  1. Literature—Philosophy 2. Criticism
  —France
  I. Title II. Carter, R.
  801   PN45
  ISBN 0 521 23036 5
  ISBN 0 521 29777 X Pbk

Contents

Contents

Sources and acknowledgements

The following are the sources of the essays in this collection. The Editor and Publishers wish to thank the authors and the publishers mentioned for their permission to publish these essays.

The Introduction, 'French poetics today', has not previously been published.

1 'Critique et poétique', in *Figures III* (Seuil, Paris, 1972), pp. 9–11.

2 'L'effet du réel', in *Communications*, 11 (Seuil, Paris, 1968), pp. 84–9.

3 'Modèles de la phrase littéraire', in *Problèmes de l'analyse textuelle* (Didier, Paris, 1971), pp. 133–48.

4 'Stratégie de la forme', in *Poétique*, 27 (Seuil, Paris, 1976), pp. 257–81.

5 'Théorie de la figure', in *Communications*, 16 (Seuil, Paris, 1970), pp. 3–25.

6 'Parallélisme et déviations en poésie', in *Langue, discours, société: Pour Emile Benveniste*, ed. J. Kristeva, J-Cl. Milner and N. Ruwet (Seuil, Paris, 1975), pp. 307–51.

7 'La notion de motif' has not previously been published.

8 'Qu'est-ce qu'une description?', in *Poétique*, 12 (Seuil, Paris, 1972), pp. 465–85.

9 'De la circularité du chant', in *Poétique*, 2 (Seuil, Paris, 1970), pp. 129–40.

10 'Le pacte autobiographique', in *Le pacte autobiographique* (Seuil, Paris, 1975), pp. 13–46.

11 'Une complication du texte: les *Illuminations*', in *Les genres du discours* (Seuil, Paris, 1978).

Introduction

French poetics today

TZVETAN TODOROV

I

Let me start with some remarks concerning each of the words in the title of this introduction.

Today is evidently a synecdoche for 'recent': the texts which follow, and which are the subject of this introduction, were ·written over the last ten years, between 1968 and 1978. This period was not chosen at random: before 1968 there were only sporadic publications in the area of poetics; today, however, it is reasonable to say, the time has arrived for a preliminary assessment.

French refers to the language of publication, not to the nationality of the authors. I realized after the fact that, of the eleven texts assembled here, only six are by authors who are French both by nationality and by birth. This proportion gives, I would think, a rather accurate idea of the 'French' participation in the world of publication in French.

Poetics, last of all, is a term I will deal with in more detail below. All that need be said at present is that it will be used as a synonym of 'theory of literature', and thus two other meanings it has, related to the first, will not be relevant here; these are: 'theory of poetry', as opposed to the theory of prose, and 'system of devices characteristic of the work of a writer', as when we speak of 'the poetics of Hugo', for example.

To indicate now the domain formed by the intersection of the three words in our title, I will comment briefly on the texts below, following the order and the groupings which I have imposed on them. I hasten to add that the assigning of each text to one of the headings involves a certain amount of arbitrariness, and that in fact each study raises problems which fall under one or more of the other headings.

II

1 Scope

The first question to be raised, and the most basic, since its answer is what

T. Todorov

permits the constitution of a domain of study, concerns the definition of poetics. It is treated here in just one text which, although short, synthesizes the results of more extensive evolving discussion.

Poetics, as it is understood here, is constituted by three kinds of choice, and develops from three types of opposition.

First of all, and this is the most important aspect, poetics is opposed to interpretation, or, to use the term common in literary studies, to criticism; this is simply a concrete case of the dichotomy between the general and the particular. The object of interpretation is each of the individual works which together make up literature; the object of poetics is the general laws which govern the functioning of literature, its forms and varieties (it thus presupposes the existence of such laws). I am convinced that it is impossible to speak of literature without having as point of departure a poetics, a general theory of literary discourse; the difference between the authors, or periods, which proclaim a poetics and those which renounce one (and there are many of the latter) lies not in whether a poetics is present or absent, but rather in whether there is acceptance of it, or failure to take it into account. The 'classics' invoked a poetics, the 'romantics' were ignorant of any; but there is a romantic poetics just as there is a classic one. The opposition between poetics and criticism, as well as the other oppositions to be mentioned below, is not of the value-assigning, exclusive variety (the *others* do that, but *we* do this); it involves a necessary complementarity. In practice, a piece of writing often mixes the two kinds of attitude, but the distinction is necessary and easy to establish in theory.

Second, poetics has its own way of carving out its object of study: that object is the literary text, or discourse, rather than the process by which it is produced or received. Speaking of the totality of disciplines which have the arts as object, René Passeron recently proposed the following classification: poietics, or the study of production; the sciences of art, hence of works of art, including poetics, musicology, etc.; and aesthetics in the etymological sense – the study of the reception or perception of works of art. Poetics, then, is primarily concerned with the verbal structures which are to be found in works of literature, and in this way it is related to linguistics, whose subject matter is also the verbal, but from a quite different point of view. However, this opposition is less sharp than the preceding one; it might be said that the preceding one is qualitative, while this one is merely quantitative. In fact, it is not evident that a theory of literary works is possible which does not take into account, or which does not deal, whether intentionally or not, with problems of production and reception; and it will be seen below that the question of the formal sources of the work, or of the reader's contract, is important. The opposition, in other words, concerns two poles of attraction, two predominant orientations, rather than a rigid exclusion.

2

Third and last, the object of poetics is furnished by literary discourse, as opposed to other types of discourse. To my mind this is the least important distinction, so minor that, for most of the authors represented below, including myself, it is irrelevant – or rather it is relevant not to poetics, to the theory of discourse, but to the history of culture. Others, however, keep the distinction, and in this compilation will be found two kinds of answer to the question of how specific literary discourse is. The first, a classical one in that it is based on the idea of a norm, is defended here by Jean Cohen: it says that poetry represents a systematic deviation from the rules of language. The second is romantic, in that it defines poetry as over-structured discourse; it is represented here in its restricted (Jakobsonian) form by Nicolas Ruwet, who envisages supplementary constraints that are syntactic in nature, and intratextual (in short, repetitions). In its generalized form it is represented by Michael Riffaterre, who calls it 'overdetermination', and who includes paradigmatic and intertextual relations (for example, clichés). As for myself, I prefer to think that I am concerned with overdetermined, or deviant, discourse, without attempting to make this part of a definition of literature. Poetics is for me a theory of discourse, and the fact – whatever its importance – that poetics deals with works of literature is, from this point of view, not distinctive.

The discourse of poetics has existed at least since Aristotle; however, it is not an accident that our own epoch is a period of expansion. In turn, this fact has an explanation in terms of historical analysis. The classical world, dominated by the notion of a unique norm, does not provide sufficient room for a comfortable development of the theory of *discourses*, nor does the romantic outlook, which exalts the individual, the particular, as its supreme value, and refuses to admit the existence of transcendental forms (to oversimplify enormously). Poetics implies a recognition of differences free of any value judgements; at the same time it requires awareness of the unanalysability and irreducibility of the particular. Is it not precisely these two features which characterize our present-day mental universe, which refuses both naive universalism and extreme individualism, in the hope of attaining a way of thinking that is *typological*?

On the other hand, I do not find that there is much to say about the relation between poetics and structuralism; none of the texts gathered here mentions this. Particularly in France, it was under the influence of structuralism that literary studies became open to theory; however, poetics is not a method – structuralist or other – but rather a way of looking at the facts. So, since that creates the facts, it is both an object and a discipline. The concepts and hypotheses to be found in the texts presented here are not themselves what constitutes poetics, and they are destined for obsolescence; this is not true of the *orientation* they represent, which is that of the practitioner of poetics.

3

2 The process of literary creation

We now turn from the discipline – poetics – to its object – literature. Not that the texts grouped under this heading explicitly ask the question 'what is literature?', but that they raise the problem of what are the essential determining factors of the literary text. The answers which they offer, reduced to their common denominator, may be expressed in the form of a sentence with two clauses: a text is not determined by those things which it evokes, it is governed by relations which are invariably textual already. Of the three authors represented here, Roland Barthes comments on the first proposition: the fact that a thing exists does not of itself explain why it will be noted down; the 'unnecessary detail', dear to Orwell's heart, far from directly denoting the real, *symbolizes* the realist's *parti pris*. Laurent Jenny spells out the second, proposing one, or even several, typologies of intertextual relations. Michael Riffaterre, one might say, puts the comma between the two clauses, that is, articulates them.

Such a position implies two refusals. On the one hand, there is a refusal of the immanent study of the text (but this, as we have seen, is a consequence of the definition of poetics); on the other hand, there is a refusal of exogenesis, of the study of extratextual relations, and, in particular, of the representation of reality. This latter choice is unambiguously romantic (we know independently of the romantic origins of all twentieth-century formalist criticism, which is the immediate predecessor of poetics): the opposition between the classical and the romantic aesthetic might be characterized summarily as this eviction of *mimesis*, and its replacement by *poiesis*, as the most elevated of the notions describing artistic activity.

Here again, we are faced with a feature that is at once characteristic and contingent. Such a hypothesis concerning the functioning of literary discourse is not implicit in the principles of poetics, and it is easy to conceive of the appearance of a different one. At the same time, its existence is not the result of chance, but is due to the cultural and historical context in which poetics developed in France.

3 Analytical categories

Here we move into the kitchen of poetics (assuming that discussions about the grand principles take place in the drawing-room), since we must deal with the particular notions and hypotheses elaborated in poetics in order to account for the working of literature. The selection presented here, as in the following section, is more arbitrary than it was for the first two: this is because we are now in direct contact with the concrete matter of literature,

4

and all that is possible is to sample from among the many problems that have been discussed.

I have above all tried to illustrate the variety of these problems. Two of the studies below concern units smaller than the sentence which are particularly relevant to the understanding of poetry: rhetorical figures in the article by Jean Cohen, and grammatical and phonetic parallelisms in the study by Nicolas Ruwet. The connection with the descriptions proposed in linguistics is obvious, and inevitable. The other two selections deal with units that are transsentential, and which are of more relevance to fiction: the motif, studied by Claude Bremond, and the description, treated by Philippe Hamon. These two pieces have other particularities: that by Bremond is essentially critical in nature (it demonstrates clearly, I believe, that current studies in poetics are not, as is sometimes alleged, mere paraphrases, in pseudo-technical language, of long-familiar observations and hypotheses); that by Hamon is noteworthy in that it is a 'physiology' rather than an 'anatomy' of the literary text – in spite of its title, it asks less what a description is than how a description functions.

Lack of space has forced me to exclude other examples of such descriptive work: for example, the studies of metrics from a group inspired by Jacques Roubaud; other studies of rhetoric, notably those of the 'Mu' group at the university of Liège; of poetic onomastics, by François Rigolot; of reflexive narrative, by Lucien Dällenbach; of narrative techniques in general, with an especially large number of studies, of which Gérard Genette has given a synthesis in his 'Discours du récit' (*Figures III*); my own work on the symbol; etc.

The concepts and hypotheses which have been developed in this domain are no doubt fated to be replaced by others, as a result of the process of discussion already begun, but is this regrettable? The reader will notice, in fact, that even among the studies in this book there remain disagreements on certain points. Thus Cohen tends to interpret parallelisms as attenuated deviations, while Ruwet treats deviations as a preliminary stage of parallelisms: a difference which is clearly due to different choices within the ideological frameworks of the authors, 'classical' in the first case, 'romantic' in the second. Curiously, however, this impulse to illustrate an *a priori* thesis deprives neither study of its descriptive interest.

4 Genres and models

What we have said about poetics so far has not distinguished it in any way, as far as its structure is concerned, from the general theory of discourses of any type, and there was no reason to make such a distinction. Nevertheless, from an alternative point of view, a difference does appear, and an important

5

one. If I develop a theory of everyday discourse, for example, what I have available is not a corpus, but a capacity to produce and recognize the utterances which belong to this type of discourse. That is not the case with literature: literary works exist, and those existing works are what we want to understand, even if understanding them requires imagining works which are merely 'possible' or 'virtual'. For this reason, poetics is never free of its relationship, stronger here than in any other area, to description and to history. This interaction with the history of literature and interpretation is mediated especially through the notion of the *genre*. If we wanted to continue to spin out the domestic metaphor, we could say that, after the drawing-room and the kitchen, we now come to the bedroom, where the really important things happen, and we are face to face with Literature herself.

A genre is a class of texts which has a historically attested existence. It is an ambiguous entity, on the level of analysis: on the one hand it is empirical, since it can be situated in space and time, its exemplifications can be listed, testimony as to its relevance for producers (writers) and receivers (readers) of texts can be collected; on the other hand it is theoretical, because it should be possible, ideally (that is, if the descriptive apparatus of poetics were rich enough), to deduce the genres from the combinatory possibilities of the characteristic features of literary discourse. The current notion of genre is, thus, rather different from preceding ones: with the classics, it was a norm invoked to condemn deviations; for the romantics, each work had its own genre, and the notion was thus deprived of all interest. A modern theory of genres refuses both a rigid hierarchy based on *a priori* value judgements and a blind empiricism which fails to recognize, behind the particular historical instances, the transcendent categories of literary discourse.

Discussion and debate concerning the genres has been abundant in France in recent years, and will continue. I have chosen as an illustration the study of autobiography by Philippe Lejeune, which is an example, rather than a theoretical discussion; but it is, so to speak, an exemplary example. It will be seen how he establishes a balance between historical and theoretical requirements, and also how the theory of the text in itself spills over into pragmatic considerations.

The other two texts presented here have a more limited goal. They adopt an inductive approach, focussing on the stylistic or thematic procedures of two limited sets of texts: the *chanson* of the *trouvères*, in the case of Paul Zumthor, and the poems making up the *Illuminations*, in my own case. These articles also illustrate the constant, and indispensable, back-and-forth movement between down-to-earth empirical work and speculation. For although both are essentially descriptive, the first points towards a conception of literature itself, and the second towards a theory of interpretation. This is the reason why I have left them in the position of a conclusion.

III

I must now make a few more technical remarks on how this collection is made up.

Since it was by definition impossible to be exhaustive, my primary concern was to bring out the variety of work being done, and it is not an accident that each author is represented by a single text. But this variety was limited, in the first place, quantitatively, because of space limitations (it has not been possible to include, for example, any of the studies, now numerous, bearing on the history of poetics); it was also limited qualitatively, because of the desirability of having a more coherent whole. I have left aside studies that have been quite influential, in France and abroad, both for the evolution of poetics, and more generally, because they were done with an outlook and with goals other than those of poetics.

The authors of the pieces to follow belong to three micro-generations, if we consider the date at which their research in poetics began rather than their date of birth: those who preceded, and laid the ground for the current renaissance in poetics (Barthes, Zumthor, Riffaterre), those who developed with it (Genette, Cohen, Ruwet, Bremond, and myself), and those who followed (Lejeune, Hamon, Jenny).

All the texts were first published autonomously: they are not extracts of larger works; nor have any been previously translated into English. Within each section, they are arranged in systematic rather than chronological order.

At the end of the book will be found a short biography of each author and a note of his other publications. For more extensive bibliographies, the reader might consult the *Dictionnaire encyclopédique des sciences du langage* by O. Ducrot and T. Todorov (Paris, Seuil, 1972), and a more recent source, the review *Poétique*, 30 (April 1977), which contains three annotated bibliographies: 'Le texte poétique', 211–25; 'Analyse du récit', 226–59; 'Cinéma et narration', 260–2. Two surveys recently published in English may also be useful: R. Scholes, *Structuralism in Literature* (New Haven, Yale University Press, 1974); and J. Culler, *Structuralist Poetics* (London, Routledge and Kegan Paul, 1975). A presentation of the field itself, rather than of the work done in poetics, and which was written before recent developments, is my *Poétique* (Paris, Seuil, 1968, second revised edition published separately in 1973).

Part I

1. Criticism and poetics

GÉRARD GENETTE

A few years ago literary consciousness in France seemed deep in a process of involution somewhat disquieting to observe – with skirmishes between the proponents of literary history and those favouring the 'nouvelle critique'; obscure debates, even within the new criticism itself, between the 'old new', existential and thematic, and the 'new new', whose inspiration was formalist or structuralist; and an unhealthy proliferation of studies and surveys on the tendencies and methods, thoroughfares and blind alleys of criticism. From scission to scission, and from reduction to reduction, literary studies seemed to turn their observational tools evermore inward, to be immured in a self-examination that was narcissistic, sterile and ultimately destructive – doomed to realize the prophecy uttered in 1928 by Valéry: 'Where is criticism headed? To its ruin, I hope.'

This unfortunate situation may, however, be more apparent than real. For, as Proust's thought in *Contre Sainte-Beuve* demonstrates, any reflection on criticism that is at all serious necessarily sets going a reflection on literature itself. Criticism may be purely rule-of-thumb, naive, intuitive, and undisciplined, but *metacriticism* always implies some broader idea of what literature is, and this implicit conception cannot go for long without explicit formulation. In this way, perhaps, out of a kind of evil there may arise a kind of good: from a few years of speculation or ratiocination about criticism may come what we have so evidently lacked for more than a century – so that the consciousness of this lack seems itself to have abandoned us. An apparent dead end of criticism may in fact lead to the rebirth of *literary theory*.

It is indeed appropriate to speak of rebirth. Under the names of *poetics* and *rhetoric*, the theory of 'genres' and, more generally, the theory of discourse, go back, as we all know, to remote antiquity. From Aristotle to La Harpe, they occupied a place in the literary thinking of the Occident, down to the appearance of romanticism. But romanticism, by shifting attention from forms and genres to the 'individual creator', displaced general reflection of this kind in favour of a *psychology of the work of art*, and from Sainte-Beuve onward, through all his avatars, what today we call criticism has always been faithful to this. Whether this psychology is reinforced (or deformed) by historical perspective, by psychoanalysis – Freudian, Jungian, Bachelardian,

8

or other – or by sociology, Marxist or not; whether it is oriented more towards the author or towards the reader (the critic himself); or whether it attempts rather to confine itself within the problematic 'immanence' of the work, the essential function of criticism is never fundamentally modified. It is always seen to be the maintenance of a dialogue between a text and a *psyche*, conscious and/or unconscious, individual and/or collective, creative and/or receptive.

The structuralist project itself may have done no more than add a nuance to this picture, at least insofar as it consists in the decision to study 'the structure' (or 'the structures') of a work, considered in a somewhat fetishistic manner as a self-contained, finished, *absolute* 'object'. This inevitably 'motivates' the closedness (by 'accounting for' it with the procedures of structural analysis) and thereby 'motivates' also the decision (which was perhaps arbitrary) or the circumstance (which was perhaps fortuitous) which established it. This is to forget Valéry's warning that the idea of a literary work as something finished comes under the heading of 'fatigue or superstition'. In his debate with literary history, the modern critic has for half a century been concerned to separate the notions of *work* and *author*, with the quite comprehensible tactical aim of opposing the former to the latter, who was responsible for so many excesses and sometimes pointless activities. We are beginning to perceive today that these notions are linked, and that any form of critical activity is necessarily caught in the orbit of their reciprocal attraction.

It is also becoming apparent that its status as a work does not exhaust the reality, or even the 'literariness', of the literary text, and that, moreover, the existence of a work (its immanence) presupposes the existence of a large number of phenomena transcendent to it, which are the concern of linguistics, stylistics, semiology, discourse analysis, narrative logic, the thematics of genres and periods, etc. Criticism is in the uncomfortable situation of being able, *as criticism*, neither to do without such phenomena nor to master them. It is thus required to admit the necessity, in order fully to accomplish its task, of a discipline dealing with these kinds of studies which are not connected with the idiosyncratic properties of particular works, and which can only be a general theory of literary forms – call it a *poetics*.

It is, perhaps, a secondary question whether or not such a discipline should seek to become a 'science' of literature, with the unpleasant connotations that premature use of such a word in such a context may have; but it is at least certain that it alone *could* claim to be such, since, as everyone knows (but as our positivist tradition, worshipping 'facts' and indifferent to laws, seems to have forgotten long ago), no 'science' is possible except a 'general' one. But what is in question here is less the study of forms and genres as this was understood by the rhetoric and poetics of the classical period, which

9

were always inclined, from Aristotle onward, to set up tradition as a norm and to canonize what exists, than the exploration of the various *possibilities of discourse*, with respect to which works already written and forms already exemplified appear merely as so many particular cases beyond which loom other predictable, or deducible, combinations. This is one of the interpretations which can be given to the celebrated formulas of Roman Jakobson who proposes as the object of literary studies not literature but literarity, not poetry but the poetic function: more generally, the object of theory is to be not just the *real*, but the *virtual* – all that is potentially literary. This opposition between an *open* poetics and the closed poetics of the classical tradition indicates clearly that what is at issue here is not, as might perhaps be thought, a return to the precritical past: literary theory, on the contrary, will be modern, and bound up with the modernity of literature, or will be nothing at all.

When introducing his programme for the teaching of poetics, Valéry declared with a salutary, and, all in all, justified insolence, that the object of this teaching, 'far from being substituted for or opposed to the teaching of literary history, should be to give to the latter simultaneously an introduction, a sense, and a purpose'. The relations between poetics and criticism could be of the same nature, with the difference – capital – that Valéry's poetics expected next to nothing in return from literary history, termed a 'vast fake', while literary theory has much to learn from the specific studies of criticism. While literary history is in no sense a fake, nevertheless it is clearly, like the philological techniques of deciphering and establishing a text (and in reality much more so), an *ancillary* discipline for the study of literature, for it only explores (through biography, the study of sources and influences, of the genesis and the 'career' of literary works, etc.) the secondary aspects. Criticism, on the other hand, is and will remain a fundamental approach, and it can be predicted that the future of literary studies resides essentially in the exchange and the necessary cross-fertilization between criticism and poetics – based on an awareness and exploitation of their *complementarity*.

Part II

2. The reality effect

ROLAND BARTHES

When Flaubert, describing the room occupied by Madame Aubain, Félicité's mistress, tells us that 'on an old piano, under a barometer, there was a pyramid of boxes and cartons',[1] or when Michelet, describing the death of Charlotte Corday and reporting that in prison, before the arrival of the executioner, she was visited by an artist who painted her portrait, gives us the detail that 'after an hour and a half, someone knocked softly at a little door behind her',[2] these authors, like so many others, produce *notations* (data, descriptive details) which structural analysis, occupied as it is with separating out and systematizing the main articulations of narrative, ordinarily, and up to the present, has left out, either by excluding from its inventory (by simply failing to mention them) all those details which are 'superfluous' (as far as structure is concerned), or else by treating these same details (as the present author has himself attempted to do)[3] as fillers, padding (catalyses), assigned indirect functional value in that, cumulatively, they constitute an indication of characterization or atmosphere, and so can finally be salvaged as part of the structure.

It would seem, however, that if we want the analysis to be truly exhaustive (and what would any method be worth which did not account for the whole of its object, in the present case, the entire surface of the narrative fabric), to try to encompass the ultimate detail, the indivisible unit, the fleeting transition, in order to assign these a place in the structure, we will inevitably be confronted with *notations* which no function (not even the most indirect) will allow us to justify: these details are scandalous (from the point of view of structure), or, even more disturbingly, they seem to be allied with a kind of narrative *luxury*, profligate to the extent of throwing up 'useless' details and increasing the cost of narrative information. So, although it may be possible just to regard the detail of the piano as a sign of the bourgeois status of its owner, and that of the boxes as a sign of disorder and something like a reverse or fall in status, appropriately evocative of the Aubain household, there seems to be no such end in view to justify the reference to the barometer, an object which is neither incongruous nor significant, and which, therefore, at first sight, seems not to belong to the domain of the *notable*. In Michelet's sentence, also, it is difficult to account structurally for all the details: the only thing that is indispensable to the account is the statement that the executioner came after the painter. How long the sitting lasted, and the size and location of the door, are useless (but the theme of the door, and death's soft knocking, have indisputable symbolic value). Even if they are not plentiful, 'useless details' thus seem inevitable: any narrative, at least any Western narrative of the ordinary sort, has some.

Insignificant *notation* (taking 'insignificant' in the strong sense – apparently detached from the semiotic structure of the narrative)[4] – is related to description, even if the object seems to be denoted by a single word (in reality, the pure word does not exist: Flaubert's barometer is not cited as an isolated unit, it is situated, placed in a syntagm that is both referential and syntactic). This underlines the enigmatic character of any description, of which something must be said. The general structure of the narrative, at least as this has been analysed at one time or another up to the present, appears essentially *predictive*; to be extremely schematic, ignoring the numerous digressions, delays, changes of direction, or surprises which the narrative conventions add to this schema, it can be said that, at each juncture of the narrative syntagm, someone says to the hero (or to the reader, it does not matter which): if you act in this way, if you choose this alternative, then this is what will happen (the *reported* nature of these predictions does not alter their practical effect). Description is quite different: it has no predictive aspect; it is 'analogical', its structure being purely additive, and not incorporating that circuit of choices and alternatives which makes a narration look like a vast traffic control centre, provided with referential (and not merely discursive) temporality. This is an opposition which has its importance for anthropology: when, influenced by the work of von Frisch, some imagined that bees might have a language, it had to be recognized that, while these animals might have a predictive system of dances, used in food-gathering, they possess nothing resembling a *description*.[5] Description thus appears to be a characteristic of so-called higher languages, in that, seemingly paradoxically, it is not justified by any purpose of action or communication. The singularity of the description (or of the 'useless detail') in the narrative fabric, its isolatedness, brings up a question of primary importance for the structural analysis of narrative. This question is the following: is everything in the narrative meaningful, significant? And if not, if there exist insignificant stretches, what is, so to speak, the ultimate significance of this insignificance?

It should first be recalled that Western culture, in one of its major currents, has certainly not left description without a meaning, but has in fact assigned to it an end perfectly well recognized by the institution of literature. This current is rhetoric, and the end is 'beauty': description has long had an aesthetic function. Very early in antiquity, to the two explicitly functional genres of oratory – legal and political discourse – was added a third, epideictic discourse, the set speech whose goal was to excite the admiration of the audience (and not to persuade it); and this genre, whatever the rituals governing its use – whether praise of a hero or an obituary – contained the seeds of the notion of an aesthetic purpose in language. In Alexandrian neo-rhetoric of the second century A.D. there was an infatuation for the *ekphrasis*, a polished piece, and detachable (thus having its own purpose, independent of any general function), whose object was to describe places, times, people or works of art; and this tradition was maintained down through the Middle Ages. As Curtius[6] has emphasized, throughout this period description was not constrained by any desire for realism; truth, or even verisimilitude, was of little moment – nobody was bothered when lions or olive trees were placed in a northern landscape. The only constraints that mattered were descriptive ones; plausibility was not referential, but overtly discursive; it was the rules of the discourse genre which laid down the law.

Moving ahead to Flaubert, we see that the aesthetic intention of description is still very strong. In *Madame Bovary*, the description of Rouen (a real referent if there ever was one) is subjected to the tyrannical constraints of what must be called aesthetic plausibility, as is attested by the corrections made in this passage in the course of six successive versions.[7] We note first of all that the corrections are in no way due to closer attention to the model: Rouen, as perceived by Flaubert, stays the same, or more exactly, if it changes a little from one version to the next, this is only because it was necessary to tighten up an image or avoid a phonetic redundancy condemned by the rules of *le beau style*, or else to create the appropriate environment for some happy but quite contingent expressive find.[8] Next we see that the descriptive fabric, which at first glance seems to assign great importance (by its length and attention to detail) to the object *Rouen*, is really no more than a kind of background or setting meant to receive the jewels of a few precious metaphors, the neutral matter enveloping the precious symbolic ingredients, as if, in Rouen, all that was important was the rhetorical figures available for describing what one sees, as if Rouen was only notable via its substitutions ('the masts like a forest of needles, the islands like great immobile black fish, the clouds like aerial waves silently breaking against a cliff'). Lastly, one sees that the entire description *is constructed* so as to associate Rouen with a painting: it is a painted scene taken on by language ('Thus, seen from above, the entire landscape looked as motionless as a painting'). The writer fulfils here the definition given by Plato of the artist: a maker in the third degree, since he imitates what is already the simulation of an essence.[9] So although the description of Rouen is perfectly 'irrelevant' to the narrative structure of *Madame Bovary* (it can be attached to no functional sequence, nor to any signified (*signifié*) of characterization, atmosphere, or information), it is in no way shocking, being justified, if not by the logic of the work, at least by the laws of literature; it has a meaning, but that meaning is given by its conformity, not to the object of description, but to the cultural rules governing representation.

Nevertheless, the aesthetic intention of Flaubertian description is totally interwoven with the imperatives of 'realism', as if exactitude of reference, superior or indifferent to all other functions, of itself commanded and justified description of the referent, or, in the case of a description reduced to a single word, its denotation. Here aesthetic constraints are impregnated – at least as an alibi – with referential constraints: it is probable that, if one had arrived at Rouen by stagecoach, the view one would have had descending the hill road which leads to the city would not have been 'objectively' different from the panorama described by Flaubert. This mixing, this interweaving of constraints, has two advantages: on the one hand the aesthetic function, by conferring a meaning on the set piece, is a safeguard against a downward spiral into endless detail. For, when discourse is no longer guided and limited by the structural imperatives of the story (functions and signals), there is nothing to tell the writer why he should stop descriptive details at one point rather than another: if it was not subject to aesthetic or rhetorical choice, any 'seeing' would be inexhaustible by discourse; there would always be some corner, some detail, some nuance of location or colour to add. On the other hand, by stating the referent to be real, and by pretending to follow it slavishly, realistic description avoids being seduced into fantasizing (a precaution which was believed necessary for the 'objectivity' of the account). Classical rhetoric had in a sense institutionalized the fantasy under the name of a particular figure, hypotyposis, whose function was to 'place things before the hearer's eyes', not in a neutral manner, merely reporting, but by giving to the scene all the radiance of desire (this was a division of vividly illumined discourse, with prismatic outlines: the *illustris oratio*). Having proclaimed its renunciation of the constraints of the rhetorical code, realism had to find a new reason to describe.

What the irreducible residues of functional analysis have in common is that they denote what is commonly called 'concrete reality' (casual movements, transitory attitudes, insignificant objects, redundant words). Unvarnished 'representation' of 'reality', a naked account of 'what is' (or was), thus looks like a resistance to meaning, a resistance which confirms the great mythical opposition between the true-to-life (the living) and the intelligible. It suffices to recall that for the ideology of our time, obsessive reference to the 'concrete' (in what is grandiloquently asked of the sciences of man, of literature, of behaviour) is always brandished as a weapon against meaning, as if there were some indisputable law that what is truly alive could not signify – and vice versa. The resistance of 'reality' (in its written form, of course) to structure is quite limited in fictional narrative, which by definition is constructed on a model which has, on the whole, no other constraints than those of intelligibility. But this same 'reality' becomes the essential reference in historical narrative, which is supposed to report 'what really happened'. What does it matter that a detail has no function in the account as long as it denotes 'what took place'? 'Concrete reality' becomes a sufficient justification for what is said. History (historical discourse: *historia rerum gestarum*) is in fact the model for those narratives which accept, as a filling for the gaps in their functions, *notations* which are structurally superfluous. It is logical, therefore, that realism in literature should have been, give or take a few decades, contemporaneous with the reign of 'objective' history, to which should be added the present-day development of techniques, activities, and institutions based on an endless need to authenticate the 'real': photography (direct evidence of 'what was there'), reportage, exhibitions of ancient objects (the success of the Tutankhamun show is a sufficient indication), tours to monuments and historical sites. All this demonstrates that the 'real' is assumed not to need any independent justification, that it is powerful enough to negate any notion of 'function', that it can be expressed without there being any need for it to be integrated into a structure, and that the *having-been-there* of things is a sufficient reason for speaking of them.

Since antiquity, the 'real' and history have gone together (seemingly truthful), but this helped to oppose it to the 'vraisemblable' that is, to the very nature of narrative (imitation or 'poetry'). The whole of classical culture was for centuries nourished by the idea that there could be no contamination of the 'vraisemblable' by the real. At first because what is 'vraisemblable' is never other than the thinkable: it is entirely subject to (public) opinion. Nicole said: 'One must not view things as they are in themselves, nor as he who speaks or writes knows them to be, but only in relation to what the reader or the hearer knows of them.'[10] Then because it was thought that what is 'vraisemblable' is general and not particular, as is history (hence the tendency, in classical texts, to functionalize every detail, to produce strong structures and, it would seem, to leave no notation which is justified only by its conformity to 'reality'). Finally because, with the 'vraisemblable', the opposite is never impossible, since description is founded on majority, but not unanimous, opinion. The motto implicitly prefacing all classical discourse (obeying the ancients' 'vraisemblance') is: *Esto* (Let there be, suppose . . .). The kind of 'real', fragmented, interstitial descriptive *notation* we are dealing with here does not appeal to this implicit introduction, and it takes its place in the structural fabric with no hint of such a hypothetical qualification. Just for that reason, there is a break between the old 'vraisemblance' and modern realism; but for that reason also, a new 'vraisemblance' is born, which is precisely what is called 'realism' (taking

15

this term to refer to any discourse which accepts statements whose only justification is their referent).

Semiotically, the 'concrete detail' is constituted by the *direct* collusion of a referent and a signifier; the signified is expelled from the sign, and along with it, of course, there is eliminated the possibility of developing a *form of the signified*, that is, the narrative structure itself. (Realist literature is, to be sure, narrative, but that is because its realism is only fragmentary, erratic, restricted to 'details', and because the most realistic narrative imaginable unfolds in an unrealistic manner.) This is what might be called the *referential illusion*.[11] The truth behind this illusion is this: eliminated from the realist utterance as a signified of denotation, the 'real' slips back in as a signified of connotation; for at the very moment when these details are supposed to denote reality directly, all that they do, tacitly, is signify it. Flaubert's barometer, Michelet's little door, say, in the last analysis, only this: *we are the real*. It is the category of the 'real', and not its various contents, which is being signified; in other words, the very absence of the signified, to the advantage of the referent, standing alone, becomes the true signifier of realism. An 'effet de réel', (a reality effect) is produced, which is the basis of that unavowed 'vraisemblance' which forms the aesthetic of all the standard works of modernity.

This new 'vraisemblance' is very different from the old, for it is neither a respect for the 'laws of the genre', nor even a disguise for them, but arises rather from an intention to alter the tripartite nature of the sign so as to make the descriptive notation a pure encounter between the object and its expression. The disintegration of the sign – which seems in fact to be the major concern of modernism – is indeed present in the realist enterprise, but in a somewhat regressive manner, since it is accomplished in the name of referential plenitude, while on the contrary the goal today is to empty the sign and to push back its object to infinity to the point of calling into question, in radical fashion, the age-old aesthetic of 'representation'.

Notes

1. G. Flaubert, *Un Coeur Simple*, in *Trois Contes* (Paris, Charpentier-Fasquelle, 1893), p. 4.
2. J. Michelet, *Histoire de France, La Révolution*, vol. v (Lausanne, Éditions Rencontre, 1967), p. 292.
3. 'Introduction à l'analyse structurale des récits', *Communications* 8 (Nov. 1966), pp. 1–27.
4. In this brief survey, we give no examples of 'insignificant' *notation*, since the insignificant can be illustrated only within the framework of a very large structure: when cited, a *notation* is neither significant nor insignificant: it requires a previously analysed context.

5. F. Bresson, 'La Signification', in *Problèmes de psycho-linguistique* (Paris, P.U.F., 1963).

6. E. R. Curtius, *La Littérature européenne et le Moyen Age latin* (Paris, P.U.F., 1956), ch. 10.

7. The six successive versions of this description are given by A. Albalat in *Le Travail du style* (Paris, A. Colin, 1903), pp. 72ff.

8. The mechanism is well noted by Valéry, in *Littérature*, when he comments on a line of Baudelaire's: 'The servant with the big heart . . .' ('This line *came* to Baudelaire . . . And Baudelaire continued. He buried the cook in a lawn, which goes against the custom, but goes with the rhyme . . .').

9. Plato, *Republic* x, 599.

10. Cited by R. Bray in *Formation de la doctrine classique* (Paris, Nizet, 1963), p. 208.

11. The illusion is clearly illustrated by the programme which Thiers established for the historian: 'To be simply true, to be as things themselves are, to be nothing more than them, to be nothing other than by them, like them, as much as them' (cited by C. Jullian, *Historiens français du XIXe siècle* (Paris, Hachette, no date), p. lxiii).

3. Models of the literary sentence

MICHAEL RIFFATERRE

Any model of the literary sentence must account for the *literariness* of this kind of sentence,[1] that is, for the formal characteristics resulting from the particularities of linguistic communication in literature. What these particularities amount to is this: in the act of literary communication only two factors are present – the text and the reader. From the text the reader reconstitutes the factors which are absent: the author, the reality to which the text refers or seems to refer, and the code used in the message (as the lexical and semantic corpus of reference, which is the verbal representation of the socio-cultural corpus, of the mythology constituted by the stock of commonplaces). The literary sentence must accordingly be of a nature that allows such reconstitution. Conveying a message, telling a story, but also at the same time setting the scene, introducing the protagonists and explaining their motives, it must be at once action and representation.

Three rules seem to me to govern the generation of sentences that satisfy the conditions just outlined. First, the rule of *overdetermination*, through which the sentence brings about the adherence of the reader. Second, the rule of *conversion*, which allows the sentence to be treated as a stylistic unit. Third, the rule of *expansion*, which expresses the transformation of an implicit motivation to an explicit one, of the narrative to the descriptive.

I will deal first with the mechanism of *overdetermination*. The components of the literary sentence are bound to one another by the syntagm, as with any sentence, but these relations are reinforced by others, which are formal or semantic. Each word thus appears multiply necessary; its relations with other words seem multiply compelling.[2] Instead of the meaning being based on reference by the signifier to the signified, it resides in the reference of the signifier to other signifiers, which creates *the illusion that the arbitrariness of the sign is reduced*. In reality, it is only shifted from one word to others, but, in the eyes of the reader, the sentence proceeds like a deduction, like a derivation from its initial state. To be sure, a text is decoded in two directions: in the direction of the initial reading, following the normal word order; and in the opposite direction (retroactively), with the meaning of what has been read being constantly modified by what one is currently reading. But in both kinds of reading, the reader has the same feeling that there is a reduction of arbitrariness. In retroactive reading, it is the initial utterance which seems to be confirmed by what is derived from it. In the first, left-to-right reading, it is the derivation which is made convincing or 'vraisemblable' (seemingly truthful) because, since it proceeds in terms of verbal associations to which we are accustomed, it conforms to our expectations.

These associations are well known: formal similarities, including puns, membership in the same synonymy or antonymy paradigm, in short, all the phenomena involving transfer of similarity on the syntagmatic level for which Roman Jakobson has developed the theory.[3] However, these phenomena do not necessarily concern the sentence, for they can also be observed on a smaller or larger scale.

I will therefore examine facts which are less familiar, but which concern only the sentence. What I have in mind are the cases where overdetermination results from a sentence's having been superimposed on other preexisting sentences – sentences which occur in other texts, or stereotypes belonging to the linguistic corpus. From these, the literary sentence is generated by the formation of calques, by polarization, or simply by the actualizing of potential sequences.

The *calque* is based on a cliché. Consider for instance the cliché: 'Il a passé (il passera) beaucoup d'eau sous le pont depuis que (avant que) . . .' (a lot of water has passed/will pass under the bridge since/before . . .). From this Lautréamont derives a sentence whose functions are undeniably literary. Mervyn, pursued by Maldoror, comes home and falls unconscious in the mansion of the English lord who is his father. The noble lord, old but still vigorous, declares that a lot of water will pass under the bridge before his strength gives out, and that he will avenge his son. This statement is in English, or rather, the text reports his words in French and simultaneously constitutes an oblique representation of the English language:[4]

Il parle dans une langue étrangère, et chacun l'écoute dans un recueillement respectueux: 'Qui a mis le garçon dans cet état? La Tamise brumeuse charriera encore une quantité notable de limon avant que mes forces soient complètement épuisées . . .'
(He speaks in a foreign language, and everyone listens with respectful solemnity: 'Who has put the boy into such a state? The foggy Thames will yet convey a noteworthy amount of mud before my forces are completely exhausted . . .')

This is not merely a word-for-word stylistic transposition, but rather the transformation of a minimal sentence, the cliché, into a sentence which is understandable on its own by reference to the really existing Thames, but whose true meaning (a lot of time will pass) is given by the reference to time. Not to real time, however, but to usual, already consecrated signifiers for the signified 'time'. The literary function of the sentence in this context is precisely due to this double reading. On the one hand, on the narrative level, in the plot, the sentence transcribes the words of the protagonist. On the other hand, on the representational level, it confirms the stage direction (*he speaks a foreign language*):[5] it is a *mimesis* of British behaviour. In addition, the calque has a metalinguistic function, as a parody of the society novel, whose aristocratic characters have a hyperbolic variant: the British gentleman. The calque thus defines the utterance first as an utterance and then as verbal play.[6]

The calque may equally well concern the proverb, which is a particular case, archaic and gnomic in nature, of the cliché: the maxim (a literary genre whose characteristics include the fact that the text is coextensive with the sentence) is frequently a transformation of the proverb.[7]

Another specific case of the cliché is the *citation*. It is nothing other than a cliché with a signature.[8] I will take as example this line from Abbé Delille, which ends a moving account of the September Massacres:[9]

Le meurtre insatiable a lassé les bourreaux.
(Insatiable murder has tired the executioners.)

The sentence contains a personification of Murder and the metaphor *bourreaux* (executioners). Moreover, the syntagm superimposes on the predicative relation a relation of equivalence: the antinomy 'insatiable'/'lassé'; and the agentive nouns are synonyms, for 'bourreau' is linked by metonymy to 'meurtre'. Such a complex of relationships is more than enough to draw attention to the form of the message – this in itself is a characteristic of literary communication. But along with this linear decoding, the utterance imposes another implicit reading, that of Juvenal's *lassata necdum satiata*. By analogical equivalence Murder thus becomes a Messalina whose lovers would be the bloodthirsty revolutionaries, with their thirst for blood consequently being transposed into erotic terms. The relation is not completely parallel to that of the Latin original; for that, the victims would have to be the lovers of Murder.[10] Be that as it may, this Murder–Messalina gives the line an effectiveness far beyond that which the grammatical relations would contribute if they were perceived only on the textual level instead of being read simultaneously on two levels. It contributes to this effectiveness that the calque, faithful to the aesthetics of the *imitatio*, gives the reader the pleasant illusion of belonging to the same cultural elite as the author[11] – no doubt a rationalization, but one which bears witness to closer contact with the text.

The literariness of the sentence is thus here due to the fact that it is a partial quotation, or, more precisely, a variant of a structure for which there already exists a renowned variant in literary history. This kind of calque is extremely frequent. If we are less aware of it at present, this is because it is no longer connected with an aesthetic, as it was in classical literature.

The second variety of intertextual overdetermination is *polarization*.

Among the relations of synonymy, metonymy, and antonymy which organize the universe of meanings just one – association by contrast – defines a structural relation which is clear, immediately perceptible, and perceived without ambiguity. For this reason the lexicon abounds in binary stereotypes whose terms are in opposition, one member of the pair counterbalancing and completing the other. This favoured relation is so powerful that it generates sentences which, literally, exist only to introduce the pair of polar items. Such sentences are constructed teleologically, just as certain anecdotes have as their only *raison d'être* the fact that they lead up to the final line or allow a pun. Binariness can therefore be considered as a matrix for verbal associations, a mould for a whole system of motivation which can be put into operation to accentuate the polarity of contrasts. Conversely, the constructions which express the contrasts receive a kind of consecration from this polarization.

This is the case, for example, with the colour words 'vert' and 'rouge'. They are definitely coupled due to the fact that green and red are complementary colours. Hence we find, in Baudelaire:[12]

> Delacroix, lac de sang hanté des mauvais anges,
> Ombragé par un bois de sapins toujours vert

(Delacroix, lake of blood haunted by fallen angels, overshadowed by a wood of fir-trees always green)

It does not matter much that Baudelaire thought he was explaining this image by tracing the sentence back to the mould from which it issued: '*lake of blood*: red; *haunted by evil angels*: the supernatural; *a wood always green*: green, the complement of red'.[13]

The point is that his translation is *not* literary. What does matter is that this opposition, so simple and natural, could generate such a romantic landscape. A landscape was required by the context, and the characteristic green of Delacroix, in the code of landscape, could only be vegetation. But what is striking is that this green has produced, rather than any other tree, firs, a hyperbole of greenness. And, among all the possible reds, this *vert* has called up the most extreme – this dramatic 'lac de sang', a hyperbole of redness.[14] The generative process has followed the channel cut by the preexisting cliché 'mare de sang' (pool of blood), with polarization affecting also 'mare', hyperbolized into 'lac'.[15] The sentence follows the line of least resistance of stereotypical associations.[16] It suffices that there exists a cliché making green the colour of hope for our opposition to dictate to Baudelaire the sentence: 'cette sanglante et farouche désolation, à peine compensée par le vert sombre de l'espérance'. (This bloody and wild desolation, barely compensated by the dark green of hope.)[17] Since the sense requires attenuation of the opposition (what is involved is a view coloured by the depression of *spleen*), the verb expressing the colour polarity ('compensée') is cancelled by its adverb ('à peine'), and this leads to a parallel alteration of the colour, and thus of its symbolism: the green has darkened.[18] A preestablished metaphorical opposition, whether modified or not, thus functions as metaphorical demonstration of the 'truth' of the utterance. It is this kind of 'demonstration', and nothing else, which gives its realism to the king exhausted by debauchery in the third *Spleen*:

> ... ce cadavre hébété
> Où coule au lieu de sang l'eau verte du Léthé.
> (... this exhausted corpse in which flows instead of blood the green water of Lethe.)

The substitution of water for blood is expressed both grammatically ('au lieu de') and allegorically ('Léthé'), but what consecrates, so to speak, the devitalization of the blood, the transformation of the veins, vessels of life, into dismal streams ('funèbres ruisseaux'),[19] is this 'vert' which destroys the red of vitality.[20]

It can happen that the lexical coupling is strong enough to be symbolic by itself. The semanticized syntagm will then be able to generate a 'story', like the love of two schoolmates recounted by André Pieyre de Mandiargues: 'He green ink, she red, they shake their fountain pens.'[21]

We must still consider the most important of the three kinds of overdetermination: *the actualization of descriptive systems*. I propose this term, which is narrower than 'semantic' or 'associative' field, to designate an ideal model to which we conform (positively or negatively, totally or partially) our references to a given signified.[22] The descriptive system is composed of signifiers associated with one another in accordance with the structure of a central signified, these associations themselves being clichéd and so well linked together that any signifier of the system can serve as a metonym for the whole. Thus, for example, the signified 'roi' can trigger the development of numerous associative chains. Taken pejoratively, for instance, 'roi' is at the centre of a system whose satellites are words like 'courtisan', 'bouffon', stereotypes of the solitude, *ennui*, powerlessness of the all-powerful king. The associative sequences vary according to the seme or semes of 'roi' that is or are selected by the context in which the kernel word appears. Their unfolding offers to the reader relations which are familiar to him, and give him the impression that they respond to some obvious truth, since they respond to his expectations. This results in convincing descriptions, for they suggest that their object is exemplary, a type, the raw material of literature. The entire third *Spleen* of Baudelaire, for example, is exclusively built on the actualization of this system of 'roi'.

In the simplest case, the descriptive system resembles a dictionary definition. We find this with the romantic theme of the harmonica, whose constants are given by the definition of the word itself. What is involved is not the modern instrument, the mouth organ, but the *Glasharmonika*, which was so popular in the Germany of Werther, and was made of glasses filled with varying amounts of water that sounded when the player rubbed the edges with his moist finger. Contemporary definitions always mention the almost painful effect produced by the vibrations of the harmonica on the nerves; its music accompanied Illuminist rites, and Madame de Staël observed the 'correspondences' between this music and romantic states of mind.[23] Thus the word generates images of gloomy spirituality,[24] such as this sentence from the *Vie de Rancé*, where Chateaubriand evokes the polemics which the Trappist reformer conducted even from retirement, and even when that meant later repentance and refuge in prayer:[25]

Au reste Rancé, tout vieux et tout malade qu'il était, ne déclinait jamais le combat, mais aussitôt qu'il avait repoussé un coup, il plongeait dans la pénitence: *on n'entendait plus qu'une voix au fond des flots, comme ces sons de l'harmonica, produits de l'eau et du cristal, qui font mal.*

(Moreover Rancé, old and sick as he was, never refused a fight, but as soon as he had repelled an attack, he immersed himself in penitence: all that could then be heard was a voice from beneath the waves, like those sounds of the harmonica, products of water and crystal, which cause pain.)

The sentence is a calque on the definition, as it stands: *'produits de l'eau et du cristal, qui font mal'*. Except for 'cristal', which is a stylistic sublimation of 'verre'. This is a sublimation which is neither gratuitous nor merely ornamental, but a necessary consequence of the symbolism assigned by the context to 'harmonica': as a hyperbole of 'verre', 'cristal' is an amplification of semes like 'transparence', 'fragilité', and, here, 'vibratilité'. The hyperbole is thus, in the paradigm of possible substitutes for 'verre', the *lexical* source of musical vibrations, and consequently, in the syntagm, the *descriptive* source of their action on the nerves.[26] The relative modifier, actualizing a common-place of contemporary descriptions of the instrument, takes us back to the starting point of the image: the voice is melodious but full of pain,[27] and hence, in this context, penitent. Moreover, the sentence is, so to speak, doubly overdetermined, for 'harmonica' is also related to 'pénitence' through 'eau', since this harmonious water is the water of penitence as well. The image is thus the result of coincidence or interference between the definition of 'harmonica' and the cliché 'se plonger dans' ('la méditation', 'le désespoir', etc.); taking 'plonger' literally (as the absence of the reflexive 'se' indicates we should), the cliché transforms 'pénitence' into a substitute for 'eau' – this is a syntagmatic fact, since the two words occupy the same slot in the construction. The sentence yields 'flots', accordingly, just as 'dans' (in), coinciding with the seme 'retraite' (retirement, retreat) contained in 'pénitence', generates the hyperbolic 'au fond des'. Between these 'flots

23

douloureux' and the 'eau' of the instrument, the source of melancholy harmonies, the metonymic equivalence can easily be established.

Actualization of the descriptive systems of a word does not necessarily depend on the physical presence of the word in the sentence. On the contrary, it is even easier to observe it if the sentence is, literally, the transformation of this word: if the sentence is a periphrasis. In fact, *periphrasis* or circumlocution is the extreme case of the overdetermination of grammatical relations by semantic relations: whether narrative or description, all it does is develop for the length of a syntagm what is already present in its entirety in the semes of the word of which the periphrasis is the transformation, and in the functions which that word would have had in the context where it has been replaced. Thus, for instance, Lamartine writes:[28]

> Tu chantais au berceau l'amoureuse complainte
> Qui le force au sommeil
(You sang to the cradle the amorous complaint which forces it to slumber)

and we understand effortlessly that this is the literary equivalent of the sentence 'tu chantais une berceuse' (you sang a lullaby).

We recognize this literariness by the conventionality of the substitution, for at the moment when we understand the meaning of the utterance we feel that this way of expressing it by words used inappropriately ('berceau', and the periphrasis itself) belongs to a traditional aesthetics which occupies a quite specific place in literary history. However, this historical explanation only accounts for how the reader knows that he perceives a phenomenon. We must still explain the perception itself: first of all, it is evident that the substitution functions as a riddle – whereas in the sentences generated by the descriptive system of a word, this word-kernel remains present (as in the example of 'harmonica'), in periphrasis it disappears. Secondly, the existence of this riddle is perceived because the reader is confronted by phenomena of ungrammaticality. This is, then, the linguistic mechanism behind literariness: because these phenomena prevent the reader from understanding, he is forced to resort to the hypothesis that a figurative sense is involved. He can only understand 'tu chantais au berceau' by supposing that with 'berceau' the container is substituted for the contained. It follows that the rule governing the idiolect of this sentence must be formulated as follows: the object complement designates a melody, and the signifier of the signified 'melody' is to be obtained, in the absence of the appropriate word, by taking the intersection of the semic system of 'mélodie' and of 'bébé'. 'Tu chantais au berceau', a syntagm whose relevance is only implicit, plays obliquely the role which 'harmonica' played directly.

Determined in this way, the sentence realizes the essential conditions of the potentially present 'berceuse', which are a song for putting someone to sleep, the singer of that song, the child to whom it is sung, the sleep that results from it. As opposed to what happens in the case of 'tu chantais une berceuse', here a description is added to the utterance. The addressee of the act of singing the lullaby is represented by 'berceau': thus to the syntactic connection is added a metonymic one (there would have been paronomasia if the word 'berceuse' had been explicit). To this stylistic effect is added 'l'amoureuse complainte', which expresses two semes of 'berceuse': first, the seme 'maternal love' (or at least 'protective love') that grounds the relation 'berceur–bercé' (cradle-rocker – rocked, lulled); second, the seme 'melancholy'.[29] But this development is only possible because 'amoureuse complainte' is the direct object of a verb whose meaning is inflected by 'berceau'. The equivalence between 'amoureuse complainte' and 'berceuse' is thus indeed a fact about the sentence. Finally, the relative clause spells out the seme 'dormitive virtue' of the word 'berceuse'. This has a threefold function. On the level of the sentence, the relative clause terminates the transformation, completes the replacement of the word-kernel by its defini-tion. Consequently, it constitutes a stylistic structural unit, because it makes the reader conscious of a pause, of the end of a period. On the representa-tional level, it terminates the scene and gives, at last, its narrative *telos*: 'sommeil', (sleep), the teleological justification of 'chantais' (sang). On the stylistic level, 'forcer au sommeil' is related to clichés like 'lutter contre le sommeil', 'vaincu par le sommeil' (to struggle against sleep, conquered by sleep) etc., clichés whose effectiveness comes from their fusing of contradic-tory semes: the archetype 'faire une douce violence' (doing gentle violence) is thus the activating element of this sentence-ending.

Let us consider now the second of the rules which govern the generation of the literary sentence: the rule of *conversion*. It applies to cases where the sentence is produced by a simultaneous transformation of all its components – all the meaningful elements being affected by the modification of a single factor (or at least those of its elements which actualize a thematic structure). Let us note in passing that it is this global convertibility which enables the sentence to be regarded as a micro-idiolect.

Hugo writes, for example, the sentence 'Ce livre [. . .] existe solitairement et forme un tout' (This book . . . exists in isolation and forms a whole). Then he changes the 't' of 'solitairement' to 'd', this modification transforming the components of the rest of the sentence, and he obtains: '(Ce livre) existe solidairement et fait partie d'un ensemble' (This book exists in association and forms part of a whole). The original and its transformation are kept side by side in the text to indicate the 'double character' of the *Légende des Siècles*.[30]

The cliché, because it is frozen, lends itself admirably to these global conversions: someone, for example, rewrites the familiar English expression 'You need it like a hole in the head' as 'You need it like a crevice in the

25

cranium'.[31] As *hole* and *head* belong to an alliterative paradigm of words with initial /h/, it was sufficient to find their semantic equivalents in a paradigm with initial /kr/. The conversion factor is a parodic recourse to technical language. Or consider the sentence: 'fléchissez vos deux genoux et priez pour les morts' (bend both your knees and pray for the dead), where the words are bound together only by the syntax and by their common semantic field. Lautréamont rewrites this sentence giving to each word a mark of technical status:[32]

Inclinez la binarité de vos rotules vers la terre et entonnez un chant d'outre-tombe. (Incline the binarity of your rotulae toward the earth and intone a chant from the beyond.)

The literariness of this sentence derives from its twofold nature. On the one hand, it is a message (a request from the author to his readers); on the other hand, it is a comment on this message. As it passes from one word to the next, the sentence creates a meaning. By imposing on these words a formally unmotivated constant, a sort of morphological masquerade, the sentence devalues, destroys, that meaning.

The assigning of value (positive, or, as in this passage, negative) affects the sentence as a whole: the entire sentence forms a single stylistic unit. If we describe the phenomenon in semantic terms, we observe that there are two meanings, one obtained by progressive decoding of the sentence, the other resulting from a simultaneous apprehension of the formal constants of the sentence. In the Lautréamont example, the global meaning is a negation of the discourse meaning – a negation of the exhortation to prayer. The irony is thus situated in the play between the decoding of the sentence as a sequence of signs and its decoding as a single sign.

Of course, the irony and humour of the preceding examples are just particular cases of the positive or negative assigning of value to the sentence. Such value assignment, in fact, profoundly modifies the semantic structure: the words, instead of having meaning as a function of their respective referents and signifieds, have meaning according to the mark which is affixed to them. This can be observed in the following sentence from a prose poem of Baudelaire's:[33]

[Il y avait] de vieilles mères portant des avortons accrochés à leurs mamelles exténuées. ([There were] old mothers carrying abortions hooked onto their emaciated dugs)

The sentence is not generated by spelling out of the semes of the signifier 'vieille mère' (which would exclude breast-feeding and any genuine relation with an infant;[34] the relations indicated in the text might be derivable, at most, from a descriptive system for 'famine'). Nor does there exist any associative chain which would allow us to derive 'accroché' from the word 'avorton'. In reality, the pejorative continuity of the sentence results from reversal of the + sign to the − sign, a reversal dictated by the context. The preceding paragraph describes Satan's stomach, on which there are tattooed 'de petites figures mouvantes représentant les formes nombreuses de la misère universelle' (small moving figures representing the numerous forms of universal misery). In the midst of these necessarily pejorative forms, our sentence is nothing more than the negative of a clichéd portrait of a mother, which, in its normal positive version, would be 'des mères portant des nourrissons suspendus à leur seins' (mothers carrying sucklings suspended from their breasts). The effect of negation is enhanced by a polarization which, for each term, increases the distance between its variant before the conversion and its variant after. 'Mère' in its maximally positive version being 'jeune mère', we get 'vieille mère'. 'Nourrisson', which is so often associated with the cliché 'plein (éclatant) de santé', generates 'avorton'. 'Suspendus', an image of positive dependence (cf. 'La Vache' of *Voix Intérieures*: 'O mère universelle! indulgente Nature! . . . Nous sommes là . . . Pendus de toutes parts à ta forte mamelle! . . . À tes sources sans fin désaltérant nos coeurs.' (O universal mother! indulgent Nature! . . . We are there . . . Hanging everywhere from thy strong breast! . . . From thy endless springs quenching our hearts' thirst))[35] thus gives 'accrochés', an image of frustrated obstinacy, with emphasis on the frustration, etc. The sentence is, therefore, not made up of realistic observations, and has meaning only through its negative character, a descriptive system normally reserved for the expression of joy being converted to a variant of 'misère universelle'.

Conversion is paradigmatic transformation. I have still to analyse syntagmatic transformation. To this type is applied the rule of *expansion*, which will be formulated thus: given a minimal (nuclear, matrix) sentence, each of its components generates a more complex form. Such is the case in this portrait of Nerval by Théophile Gautier:

Cet esprit était une hirondelle apode. Il était tout ailes et n'avait pas de pieds, tout au plus une imperceptible griffe pour se suspendre un moment aux choses et reprendre haleine; il allait, venait, faisait de brusques zigzags aux angles imprévus, montait, descendait, montait plutôt, planait et se mouvait dans le milieu fluide avec la joie et la liberté d'un être qui est dans son élément.[36]
(This sprite was an apodiform swallow. He was all wings and had no feet, at most an imperceptible claw to hang on to things for a moment and catch his breath; he went, came, made sudden zigzags at unforeseen angles, rose, fell, or rather rose, glided, and moved in the fluid medium with the joy and freedom of a being who is in his element.)

The first sentence ('cet esprit était une hirondelle apode') makes explicit all the semes of 'esprit' by which it is opposed to heavy matter and which have given birth to so many poems in which soaring flight expresses metaphorically the notion of spiritual elevation. This is reinforced by 'apode': instead of a simple metaphor for the poet as bird, 'hirondelle' becomes its hyperbole; without feet, there is no risk that he will be 'exilé sur le sol' like Baudelaire's albatross. This foregrounding, this stylistic overload of explicitness then triggers the expansion of the initial sentence into the two following sentences. The former is thus retroactively perceived as a minimal form. Each of the components of the sentences developed on the basis of this model is repeated at least twice, first simply set out, given, and then illustrated, motivated: 'tout ailes' generates 'pas de pieds', 'zigzags' first yields 'angles imprévus', then the group 'il allait, venait' and its homologues, also binary, etc. Of course the motivation is only apparent, a result of the geometry of the sentence. This example is relatively simple, because it can be reduced to a series of repetitions, each phrase generating its homologue, in order of increasing complexity.

In the majority of cases, a pronoun becomes a noun, a noun becomes a noun phrase, an adjective becomes a relative clause, etc., with each of the resulting constituents being able to produce another by adjunction or embedding. The verb is a special case: it is transformed so that the state or process that it expresses may be represented in dramatic or dynamic form, or at least in a form which can be concretely imagined, in terms of sensory perceptions. Thus, in a passage of *L'Eve future* where Villiers de l'Isle-Adam describes Thomas Edison, the inventor pushes a button to start his phonograph:[37] '[il] gratifia d'une chiquenaude le pas de vis de la plaque vibrante' (he presented the screw thread of the resonating plate with a flick of the finger). This descriptive mannerism is not gratuitous: it actualizes an antithetical structure – the archetype of the imperceptible movement which is enough to set a complicated mechanism into action – a structure evidenced in various clichés of literary *mimesis* of the machine, and of the science fiction novel.

Expansion is thus the mechanism by which a sentence changes from narrative to descriptive, from an unmotivated utterance to a representation which is credible, or as capable of inducing emotions as the thing represented.

One last example will illustrate the way expansion generates forms of increasing complexity:[38]

> Les yeux fixés sur moi, comme un tigre dompté,
> D'un air vague et rêveur elle essayait des poses,
> 15 Et la candeur unie à la lubricité
> Donnait un charme neuf à ses métamorphoses;
>
> Et son bras et sa jambe, et sa cuisse et ses reins,
> Polis comme de l'huile, onduleux comme un cygne,
> Passaient devant mes yeux clairvoyants et sereins;
> 20 Et son ventre et ses seins, ces grappes de ma vigne,

S'avançaient, plus câlins que les Anges du mal,
Pour troubler le repos où mon âme était mise,
Et pour la déranger du rocher de cristal
Où, calme et solitaire, elle s'était assise.

(Her eyes fixed upon me, like a tamed tiger, with a vague and dreamy air she was trying poses, and candour joined to lubricity gave a new charm to her metamorphoses; and her arm and her leg, and her thigh and her back, polished like oil, sinuous as a swan, passed before my clear-sighted and serene gaze; and her belly and her breasts, those clusters of my vine, moved closer, more coaxing than the Angels of evil, to disturb the repose of my soul, and to budge it from the rock of crystal where, calm and solitary, it had seated itself.)

Baudelaire is describing a hackneyed bedroom scene that can be somewhat crudely summarized like this: 'She was striking erotic poses to excite me.' In fact this nuclear sentence can be found, in minimal form, in the text itself, two lines before the sentences which are derived from it: 'elle essayait des poses' (line 14). In the first derived sentence (17–18), the transformation of the pronoun 'elle' generates an accumulation of metonymic representations of woman as an object of desire: her charms (17). This first expansion determines a second – the adjectives of line 18. Each of these adjectives in turn generates its own description, backed up by a comparison. The comparison is functional, since it confirms the transferral of 'bras', 'jambes', etc., from the class 'body parts' to the class 'erotic object'. This type of comparison involves a circular structure which helps make the sentence into a closed system. A transformation takes place which is the inverse of that which produces an adjective out of a noun by making explicit one of the semes of that noun: here there is generation of the noun on the basis of the adjective, with the sole restriction that the final noun must be different from the initial noun. With its positive value increasing at each step, the seme 'voluptuously lithe' goes from the 'reins' of the girl to 'onduleux' to 'cygne', with the slight complication that the swan here is a metonymy for a swan's neck, so that there is a transfer to that part, which explicitly represents the seme, of all the affective weight that comes with the concept 'swan'. As for the verbal matrix 'prendre des poses', it is first rewritten in dynamic terms: 'passaient devant mes yeux' (19); then, in the second derived sentence, in dramatic terms: 's'avançaient' (21), where simple exhibitionism is metamorphosed into sensual challenge.[39]

The male, the voyeur, since he is the one being tempted, is defined in the narrative sequence by a bifurcation of possibilities: he is suspended between yielding and not yielding to the temptation. The proairetic choice is made in virtue of the rule of polarization: it is clearly more interesting that he should not yield, that his resistance should prolong the erotic play. This explains the 'yeux clairvoyants et sereins' (19).

The second derived sentence (20–4) is an expansion of the second degree, and a sort of hyperbole of the first sentence, which is its matrix (in transformational terms) and also its microcontext (in terms of stylistic structure). The paradigm of the seductress' metonymic attractions reaches its culminating point with 'ventre' and 'seins', which are emphasized by 'ces grappes de ma vigne'. The metaphor comes from the Song of Songs, of course, but it also adds to the seme 'woman' that of 'possession', and turns the mistress into a slave.[40]

Instead of the adjectives reinforced by comparisons of the first derived sentence, here we find metaphorical appositions. Finally, the opposition between temptress and tempted is doubly polarized: first, instead of being reinforced by simple comparisons, it is presented in the form of a conflict between two personifications ('Anges', 'âme'), a spiritual duel closer to the confrontations of Satan and the anchorite than to amorous jousting. Second, there is a transfer from the narrative to the descriptive: the sentence engenders an allegory[41] by following the easy path of two stereotypes (firstly, a commonplace, that of the symbolic figure who is seated and lost in a reverie, a frequent emblem of contemplation with the Romantics; secondly, since the sitter needs something to sit on, and this attribute of the allegory should be positive, as is the allegory itself, we have the equivalent of a revitalized cliché, with the expression for rock crystal, 'cristal de roche', being reversed to 'rocher de cristal').

Generated as it is from the starting point of a minimal sentence whose components are given unadornedly, and are acceptable ('vraisemblable') simply because what motivates them remains implicit,[42] the literary sentence thus tends to be a sequence of explanatory and demonstrative syntagms, driving arbitrariness ever farther before them, from clause to clause. The transformation of simple components into complex representations makes the literary sentence the grammatical equivalent of an allegory loaded with symbolic attributes.

Notes

1. The studies dealing with the literary sentence all neglect literariness: if they bear on the style of an author, they talk about statistics, or grammar, or are only interested in characteristics (rhythm, word order, etc.) of that style, not of the sentence. If they bear on the sentence as such, they try in vain to list exhaustively possible word combinations, or else present word order facts which are the same for larger and smaller units than the sentence.
2. Concerning these multiple relationships (in particular the interaction of linguistic and thematic structures and of the descriptive system) which seem to me to constitute overdetermination, see my 'Le Poème comme representation', *Poétique* 4 (1970), pp. 401–18.
3. See, for example, the associations listed in J. Dubois, F. Edeline, J. M. Klinkenberg, etc. *Rhétorique Générale* (Paris, Larousse, 1970), pp. 118–19.

4. Lautréamont, *Chants de Maldoror*, chant vi (2), Walzer edn (Paris, Pléiade), p. 227.
5. A stage direction corroborated further on by the words 'commodore', for the father, and 'la sensible Londonienne', for the mother. Perhaps 'le garçon' should be read as an anglicism ('the boy') for 'cet enfant'.
6. On the role of the cliché in literature, see my *Essais de stylistique structurale* (Paris, Flammarion, 1971), pp. 161–81.
7. On the functioning of the maxim in general, see Serge Meleuc, 'Structure de la maxime', *Langages* 13 (March 1969), pp. 69–99.
8. It suffices that the reader recognize a citation; it is not necessary that he identify its author (cf. the notion of 'prélèvement' in Julia Kristeva, *Sémiotikè, recherches pour une sémanalyse* (Paris, Seuil, 1969), pp. 332–4).
9. 'L'imagination', chant iii, *Oeuvres complètes*, 6th edn (Paris, F. Didot, 1840), p. 132, col. 2.
10. This obscene variant of the 'bourreau–victime' relation can be found also in the slang metaphor which calls the guillotine 'la veuve' (the widow), and in the literary version of the myth of the devouress who kills her lovers, like Queen Margot in *La Tour de Nesle*, etc.
11. The recognition is facilitated for the post-Baudelarian reader by the *sed non satiata* of the *Fleurs du mal*. There was little problem for Delille's contemporaries; Baudelaire, writing later, felt it necessary to replace the *necdum* of Juvenal for a *sed non* more likely to be understood by all.
12. *Fleurs du mal*, vi, 'Les Phares', lines 29–30.
13. Baudelaire, *Exposition universelle de 1855*, iii (Le Dantec–Pichois edn (Paris, Pléiade), p. 973). Cf. 'si l'ombre est verte et une lumière rouge, trouver du premier coup une harmonie de vert et de rouge, l'un obscur, l'autre lumineux' (if the shadow is green and a light is red, find straight away a harmony of green and red, one dark, the other luminous) (*Salon de 1845*, ibid., p. 817; cf. p. 816: 'pondération du vert et du rouge'; and *Salon de 1846*, iii, p. 883; 'un cabaret mi-parti de vert et de rouge crus, qui étaient pour mes yeux une douleur délicieuse' (a cabaret half green and half red, both garish, which were for my eyes a delicious pain)).
14. It might be objected that, on the level of the signifieds, there is a natural contiguity of firs and mountain lakes. But real firs do not make the lakes they surround look like blood. When Baudelaire speaks of these lakes without mentioning fir-trees, their water is 'noire' or 'sombre' (*Petits Poèmes en prose*, xv, 'Le Gâteau', and, in his juvenilia, 'Incompatibilité'). No polarization from *vert*, no transformation from water to blood.
15. The 'sang' has contaminated the 'anges', which become 'mauvais anges'. In 'Incompatibilité', where there is no blood, the angel of the lake remains beneficent.
16. Cf. the following, where the cliché structures the sentence on the syntactic level and, on the graphemic level (italics), gives it humorous value (the topic is the critical savaging of a painter): 'Ah! les chevaux *roses*, ah! les paysans lilas, ah! les fumées *rouges* (quelle audace, une fumée rouge!) ont été traités d'une *verte* façon' (Ah! the *pink* horses, ah! the lilac peasants, ah! the *red* smoke (what boldness, red smoke!) have been treated in *green* [i.e. crude, shocking] fashion): Baudelaire, *Salon de 1859* (Pléiade, p. 1049).
17. Baudelaire, *Salon de 1846*, iv (Pléiade, p. 894).
18. There is an analogous alteration in 'La Muse malade' of Baudelaire: 'Le succube verdâtre et le rose lutin' (the greenish succubus and the pink imp). The word

31

'lutin', because it has a positive connotation, transforms the symbolically ambiguous 'rouge' into the meliorative 'rose'. Conversely, the 'vert' of 'succube' (which has a negative value) acquires a pejorative suffix. Cf. Gautier, 'Comédie de la Mort', lines 97–8: 'Le flot a . . . couvert de son linceul *verdâtre* . . . les rougeurs de *rose*' (the waves have covered with their greenish winding-sheet . . . the rednesses of pink [of drowned youths]). This interpretation seems to me more justified than the exegesis by Michel Butor of the Baudelairian 'rose' and 'vert' (*Histoire Extraordinaire*, pp. 244–8).

19. Baudelaire, *Fleurs*, 'A Théodore de Banville'.

20. The blood changed into water is also a calque on a familiar cliché. The opposition of 'rouge' and 'vert' can create an *ad hoc* reality: a 'natural' green can generate a 'verbal' red, as in this example from Gautier, *Poésies diverses 1838–45*, 'A trois paysagistes': 'artistes souverains/Amants des chênes verts et des rouges terrains' (sovereign artists/Lovers of green oaks and red earth).

21. *Dans les années sordides*, 'Les yeux gelés' (*L'Age de craie*, Coll. Poésie, NRF, p. 94).

22. I have studied various applications (and implications) of the concept of descriptive system in three recent essays: 'Le Poème comme représentation' (see n. 2); 'Sémantique du poème' *Cahiers de l'Assoc. Intern. des Etudes Françaises*, 23 (1971) (communication to the congress of July 1970); and 'The stylistic approach to literary history' *New Literary History* 2 (1) (Fall 1970). In a study dating from 1966, included in my *Essais de stylistique structurale*, pp. 213–21, I spoke of *code*: it seems to me now that this term should be restricted to the descriptive system already encoded (actualized) in a text as a vehicle for metaphor.

23. *De la littérature* I, ch. xi (Van Tieghem edn, vol. I, p. 185): 'Le frémissement que produisent dans tout notre être de certaines beautés de la nature, [. . .]; l'émotion que nous causent les vers qui nous retracent cette sensation, [ont] beaucoup d'analogie avec l'effet de l'harmonica. L'âme, doucement ébranlée, se plaît dans la prolongation de cet état, aussi longtemps qu'il lui est possible de le supporter.' (The shudder that certain beauties of nature produce in all our being . . .; the emotion which the verses which retrace this sensation for us cause, (have) a great deal of analogy with the effect of the harmonica. The soul, gently shaken, takes pleasure in the prolonging of this state, for as long as it is possible to stand it.) Cf. George Sand, *La Comtesse de Rudolstadt* IV, ch. x (Potter edn, vol. IV, p. 263, n. 1): 'Les imaginations poétiques voulurent y voir l'audition des voix surnaturelles [. . .] Les néophytes des sociétés secrètes [. . .] en étaient si fortement impressionnés que plusieurs tombaient en extase.' (Those with a poetic imagination thought they heard in it supernatural voices . . . neophytes of secret societies . . . were so strongly impressed by it that several fell into a state of ecstasy.)

24. Chateaubriand speaks elsewhere of the 'plaintes d'une harmonica divine, ces vibrations qui n'ont rien de terrestre' (laments of a divine harmonica, those vibrations which have nothing of the terrestrial) (*Les Natchez* IV, (Chinard edn, p. 174)).

25. *Vie de Rancé* (Letessier edn, p. 338).

26. Cf. Baudelaire, *Choix de maximes consolantes sur l'amour* (1846) (Pléiade, p. 471): 'Poètes hoffmaniques que l'harmonica fait danser dans les régions du cristal, et que le violon déchire comme une lame qui cherche le coeur' (Hoffmanesque poets whom the harmonica makes dance in the regions of crystal, and whom the violin rends like a blade searching the heart).

27. Because he does not recognize this ambivalence of pleasure and pain attaching to the glass harmonica, J.-P. Richard, who takes the instrument to be the modern

mouth organ, does not grasp the basic unity of these superficially contradictory semes, and appeals to useless hypotheses about the sensitivity of Chateaubriand (*Paysage de Chateaubriand* (1967), pp. 79–80). Everything is in the descriptive system, and it is everything in the sentence.

28. Lamartine, *Recueillements poétiques*, xxviii, 'A Mlle Delphine Gay' (Guyard edn (Paris, Pléiade), p. 523).

29. This seme is attested in the Latin *nenia*, meaning both 'lullaby' and 'funeral hymn'. If Apollinaire was able to use 'nénie' in French in both senses, this is not only because 'nénie' is given both meanings in the dictionary, but also because 'berceuse', for which 'nénie' is the substitute, preserves something of this ambivalence: 'La mer et ses nénies dorlotent tes noyés' (The sea and its neniae coddle your drowned) (*Le Guetteur mélancolique*, 'Au prolétaire'). The comparison was suggested to me by the subtle exegesis of 'Larron' in J.-Cl. Chevalier, *Alcools d'Apollinaire, Essai d'analyse des formes poétiques* (Paris, 1970) p. 53, n. 19.

30. 'Double caractère' is the expression introducing the double sentence, before and after the conversion: preface to *La Légende des siècles* (Truchet edn (Paris, Pléiade), p. 3).

31. From a letter to the editor of the *New York Post*, 29 May 1969: this is a paraliterary 'genre' at best, no doubt, but the parody centres the communicative act on the form of the message, and this makes it an example of Jakobson's poetic function.

32. *Chants de Maldoror*, chant v (6) (Pléiade, p. 206).

33. *Petits Poèmes en prose*, xxi, 'Les Tentations' (Kopp edn, p. 60).

34. Because descriptive systems are built on signifiers and not on referents. Systems can be mutually exclusive even though they cover a single category in the real world, like 'maternity'. The system 'mother', whose hyperbole is 'young mother', is opposed to the system 'old mother'. In the latter, for example, the mother–child relationship is reversed, since it is the child who protects and nourishes, or fails to do so. The system is complicated in the negative: if there is ingratitude, 'prodigal son' is related to 'father' rather than to 'mother', and in the case of a death the relation belongs with the system *mater dolorosa*, etc.

35. Cf. Baudelaire, *Fleurs du mal*, 'J'aime le souvenir de ces époques nues' (I love the memory of these naked eras); 'Cybèle . . . louve au coeur gonflé de tendresses communes, Suspendait l'univers à ses tétines brunes' ('suspendait' was corrected in proof to 'abreuvait': slaked) (Cybèle . . . she-wolf with a heart swollen with common tendernesses, suspended the universe from her brown dugs).

36. Th. Gautier, *Histoire du Romantisme*, ch. 8 (Paris, Fasquelle), p. 71.

37. *L'Eve Future*, i, ch. 7 (Paris, Pauvert), p. 27.

38. *Fleurs du mal*, 'Les Bijoux'.

39. Everything is as it would be if the expansion realized in dramatic form the etymological seme 'appât' (bait) related to the 'appas' (charms) enumerated in line 17.

40. Cf. lines 2–4: 'Elle n'avait gardé que ses bijoux sonores/Dont le riche attirail lui donnait l'air vainqueur/Qu'ont dans leur jours heureux les esclaves des Mores' (She had kept on only her sonorous jewels whose rich show gave her the conquering air possessed by the slaves of the Moors in their happy days).

41. Allegory is a typical case of expansion, and it is, among all the figures, of which the majority only involve groups of words, that which concerns the most complex syntagms. Dumarsais had already noted its connection with the prolonged metaphor (*Des Tropes*, ii, ch. 12).

42. Cf., on motivation, and on zero motivation as motivation, in the *récit*, Gérard Genette, *Figures II*, pp. 96–9.

4. The strategy of form

LAURENT JENNY

I

Implicit and explicit intertextuality

When Mallarmé wrote: 'In just about every book there occurs the fusion of some deliberate repetition', he was emphasizing a phenomenon which, far from being an oddity of books, an echo effect, or an interference of no consequence, is the defining condition for literary readability. Without intertextuality, a literary work would simply be unintelligible, like speech in a language one has not yet learned. We grasp the meaning and structure of a literary work only through its relation to archetypes which are themselves abstracted from long series of texts of which they are, so to speak, the invariants. These archetypes, each deriving from a 'literary act', encode the usages of that 'secondary language' (Lotman) which we call 'literature'. The literary work's relation to these archetypal models is always one of realization, transformation, or transgression. To a great extent, furthermore, it is this relationship which defines it. Even if a work defines itself as having no features in common with existing genres, far from denying its awareness of the cultural context, it admits it by this very act of negation. The literary work is thus unimaginable outside a system. Understanding it supposes competence in the decoding of the literary language, which can only be acquired by experience with a large number of texts: 'virginity' is thus just as inconceivable on the part of the decoder. If this aspect of the literary work has been ignored for so long, that is only because we were blinded to the code by its very obviousness. The work appeared to be independent of any code, like a slice of reality alive on the page, which, accordingly, could be related to nothing but itself. But once formal criticism becomes established on a solid base, as is the case at present, intertextuality ought to be situated in relation to the 'functioning' of literature. If every text refers implicitly to other texts, then it is first of all from a genetic point of view that the literary work is associated with intertextuality. But it is desirable to reconsider in formal terms a phenomenon which has been misunderstood by traditional 'source criticism'.

It can happen that intertextuality is not only a condition for the use of the

34

code, but is even explicitly present on the level of the formal content of this work. This is the case with all those texts which leave their relationship to other texts visible: imitations, parodies, citations, montages, plagiarisms, etc. With these the intertextual determinants of the work are of two sorts: thus, for instance, a parody is related both to the work of which it is a parody and to all the other parodies which constitute its own genre. What obviously remains problematic is the determining of the degree of explicitness of the intertextuality in a work, when it does not fall under the limiting case of literal quotation. While it is clear that structural criteria can be used to 'prove' the existence of intertextuality, in a number of cases it will be hard to determine whether the phenomenon of intertextuality in question derives from use of the code or whether it is the very matter of the work. In fact, it is easy to see that there is no incompatibility between these two statuses of an intertextual phenomenon, if the work has a strong metalinguistic tinge. Another thing which can vary is the sensitivity of readers to this 'repetition'. Their sensitivity is evidently a function of the culture and the memory of each period, but also of the formal concerns of its writers. For example, the dogma of imitation specific to the Renaissance is also an invitation to read the texts on two levels, and elucidate their intertextual relationship with the classical model. The reading habits of each age are thus also recorded in its writing habits.

Intertextuality and historical poetics

Here a problem arises in historical poetics, or, to put it differently, in the social psychology of literature. When one starts to assemble a corpus of explicit intertextuality, one soon begins to look for an ordering principle, a law. From Petronius to Joyce, through Rabelais, Cervantes, Lautréamont and the rest, periodically in the history of literature texts appear which seem to break with the monolithism of meaning and of language imbued with the cultural weight of preceding works. In the modern period, the phenomenon sometimes reaches its apogee in fabulous constructions which evoke as much the cathedral (a critical cliché for Joyce's *Ulysses*) as the architectural folly of the 'maison du facteur Cheval' (a cliché still to be invented to characterize the works of Roussel). The problem is, therefore, to determine whether this hypothetical 'periodicity' really exists, and whether it has a meaning for the history of culture. Is there a spasmodic process which causes an era to purge itself brutally of its burden of memory which has become stifling, or is this a constant phenomenon, a simple dialectic progression of forms, in which each work is formed on the basis of preceding ones? On the second view, intertextual works are not the symptom of cultural crisis, but only the result of chance and of the individual author's more or less pronounced taste for explicit intertextuality, formal reminiscence, parody, or revolt.

Harold Bloom,[1] believing in this second hypothesis, relies on a psychologizing interpretation of literary evolution. Every poet is said to suffer from an 'anxiety of influence', a veritable Oedipus complex of the creator, which leads him to modify the models to which he is sensitive by a variety of figures. Sometimes the 'follower' will prolong the work of his precursor while deflecting it towards the point which it should have attained (*Clinamen*), sometimes the intention is to create that fragment which will make it possible to consider the precursor's work as a new whole (*Tessera*), sometimes there is an effort to break radically with the 'father' (*Kenosis*), or to purge oneself of the imaginative heritage one has in common with him (*Askesis*), or to create an oeuvre which will paradoxically seem to be the source and not the result of the preceding work (*Apophrades*). With virtuosity Bloom choreographs this curious ballet of figures, which in fact he claims to be applicable only to poetry. His theory is a bizarre mixture of formal criticism and source criticism. It views literary history as no more than a succession of family conflicts, with each new generation anxious to establish its originality. This slightly simplistic posing of the problem in terms of the creator is in any case insufficient to handle intertextual phenomena of any importance: one would have to be singularly narrow-minded to claim to be able to explain the plagiarisms of Lautréamont as due to his desire for 'originality' *vis-à-vis* romanticism.

At the other extreme, McLuhan seems more convincing when he looks for the key to intertextual facts not in the history of the creative individual but in the evolution of the media. For him, all literary memory depends on the capacity for memorization of the media of an age. The renewal of information technology produces a sudden afflux of memory deposits which have an effect on the genres in fashion; before the coming of electricity:

Print as a means of retrieving the past was unrivaled in scope and intensity, and made available the entire world of antiquity, which had been only slightly accessible in manuscript form. It also made available the entire world of scholasticism, which, for the most part, had been an oral form of culture based on sententious aphorism. The new speed and repetition of the presses also poured forth the world of the illuminated manuscripts and the Books of Hours. The creation of the new reading public by the printing press meant also an entirely new world of genre in the arts. Cervantes and Rabelais explored these changes in the reading public as the effect of the mixture of genres on a colossal scale. Cervantes has Don Quixote doting on the old romances retrieved by Gutenberg; and Rabelais presents the world as a gargantuan junkheap of sludge served up for the insatiable appetites of men.[2]

The periods of intertextual crisis are thus all those which follow the introduction of new media. One might perhaps explain in these terms that the Renaissance and the beginning of the twentieth century are two key moments in literary intertextuality. It would still be necessary to analyse scrupulously the influence of each medium and, for example, to distinguish various stages within the twentieth century. There is no common measure, for instance, between the journalistic medium which influenced Dos Passos or Joyce and the audio-visual medium which determines the work of William Burroughs. McLuhan's ideas are stimulating, but they do not offer a satisfactory answer to the question raised by intertextuality. His theory appeals to a rather simple reductive mechanism, and in so doing robs intertextuality of any ideological significance. To say, in the words of the celebrated dictum, that 'the medium is the message' is to speak too hastily. Burroughs shows quite clearly that the meaning of a medium can perfectly well be deflected: the anti-media guerrilla warfare he favours makes use of the linguistic tools of those in power. We can thus not avoid asking, for each period, who it is that controls the media and how these media are used. Moreover, McLuhan (understandably, since he is not dealing with this matter) is silent on what is the very essence of intertextuality for the student of poetics: the work of assimilation and transformation which characterizes all intertextual processes. Works of literature are never mere 'memories', they rewrite what they remember, they 'influence their precursors', as Borges would put it. The intertextual attitude is thus a critical attitude, and that is what defines it. Apart from this, we willingly grant McLuhan's point that this criticism can function more easily when new media stimulate the memory of a literate audience. But the cultural significance of the phenomenon, the explanation for these moments of dilatation of form, remain to be elucidated.

There is a common factor relating approaches as fundamentally different as those of Bloom and McLuhan: each in his own way, they are seeking a law, an order governing intertextual history in the *conditions* (psychological or social) of intertextuality, and not in its *forms*. At no moment do they adopt a point of view oriented towards form. Nevertheless it is possible to ask whether it is not a given type of form which provokes intertextuality. One might, for example, propose the hypothesis that it is the most strictly or exaggeratedly encoded texts which provide matter for such 'repetition'. To support this thesis, one might fruitfully cite from the parodic intertextuality of different periods. Thus in the *Satyricon*, when Petronius has the poet Eumolpus recite a long epic poem entitled 'The Civil War', this is first of all a parody of the baroque, hispanicized style of Lucan's *Pharsalia* (hyper-coded form) and it is also a parody of the rhetoric of epic in general, for it contains many reminders of Vergil, written at a period when epic style was becoming fixed in formulas and commonplaces that were familiar to all. With Rabelais, later on, the borrowings could be traced to the highly coded forms of the scholastics, of the romances of chivalry, of the *parodia sacra*. One might try to

37

show that even when Rabelais' intertextuality contains references to a surviving popular oral tradition it still concerns forms which are rigidly encoded: *blasons*, heraldic proclamations almost legal in nature, or the patter of charlatans with its obligatory commonplaces. Skipping ahead again a few centuries to Lautréamont, it would not be hard to argue that the reason why romantic poetry and the Gothic thriller were such easy prey for the *Chants* was the hyperbolic hyper-coding characteristic of these two genres. Likewise for Joyce's *Ulysses*, where similar hyper-coding would be claimed to be responsible for the presence of languages as diverse as those of sensational journalism, Irish epic, and the Bible. However, while parody is always intertextual, intertextuality is not reducible to parody. What is to be made of the non-parodic use of intertextuality to be found in many contemporary texts ranging from *La Route des Flandres* of Claude Simon to the distinctly classical *Sac du palais d'été* of Pierre-Jean Remy, two novels which refer to texts which lack the excess of coding that would make them especially quotable? And how is hyper-coding to be defined? Will not any abandoned genre automatically seem hyper-coded simply because its coding has become apparent? The road of immanence is full of pitfalls, but it is clear that it is essential for any research in historical poetics.

Criticism and intertextuality

Intertextuality appears to us today to be essentially connected with poeticity and literary evolution, but clear awareness of the phenomenon itself is relatively recent. For the idealist critic, there were only 'influences' and 'sources' – aquatic, fluid metaphors – where formal criticism tries to discover texts. In the metaphors of criticism, when the work of literature ceases to be an elusive fluidity it becomes texture, imbrication, weave (cf., for example, the metaphors used by Barthes in *S/Z*). The slowness with which modern poetics has become aware of intertextuality is perhaps to be explained as due to a youthful excess: its obsession with immanence. Poetics was, in fact, forced to struggle equally hard against a classical tradition and a modern tendency, both of which resulted in effacement of the work, either by claiming to explain the text through learned research into the biography of its author, or by piling up critical readings borrowed from disciplines not primarily literary (history, sociology, psychoanalysis, etc.). In its reaction, poetics imprisoned itself in a narrow conception of immanence and denied that there was any need to be interested in anything beyond the text, or to articulate this with the work. This position quickly becomes untenable, as Tynianov had already seen:

Is the so-called immanent study of the work as a system, ignoring its correlations with the literary system, really possible? . . . Literary criticism uses this approach frequently and successfully for contemporary works, because the correlations of a contemporary production are an already established fact which is always presupposed.

Today our thirst for the exploration of immanent structure has been somewhat slaked. It is time to reread Tynianov, who shows the way for the inter-articulation of several systems:[3]

> The existence of a phenomenon as *literary phenomenon* depends on its differential quality (i.e. its correlation either with a literary series or with an extra-literary series) – in other words, on its function.

Tynianov goes far beyond the poets' initial intuitions of a second, secret voice in the text. His hypothesis is that every work of literature is constructed as a double network of differential relations: (1) with preexisting literary texts; (2) with non-literary systems of meaning, such as spoken languages. If we extend this idea of 'the extra-literary' to non-verbal symbolic systems, we arrive at the notion of 'intertextuality' as defined by J. Kristeva, who invented the word. If, indeed, for Kristeva 'every text is constructed as a mosaic of citations and every text is an absorption and transformation of another text', the notion of a text is significantly broadened for her. The term is synonymous with 'system of signs', whether in literary works, spoken languages, or symbolic systems, social or unconscious. Kristeva insists on this broader definition and opposes it in advance to any reductive interpretation:[4]

> The term *intertextuality* designates this transposition of one or more systems of signs into another, but since it has often been understood in the banal sense of 'source criticism' of a text, we prefer the term *transposition*, which has the advantage of indicating that the passage from one signifying system to another requires a new articulation of the thetic – of enunciative and denotative positionality.

To illustrate this process of transposition, Kristeva takes as an example the work of *representability* in Freud, which can create a mental representation on the basis of a pun. Thus the literary text becomes the site of a blending of sign systems deriving from the instinctive and the social, and it goes without saying that any reading supposes a developed theory of the individual and of his relation to the social, which goes beyond the usual ambition of the student of poetics.

We are thus the inheritors of a term which has become 'banal' and to which it is our task to give as full a meaning as possible. Contrary to what Kristeva says, intertextuality in the strict sense is not unrelated to source criticism: it designates not a confused, mysterious accumulation of influences, but the work of transformation and assimilation of various texts that is accomplished by a focal text which keeps control over the meaning. It is not hard to see that what threatens this definition with vagueness is the notion of a 'text' and the position to be adopted with respect to metaphorical uses of the term.

The boundary-lines of intertextuality

The notion of intertextuality raises immediately a delicate problem of identification. At what point can one begin to speak of the presence of a text within another in terms of intertextuality? Is one to treat in the same way a citation, a plagiarism, and a simple reminiscence? Our search ought to be less agitated than that of Saussure hunting down anagrams and looking everywhere for 'proof'. To this end, we propose to speak of intertextuality only when there can be found in a text elements exhibiting a structure created previous to the text, above the level of the lexeme, of course, but independently of the level of that structure. We distinguish this phenomenon from the presence in a text of a simple allusion or reminiscence; in other words, from occasions when there is borrowing of a textual unit abstracted from its context and inserted as if in a new textual syntagm as a paradigmatic element.

Thus we will speak of 'weak' intertextuality to characterize the allusion that Lautréamont makes to Musset by using the image of the pelican who 'gives its breast to be devoured by its young' in chant v, strophe 12, of the *Chants de Maldoror*, the stanza of the grave-digger. For any cultivated young Frenchman at the end of the nineteenth century, the reference to 'Nuit de mai' was obvious. The theme is rare enough in French poetry, the image striking and original enough (although belonging to a Christian tradition) for the poem of Musset to be visible between the lines. Nevertheless, we cannot speak of intertextuality, because the thematic role of this image is unrelated in the two texts. With Musset, the pelican has precise symbolic significance: it is the poet, finding his inspiration in pain and feeding a public greedy for his sufferings. In Lautréamont, the image is put into the mouth of the grave-digger, who uses it to illustrate the laboured topos he has set out to develop: certain pains may be intense, but we can understand them (other examples parallel to that of the pelican: the suffering of the young man who sees his beloved in the arms of his friend; the hatred of the boarding-school pupil governed night and day by 'an outcast from civilization'). From the first text to the second, we cannot even speak of negation or diversion. The symbolism of Musset's pelican is not retained, not contradicted, it is simply forgotten. Just one seme – that of pain – permits the reuse of the image in another thematic construction. Even if the romantic allusion is held up to ridicule by the overall pomposity of the discourse, there is no relation between the two texts as structured wholes.

On the other hand, the stanza of the grave-digger, as a whole, is in an *intertextual* relation with *Hamlet*, v, 1. The 'resemblance' is no longer merely a matter of an image, but extends to the whole dramatic situation: a dialogue in a graveyard between a tenebrous hero and a grave-digger at work. A network of correlations is established between the nature of the protagonists, their respective speeches, and their situation in relation to the open grave. We gradually realize that the two texts are in a relation of inversion. With Shakespeare, it is the grave-digger who is irreverent, playful (he sings: 'O a pit of clay for to be made, For such a guest is meet.'); with Lautréamont, it is the man talking to the grave-digger who invites him not to be serious ('Tu crois que creuser une fosse est un travail sérieux!' (You think that digging a grave is serious work!)). The relationship between the two discussions about the grave is more complex. In both cases, the grave-digger is found initially with 'both feet in the grave', and this leads Shakespeare's grave-digger to claim ownership, playing with the meaning of the possessive pronoun (Hamlet: Whose grave's this, sir? – Grave-digger: Mine sir . . . You lie out on't sir, and therefore 'tis not yours: for my part, I do not lie in't; and yet it is mine). The situation is exactly the reverse in Lautréamont, where it is the man speaking to the grave-digger who claims ownership, this time literally, of the grave (Maldoror: Je suis fort, je vais prendre ta place (I am strong, I will take your place)). The figure which connects these two texts is twofold: there is inversion, but also a passage from figurative to literal meaning. The same contradiction is to be found in the things said: Hamlet is horrified by death, while Maldoror sees the corpse as a genuinely pleasurable object. (Hamlet, speaking of Yorick, whose skull the grave-digger has just given him: . . . He hath borne me on his back a thousand times: and now how abhorred in my imagination it is, my gorge rises at it. Maldoror: Fossoyeur, il est beau de contempler les ruines des cités; mais il est plus beau de contempler les ruines des humains! (Grave-digger, it is beautiful to contemplate the ruins of cities; but it is still more beautiful to contemplate the ruins of human beings!).) When we consider, furthermore, that the trappings of dramatic discourse (dialogue, the aside) are to an extent transposed into the falsely lyrical poetic discourse of Lautréamont, we are forced to admit that it is an entire fictional staging which has here been borrowed, adapted, perverted and contradicted by the intertextual operation. From the first text to the second, the tone, the ideology, the very movement of the scene have changed, not randomly, but through a succession of contradictions and symmetries between the terms. In remodelling the representation to its own ends like a malleable substance, intertextuality follows pathways which sometimes evoke the effect of a dream on memory representations.

Code, genre, text

We have recognized for any textual syntagm the possibility of figuring in an intertextual relationship, without prejudice to its level of organization. This raises no difficulty as long as what is involved is a thematic structure which is easily identifiable on the level of representation, as in the case of the grave-digger. But what is to be said when the structure in question is a 'formal' one, characteristic of a genre which is no longer living? Is it possible to say that a text is in an intertextual relation with a genre? It might be objected that this would be to mingle awkwardly structures which belong to the code and structures which belong to its realization. This distinction, however, seems difficult to maintain when, as in the case of the genre, the code is limited to the specification of a certain number of structures to be realized – structures which are as much semantic as formal and which form a sort of *architext*. Genre archetypes, however abstract, still constitute textual structures, ever present to the mind of the writer. Yuri Lotman has rightly stressed the interchangeability of code and message. All languages, and *a fortiori* artistic languages, are 'modelling systems', that is, they structure the meaning, and are thus bearers of content:[5]

The language of an artistic text, of its essence, is a determined artistic model of the world, and, in that sense, it belongs by all its structure to the 'content', it is a bearer of information.

If the code loses any of its open-endedness, if it becomes closed within a structural system – as is the case with genres whose forms have ceased to be renewed – then it becomes structurally equivalent to a text. We can then speak of a relation of intertextuality between a specific work and the architext of a genre.

An attentive reading of the *Chants* reveals such interferences. In a letter to the banker Darasse, the famous one which begins 'Let me take up again what was said above . . .', Ducasse describes the *Chants* in these terms: 'It was something along the lines ('dans le genre') of Byron's Manfred.' A curious reference (coupled with one to Mickiewicz). There is not much connection between the somewhat soothing romanticism of *Manfred* and the sarcastic bombast of the *Chants*, and one might wonder what aberration has led Ducasse so to misconstrue his own creation. It is tempting to see this as a joke, in the same tone of cool mockery as the rest of the letter. On further reflection, however, we can find several reminiscences. If Maldoror, unlike Manfred, has not blighted a pure love whose memory haunts him, he shares with Byron's hero the destiny of an individual damned and dedicated to evil. They have the same preference for mountains, solitude, oceans, the same disgust with humanity (*Manfred*, II, 2: 'For if the beings, of whom I was one, – /Hating to be so, – cross'd me in my path,/I felt myself degraded back to them,/And was all clay again . . .'). This is not much, and in any case not sufficient to define the *Chants*. We have to go back and read 'dans le *genre* de Manfred'. If we take the word in its literary sense, the genre of *Manfred* is indeed stipulated by Byron's subtitle: 'a dramatic poem'. In fact *Manfred* is provided with numerous accoutrements of drama: a list of the *dramatis personae*, indications of the setting, stage directions, division into acts and scenes. The lyrical declamations of Manfred are interspersed with dramatic dialogue. It is now easier to see how the label 'dramatic poem' could define the general plan of the *Chants*, based on the exaggeration of an antithesis which is both ideological (Good and Evil) and formal (romantic poetry and its mockery). This is a complex structure where the formal antithesis constantly belies the 'seriousness' of the ideological one that structures the work on the immanent level. What Ducasse has borrowed from the genre of *Manfred*, then, is a poetic discourse perpetually stretched into a dramatic structure, to the point where certain stanzas of the *Chants* have the form of a dramatic discourse, such as the stanza of the grave-digger, but above all I, II, the strophe where Maldoror comes to tempt and massacre a virtuous family. In the edition of 1868, this passage is in the form of a drama with four characters (with a precise indication of stage business). By the following edition, Ducasse has carefully erased all the marks of a drama and made the passage a simple dialogue, as if he wanted thus to complete the job of intertextual assimilation. The intertextual relation is established here between the text of Ducasse and the architext of the dramatic poem, considered as a narrative and semantic structure capable of organizing an individual strophe as well as the work as a whole. The intertextual work has 'forgotten' in transit what is peculiar to Byron, what belongs strictly to the level of content of *Manfred*.

Transposition, languages

From the architext to the text, the relationship is established between two literary *paroles*, two realizations of 'secondary languages' (Lotman). That is, two systems of signs are brought into relation whose organization is of the same kind. In proposing the notion of 'transposition', Kristeva envisages the possibility of passage from one signifying system to another, independently of any literary or aesthetic factors. For us the question arises of whether, in the domain of literary texts, there are examples of this phenomenon, which would then represent a particular case of intertextuality. The term itself would, in such a case, be rather inadequate, since the relation would hold between two 'open' signifying systems and not between two texts.

The case is certainly not common, but one can legitimately ask whether certain works of Raymond Roussel are not based on such a relation of transposition between two languages. We know that with Roussel literary creation is based on a system of dismemberment of the signifiers. His *Impressions d'Afrique* was composed entirely on this principle. Roussel took some arbitrary sequence of words and extracted 'images' by breaking it up 'a little as if what was involved was a rebus'. Thus the words 'Napoleon premier' will be phonetically decomposed into 'nappe ollé ombre miettes' (tablecloth olé shadow crumb). From these words, Roussel elaborates a scene where Spanish women perform a seductive dance standing on a fully set table; Roussel pushes the visual illusion to the point of making this bit of representation a *real* image in the narrative: mysterious pellets thrown into the water by one of the Incomparables produce this enigmatic tableau with such clarity that all the onlookers can even see the shadows of the crumbs ('l'ombre des miettes') on the table . . . In short, Roussel resembles an inventor of rebuses, except that his rebuses remain purely verbal. What is substituted for the graphic representation is a literary representation whose only similarity with the former is verbal. The work that is accomplished is a transposition of linguistic signs to literary signs. Each word or verbal fragment yields a fragment of the representation, but in each case there is a passage from one kind of language to another: the primary verbal language is used as trigger of a secondary language. The route followed is the reverse of that taken in dream-condensation when this results in a word (cf. the examples of rebus-dreams in *Traumdeutung*, particularly the *Maistollmutz* dream).[6] While in dream-condensation mental representations come to be concentrated in the signifiers that constitute a word, in Roussel's rebus a process is adopted of *expansion* of the verbal signifier into literary signs, that is, signs whose organization is infinitely more complex than that of signs in natural languages. Two signifying systems – linked to be sure by their common linguistic material – are thus related, or, if you like, transposed one to the other. What is certain is that one signifying system is present within another, even if its operation, and its very existence, remain latent.

Status of intertextual discourse

What is characteristic of intertextuality is that it introduces a new way of reading which destroys the linearity of the text. Each intertextual reference is the occasion for an alternative: either one continues reading, taking it only as a segment like any other, integrated into the syntagmatic structure of the text, or else one turns to the source text, carrying out a sort of intellectual anamnesis where the intertextual reference appears like a paradigmatic element that has been displaced, deriving from a forgotten structure. But in fact the alternative is only present for the analyst. These two processes really operate simultaneously in intertextual reading – and in discourse – studding the text with bifurcations that gradually expand its semantic space.

Whatever the texts may be that are assimilated, the status of intertextual discourse is thus comparable to that of some *super-parole* in that the constituents of this discourse are not just words, but bits of the already said, the already organized, textual fragments. Intertextuality speaks a language whose vocabulary is the sum of all existing texts. There takes place a sort of release on the level of *parole*, a promotion to discourse of a power infinitely superior to that of everyday monologic discourse. The allusion suffices to introduce into the centralizing text a meaning, a representation, a story, a set of ideas, without there being any need to state them. The source text is there, potentially present, bearing all of its meaning without there being any need to utter it. (In dreams there is a quite analogous concentration of meaning when they are enriched by allusion to ready-made fantasies which are not recreated during sleep but which leave the illusion that they have been when the dreamer awakes.)[7] This confers on the intertext an exceptional richness and density. But in return the 'cited' text must, as it were, give up its transitivity: it no longer speaks, it is spoken. It no longer denotes, it connotes. It no longer means on its own, it acquires the status of material, as in the 'bricolage mythique' (myth-tinkering) of Lévi-Strauss, where pretransmitted messages are collected and rearranged in new combinations: 'in this incessant reconstruction using the same materials, it is always former ends which are called upon to play the role of means: signifieds change into signifiers and vice versa'.[8] But once again analysis misrepresents what happens, and it would be closer to the truth to say that the borrowed text at once denotes and refuses to denote, is transitive and intransitive, has full value as a signified and full value as a signifier. All intertextual *parole*, all intertextual reading, come from this movement.

II

Problems of integration

The problem of intertextuality is to bind together several texts in one without their destroying each other and without the intertext (we use this term in the sense of 'a text absorbing a multiplicity of texts while remaining oriented by a meaning'; the word is sometimes used by Michel Arrivé in the sense of 'a set of texts which are in a relation of intertextuality') being torn apart as a structured whole. Intertexts solve this problem with more or less success, according to the period, the intention, and the stringency of the requirements for structural integration that are assumed. It is evident, however, that these requirements become looser as the modern notion of a text becomes more encompassing. The author may even decide in advance to give up any unifying framework, as Queneau did when he presented his variations on a basic narrative theme as a series of *Exercices de style*. When the framework is maintained, the solutions to this problem range from total respect for the various texts to their quasi-disintegration in the space of the work.

1. Anagrams

This is the most virtuoso, but also the least feasible, solution to the problem of intertextuality. It consists in scattering across the space of a text the phonemes of one or more words, which are brought to the attention of the perspicacious reader by heightened redundance and by the presence of what Saussure calls *mannequins* ('words whose beginnings and ends correspond to those of the thematic word and are a clue to it').[9] The anagram may repeat a word present in the surface text, it may define the poetic theme on which the passage is built (a logogram), or the theme word may be totally absent from the visible text and yet omnipresent, as if written in invisible ink. In any case, the miracle is that one discourse is contained within another without the slightest alteration in the texts, since their coexistence is based on the perfect coincidence of their signifiers (we leave aside that bastard form of the anagram, anaphony, which makes do with approximate and incomplete assonances). However, the difficulty of establishing such coincidence of signifiers between complete texts generally limits the anagram to a single word, often a noun, and moreover one which is most often semantically related to the text where it is secretly present. It does however happen that an anagrammatic reading will discover a complete text within the text. Thus Saussure, studying an oracle of eleven lines given by Livy found in it the following cryptogram: 'Ave Camille – Ave Marce Fouri Emperator – Dictator ex Veieis triump(h)abis – Oracolom Putias Delp(h)icas – Apollo'. As Starobinski points out, the various theme-words reveal who is speaking (the god), to whom he is speaking (the emperor) and what is being spoken about (the capture of Veii), a veritable discourse within the discourse. Whether this is in fact an analect rather than an anagram, whether Saussure is in this case the inventor and not the discover, is irrelevant for us. If it was not the oracle, then it was Saussure who inscribed the text in the text – but in either case the possibility of this type of intertextuality is established.

2. The traditional narrative framework

Leaving behind such anagrammatical exploits, which Saussure in any event limited to certain Latin poetic texts, the most common variety of intertextual construction is that in which the multiplicity of discourses is accommodated in a narrative framework, which is coherent, if not traditional, and this keeps the work from following the borrowed forms in an aimless proliferation and reassures the reader. Thus, as P. Jourda has noted,[10] Rabelais organized *Pantagruel* and *Gargantua* according to the rhetoric of the romance of chivalry which were then in vogue: in three parts devoted respectively to the birth of the hero, his education, and his feats. Four centuries later, in identical fashion, Joyce inserts apparently rambling 'modulations d'écriture' (modulations of writing mode) into a narrative (*Ulysses*), which respects the unities of time and place, proceeds according to a specific plan, and where each chapter is itself highly organized.

In reality, the maintenance of strict linearity in the narrative is not at all obligatory. Chronology can disappear, and the narrative become lacunary, as long as a unity finally emerges, a structure is produced, where the intertextual materials can find a place. Such is the technique of Claude Simon – already so well domesticated that it seems classical – in his novel *La Bataille de Pharsale*. The text is slowly built up of non-isotopic (non-homogeneous) representational chunks. From these fragments a unity appears, either through the operation of secondary semantic analogies – for example, scenes linked by a mere similarity of bodily position: a football-player leaning over an opponent who is stretched out on the ground, a warrior leaning over his enemy, a lover bent over his mistress – or by narrative connections slowly established between episodes, which are repeated, prolonged, tied together – for example, the description of a jealous lover lying in wait behind a door and of an erotic scene are at first dissociated, then they are slowly brought together until the reader sees what they have in common. In this construction a whole intertextual corpus is gradually introduced: the text of a comic strip, fragments of a magazine devoted to history, recollections of translation exercises from Latin, passages of *Un Amour de Swann*, of the *Histoire de l'art* of Elie Faure, of Apuleius' *Golden Ass*, etc. Furthermore, these extracts are always narratively motivated, the conditions of their utterance are indicated, they are not left to drift with the same freedom as the representational masses which constitute the major part of this work. To achieve this, Simon places his hero in situations where he is reading: he leafs through a magazine in the train, at home he is looking for a quotation and so skims through a book, as a child he is required by his uncle to translate a passage from Caesar, etc. The forms do not invade the text freely; they remain subservient to the story. With Joyce the technique is the reverse: the 'modulations d'écriture' are unmotivated. Nothing justifies the theatrical form of the Circe episode, nor the encyclopedic presentation of Ithaca. In *Ulysses* it is the intertextual 'writings' which determine the representational content and not the reverse. This relative timidity of the author of *La Bataille de Pharsale* is to be explained as a phenomenon of compensation to maintain a balance in the economy of the work: directing his effort to the (de-)construction of the narrative, the author prefers not to add to this a heterogeneity of 'writings' liable to confuse completely a reader who is busy trying to glue together the fragments of the fiction – a job which is all the more absorbing in that it is impossible to accomplish, for numerous pieces remain unplaceable, and the totality forms a story with remaining gaps.

The main point to be retained is that intertextuality goes perfectly well into a traditional narrative framework, and that, in addition, it is perfectly capable of being adapted without alteration to modern transformations of the narrative framework, to its 'deconstruction'.

3. Alteration of the narrative framework by intertextuality

When intertextuality exhibits a certain degree of autotelism, aesthetic for example, as in certain surrealist 'narratives' (e.g. *Poisson soluble* by Breton), it sorely tries the narrative frameworks used as pretexts. As attention is concentrated on the handling of forms and techniques their importance is exaggerated, the story becomes secondary and falls into tatters, or, even more humiliatingly, is only retained as a stylistic signal that has poetic value but is functionally empty. The narrative framework becomes a 'pre-text' onto which all sorts of parasitic discourses are grafted. Intertextuality is then used as a weapon to disorganize the narrative order and destroy the realism of the account (which amounts to the same thing). Polytopy, which is characteristic of any massive use of intertextuality, can wreck in this way the most canonical of narrative frameworks – for example the fairy-tale structure which underlies sequence 37 of *Poisson soluble*.[11] However, this does not mean that the cohesion of the text disappears. Isotopies are created, as if to make up for the deficiency of the narrative structure and supply a unity to counterbalance the multiplicity of writing modes. Semantic networks spread through the text without regard to the levels of meaning (literal or figurative), or to the narrative's rhetorical structure, which is considerably deformed. The intertextual discourse is then strung on the ruins of the narrative. But at no point in the 'automatic' writing of the surrealists does intertextuality threaten the integrity of language. The words and the syntax remain untouched, guaranteeing readability.

4. Intertextuality and the disintegration of narrative

Intertextuality pushed to its most extreme consequences results in the disintegration not only of the narrative but also of the discourse. The narrative disappears, syntax explodes, the signifier itself begins to show cracks, when the assembling of texts is no longer guided by a desire to save at any cost a monologic meaning and an aesthetic unity. This is what happens in certain ultimate texts of the twentieth-century avant-garde from *Finnegans Wake* to William Burroughs' 'cut-ups'. Joyce's procedure is to create polysemic signifiers (portmanteau words), to multiply inter-discourse allusions, to remodel syntactic categories at will, keeping scattered narrative signals here and there. Burroughs chooses the procedure of intertextual *montages* which undermine the discourse, and even the word, and subject his syntax to the most aleatory of combinations. The reshaping of the signifier is no longer a painstaking task for the literary craftsman, but the product of destructive randomness. Burroughs has summarily described the techniques of the cut-up in *The Invisible Generation* and *The Electronic Revolution*.[12] The most elementary method consists in dividing the page into four sections and mixing them up. One can cut up tape-recorded fragments and shuffle them, or else 'mix' several recorded texts simultaneously. But the spirit of the cut-up can quite well be retained without the technology. The writer becomes his own electronic mixer, and Burroughs advocates a novel approach. He recommends that the writer transcribe an entire work by another author (and preferably with an old-fashioned goose quill). In the course of this dull and time-consuming task odd notes and reminiscences will begin to slip in, until the author finds himself, under the guiding influence of his experienced model, drifting off into narratives entirely his own.[13] Thus literature and stream of consciousness can be fused, with the initial text serving as an exploratory substratum. A brief cut-up by Burroughs, *Time* (1965), is a good example in that it seems to owe something to all these techniques. It is a mélange of anonymous background noise and intimate obsessions (memories of Tangiers, drugs, sexual images), in a chaotic montage of conversation overheard in the street ('Have you got the time?'), snatches of a song ('It's a long way to Tipperary . . .'), newspaper clippings, science-fiction parody ('I've just returned from a thousand-year journey through time, and I'm here to tell you what I've seen'), advertising slogans ('Cut out and keep these coupons . . .'), etc. Mostly *Time* respects the integrity of the word (except in this loop: PROCLAIM THE END OF THE PRESENT TENSE. SHOUT PRESENT. PRO THE END OF TIME). But it completely abolishes any syntactic coherence.

One cannot but wonder if, after all these acts of aggression by the text against itself, the discourse preserves any unity at all. One thing, at least, which makes it a discourse is the substance of the expression: the linearity of the signifier and the enclosed space of the page. We are disconcerted by the dynamism of a discourse consisting of anarchically mixed texts. To be sure, the narrative signals are so fragmentary that their structuring role may be considered to be non-existent. But the reader immediately realizes that he is confronted with a 'discourse fluid' infinitely more aleatory than a narrative. The words combine *malgré tout*, and even if their syntax is uncertain, the

49

reader does not stumble over them, as his reading follows its tyrannical linear path. Here and there, moreover, vague isotopies are constituted, due to the fact that the montage uses elements that are redundant, or connected, across the ellipses. This occasionally tempts us to wonder if it is not simply the materiality of the page which creates the text, if the written text is not condemned to textuality.

III

The intertextual process

Intertextual transplanting does not only create survival problems for the receiving organism. It is also a positive activity, and we must avoid viewing it as no more than a factor for disorganizing discourse – an antirhetoric bomb with effects that are more or less disastrous according to the boldness of the user. Intertextuality raises other questions: how does a text assimilate preexisting utterances? What is the relation of assimilated utterances to their initial state? Unless this process is elucidated, we are essentially left with a conception of intertextuality as the transcendent invasion by one text of another. Contemporary critical discourse, with quite diverse languages and underlying ideologies, seems to agree in viewing these text-to-text relations as transformational. Reference to generative grammar is quite general. Thus Kristeva, treating the very special corpus of the *Poésies* of Lautréamont, has proposed a classification into transformations involving oppositions with negative effect (negation, and its variants as these are admitted in language use) and transformations involving oppositions with indefinite effect (processes involving movement and condensation, such as lexical transformations, the use of homonyms, contrastive comparison, omission, segmentation of a presupposed utterance, etc.). Michel Arrivé,[14] following linguistic concepts even more closely, sees intertextual processing as using embedding, negation, passive, and deletion transformations, among others. But he hastens to add that intertextual transformations, unlike those postulated in generative grammar, always involve a modification of content. This notion of the intertextual process as a transformation seems to be needed as the basis for all reflection on the problem, but, dropping the linguistic metalanguage, it would be desirable to have an approach that is at once more naive and more concrete, which apprehends the text as the material object it is. One might thus propose that any utterance – in fact, any signifying system – involved in an intertextual process undergoes three kinds of processing whose goal is to 'normalize' it, to facilitate its insertion in a new textual whole.

1. Verbalization

The signifying substance of the text should be uniformly verbal or verbalized, even if it contains borrowings from a meaning system of the figurative type. How should this relationship be conceived between, for example, a pictorial signifying system and a verbal one, insofar as they can work together in an intertextual process, as in descriptions of a painting of the type Claude Simon favours in *La Bataille de Pharsale*? Clearly, we must consider what is common to both: their systematic character. One possibility would be to see an iconic relation between picture and text, following a traditional view in semiotics,[15] according to which the text does nothing but mimic the diagrammatic outline of the picture. In this case, the reference is still plastic, or at least spatial. One might alternatively, like J. L. Schefer,[16] adopt the opposite viewpoint: for him, the picture has no other referent than the text which expresses it. Accordingly, to describe the picture is to constitute it. The text does not duplicate it, it recovers the secret of its generation. The diagram is still a central notion. Schefer sees the picture as a double signifying system: the signifiers of the painting are themselves composed of a two-element figurative system ('figurant' and 'figuré'). As for the signified, it is only the 'diagram of the signifier'. In order to participate in an intertextual relationship with a verbal unit, the system of the picture must take the form of a verbalization of its diagram. But whichever point of view is chosen, what is clearly absent from the intertextual relation is the strictly figurative dimension; what remains is a common relational network.

Even when pictures are kept in the text, as part of the line itself, they acquire an ideographic character which brings them close to the verbal, turns them into mere word-substitutions, immediately translatable. Thus Simon, in *La Bataille de Pharsale*, replaces the word 'chemise' by a tiny drawing of a shirt that represents the object without disturbing the linear arrangement. The picture has the scale of the typography, and its soberness. It is poor not only visually, but also because it is inserted into a sentence, which robs it of all except its symbolic value, and includes it in a syntactic structure. We might also mention Döblin's novel *Berlin Alexanderplatz*: at the point where the hero enters Berlin, the chapter begins with drawings of emblems designating the public services of the city (the Department of Roads, the Fire Brigade, Transport, etc.). Here also the schematic nature of the pictures turns them into symbols, and this is made even clearer by the fact that beside each emblem is its 'translation' into words: thus, to the right of a small flag with a cross is written 'PUBLIC HEALTH', as if the author wanted to avoid having the representation become autonomous.

Verbalization thus appears to be a 'cutting down to size' of the borrowed signs. This is, first of all, true typographically, since when an utterance is taken over into a literary text the original type is never used. The process of

51

verbalization furthermore involves an effort to reduce all non-verbal foreign bodies that come into a text. In the case of the Simon and Döblin novels, it was sufficient to whittle down the signs a little, by incorporating them into a syntactic context and forcing them into the role of symbols. But if the text is intended to integrate a richer sort of representation, as in the description of a painting, direct assimilation is impossible. There is then an effort to find help for the verbalization, to couple the system of verbal signs with some system not reducible to it, for example a figurative system, which can serve as intermediary.

2. Linearization

Although intertextuality does invite the reader to a multiple reading (polysemous, paragrammatical), it is still the case that the establishing of intertextual discourse imposes on the text a linearity which on the contrary has all the rigidity of a monologue. On the reader's side, the meaning is not perceived synthetically *from the start* as would be the case with a picture or with a confluence of sounds heard simultaneously. The verbal signifier, because of its spatial extension, is accessible only gradually, even laboriously, building up the meaning step by step and cumulatively. This is what makes cut-ups an essentially literary technique: if the signifier remained acoustic, one could scramble several messages merely by superimposing them. But the cut-up, which is meant as a transcription, is confined to a unique and successive temporality, like writing in general. It is obvious, but worth emphasizing, that linearity plays an important role in making a composite text a new whole. The uniformity of the lines of a text abolishes all boundaries and separations. The insertion of material into a new text also represents a breaking up of the page or paragraph of the original text. In this way the process of transforming material from one text into another is continued. Only when this integration is most complete can an author afford the luxury of marking the borrowed text as different, as Simon does from time to time in *La Bataille de Pharsale*, in which he points up a quotation with italics.

3. Embedding

Intertextual harmonization, to be total, must not be realized solely on the formal level. It must unify form and content. To typographical coherence must be joined the elimination of combinatorial incompatibilities of texts which often have quite heterogeneous origins. Sometimes a borrowed fragment is linked to its new context by syntactic means, in a sentence whose grammaticality enhances its plausibility. Sometimes, with no special attention to the syntax, bridges are established on the basis of a certain semantic unity. Such *isotopie* is even more necessary for embedding when the transplanted texts are only fragments, often lacking an autonomous meaning in isolation (as opposed to the 'story within the story' studied by Genette).[17] In such a case, either intertextual processing will multiply the links introduced to integrate the borrowing on several levels at once, or else the intertextual fragments will profit from their ambiguity to project a range of combinatory possibilities towards the context. In either case the intertextual fragment tends to behave, not like a story within the story, but like a word of a poem in its relationship with its context, with everything that this implies concerning stylistic instability, unverifiability, incongruity. Even if it is possible to make a logical classification of embedding operations which are rather similar to those of the story within the story, it should be kept in mind that intertextuality demands *isotopies* which are much more restrictive and which create a montage which is more stylistic in nature than narrative. This montage can be based on three types of semantic relation.

Metonymic isotopy: a textual fragment is used, called on because it allows the narrative to be furthered, often with a first-hand detail. Thus, in *La Bataille de Pharsale*, the narrator as a child translates a Latin text under the watchful eye of his uncle (or father). A fragment of the text, with a line-by-line translation, is reproduced after the adult orders the child to write from dictation. Elsewhere, the same fragment (which, by a rather perverse refinement of the author is sometimes attributed to Caesar, sometimes to Livy) will have an analogical function, when it is juxtaposed with a description of an ancient mosaic.

Metaphoric isotopy: a textual fragment is brought into a context because of semantic analogy to it. Thus *La Bataille* presents successively, with no transition, a chaotic passage where the hero, betrayed by an ephemeral mistress, stands watch behind the door, and a passage borrowed from *A la recherche du temps perdu*:[18]

I was suffering like a scratch in the grey paint of the door the visible wood scratched also small ruffled splinters of a dingy yellow a ruffled line of dingy hairs coming down from the bushy chest dividing the belly in two rubbing the tips of her breasts hardened became rough at the same time that they bright pink not right-hand page *that new smile that she had given him that very evening and which now reversed mocked Swann and took on love for another with that bending of her head but under other lips.*

It is frequently the case that this kind of embedding takes on a metalinguistic hue, for these analogies are often the result of more or less conscious reflection by the author about his own work. They serve to clarify the meaning of a passage, to enrich it with the play of remembered associations, to indicate through another's voice a direction for reading to follow. In such cases it would almost be necessary to distinguish a sub-type of embeddings by *metalinguistic isotopy*, since any metalanguage establishes a certain kind of metaphoric relation with its object. Let us consider again *La Bataille de*

53

L. Jenny

Pharsale. How is a sequence of discourses such as those of pp. 118–19 to be understood: a description of someone falling from a horse during a battle (this may be about a painting by Caravaggio), an 'erotic scene', a quote from *L'Histoire de l'art* by Elie Faure: 'A painter of bacchanals also *massacre as well as love is a pretext for glorifying form, whose calm splendour is visible only to those who have grasped the indifference of Nature before massacre and love.*' While the quotation is clearly related to the two immediately preceding sequences, it also looks like a wider commentary on the novel, whose two leitmotivs are precisely an erotic scene and battle scenes – an evaluation in plastic terms by the author of his own work, using the words of another writer. It goes without saying that the two principles of embedding given above can be combined: for that to be the case in the present example, for instance, it would suffice for the introduction of the text by Faure to be narratively motivated.

Non-isotopic montage: a textual fragment is inserted in a context with no *a priori* semantic relation to it. One would look in vain for such a case in *La Bataille de Pharsale*, where, despite appearances, all the elements turn out to be strongly motivated and grouped around a few limited semantic axes. Briefly, in this construction, the textual materials undergo a sort of mutual attraction which confers an increasing coherence upon the semantic complex that is constituted by the novel. To avoid this, constant vigilance is needed, a permanent and obstinate effort at deconstruction. This is the role of montage using the cut-up technique, for example. Furthermore, it should be noted that *non-isotopie* of the montage does not automatically produce *non-isotopie* of the discourse. The linear contiguity of the text creates chance syntactic combinations, a prelude to semantic coherence. Even in the absence of such syntactic connections, unofficial meaning relations are spontaneously produced: no longer by the interaction of lexemes, but by that of the semes which compose them, indefinitely multiplying the semantic possibilities – as is true in any event for every literary text *in spite of* its *isotopie*.[19]

4. The figures of intertextuality

The three operations of intertextual processing which we have been considering bear primarily on the transformation of contextual conditioning factors. But intertextual fragments are also subject to immanent modifications. The transformations described by Kristeva for Lautréamont's *Poésies* are an example, but a rather restrictive one for our purposes, for the corpus is composed exclusively of ideological utterances. To describe modifications of fictional fragments, the adoption of the linguistic transformations proposed by Arrivé is likely to be too vague and, on the whole, slightly irrelevant. On the other hand, the stock of rhetorical figures provides the analyst with a logical matrix diversified enough to allow precise classification of the types of alterations undergone by texts in the course of intertextual processing. It is not difficult to compile a list, which we do not claim to be exhaustive.

Paronomasia: an alteration of the original text which consists in retaining the sounds while modifying the spelling, so as to give the text a new meaning. An example is the ill-handling which a passage of *La Recherche* is subjected to in *La Bataille de Pharsale*:[20]

tous laids souvenir voluptueu kil emporté de chézelle lui permetté de sefer unidé dé zatitudezardante zoupâmé kel pouvé tavoir avek d'otr desortekil enarivé taregreté chak plésir kil gougoutait oh près d'aile, etc.

Simon vandalizes the text, transcribing it with a whimsical phonetic system, with a comical emphasis on the liaisons of the spoken language, inappropriate punning, and an intentionally exaggerated disfiguring of the prose of his illustrious predecessor. For paronomasia to become an intertextual figure, all that is necessary is that it be generalized. But it must be admitted that the case is rare, and even Queneau's *Poor lay Zanglay* from *Exercices de Style* does not meet this definition, since it does not transform a specific text but only 'correct' written French.

Ellipsis: the truncated repetition of a text or architext. Simon, in *La Bataille*, plays in this fashion with the text of Elie Faure. He uses twice a sentence taken from the chapter on German artists of the Renaissance: 'Tout pour l'artiste allemand est au même plan dans la nature' (for the German artist everything is on the same plane in the natural world), but in its first occurrence, Simon follows the sentence with a passage that in Faure's book comes only thirty-five lines later: 'le détail masque toujours l'ensemble leur univers n'est pas continu mais fait de fragments juxtaposés . . .' (the detail always masks the whole their universe is not continuous but made of juxtaposed fragments). The clever splice increases the plausibility of the text, whose source, in any case, is not given. There can also be ellipsis with respect to an expected topic, resulting in a feeling of frustration on the part of the reader who is waiting impatiently for the architext to be realized. This is utilized by Lautréamont when he introduces Maldoror: 'J'établirai dans quelques lignes comment Maldoror fut bon pendant ses premières années, où il vécut heureux; c'est fait' (I will establish in a few lines how Maldoror was good during his early years, when he lived happily; done) (1, 3). Although he has presented his hero as an accursed, satanic creature, Lautréamont with splendid insolence skips over the obligatory subject of his past history (his life before the fall and the circumstances of the fall itself), which would fill several hundred pages of a traditional Gothic novel.

Amplification: the transformation of the original text by development of its semantic possibilities. This is the relation which connects the Ocean strophe of the *Chants* (1, 9) with Baudelaire's poem 'L'Homme et la mer'. Between the two texts, there is not only a reminiscence, as suggested by Kristeva, but a real intertextual relation. Lautréamont borrows the parallel between man and the sea which is the framework for Baudelaire's text. Furthermore, he takes over many themes from the poem, treating them as topoi to be amplified: the sea as the mirror of man, the bitterness of the ocean compared to that of the human spirit, the hidden riches of the waters, their tenebrous depths, etc. This borrowing is doubly ironic: Lautréamont redirects Baudelaire's parallel to make it a comparison witheringly unfavourable to humanity, and he also rewords it in an exaggerated rhetoric which discredits not only the text but also this redirecting of it. Prosaic and pseudo-scientific language undermine any poetic plausibility, as the topos balloons out of all proportion with gaseous irrelevancies:

> . . . Tu contemples ton âme
> Dans le déroulement infini de sa lame.
>
> Baudelaire (ll. 2,3)

Vieil océan, ta grandeur matérielle ne peut se comparer qu'à la mesure qu'on se fait de ce qu'il a fallu de puissance active pour engendrer la totalité de ta masse. On ne peut pas t'embrasser d'un coup d'oeil. Pour te contempler il faut que la vue tourne son télescope par un mouvement continu vers les quatre points de l'horizon, de même qu'un mathématicien, afin de résoudre une équation algébrique, est obligé d'examiner séparément les divers cas possible avant de trancher la difficulté. L'homme mange des substances nourrissantes, et fait d'autres efforts dignes d'un meilleur sort pour paraître gras. Qu'elle se gonfle tant qu'elle voudra, cette adorable grenouille. Sois tranquille, elle ne t'égalera pas en grosseur; je le suppose du moins. Je te salue, vieil Océan!

Lautréamont (1,9)

> (. . . You contemplate your soul
> In the infinite roll of its wave.)

(Old ocean, thy material size can only be compared with the estimation one makes of how much active energy was necessary to produce the totality of thy mass. One cannot embrace thee with a glance. To contemplate thee the sense of sight must turn its telescope in a continuous movement to the four points of the horizon, just as a mathematician, to solve an algebraic equation, must examine separately the various possible cases before resolving the difficulty. Man eats nourishing substances, and makes other efforts worthy of a better fate to appear fat. Let it swell as much as it wants, that adorable frog. Do not worry, it will not equal thee in girth; at least, I suppose so. Hail, old Ocean!)

Evidently amplification embroiders a text, introduces new topoi to fill the space, as is done here by the reference to the frog of Lafontaine's fable, and thus involves a non-negligible addition of meaning. Furthermore, the amplification is here coupled with semantic inversion: for the spiritual contemplation described by Baudelaire, Lautréamont substitutes a contemplation which is coarsely conceited and materialistic.

Hyperbole: the transformation of a text by superlativization of its descriptive terms. This figure is so widespread in the *Chants* that it almost takes on the value of a characteristic of the representational code. The strophe cited above seems to illustrate this formal flatulence.

Inversion: this figure affects textual elements that are so various in nature that it is worth detailed treatment. No doubt it is because of its antiphrastic value that it is particularly frequent in parodic intertextuality. Once again, the *Chants* offer numerous and varied examples.

Inversion of the situation of utterance: the content of the discourse remains stable, the addressee changes. Where Baudelaire speaks to Man ('Homme libre, toujours tu chériras la mer!' (Man, while free, you will always cherish the sea!)), Lautréamont addresses only the Ocean ('Je te salue, vieil Océan!'). In so doing, he evidently reverses the meaning of the parallel. One might similarly speak of inversion if it was the speaker of the utterance who changed.

Inversion of modifiers: the entities of the original text are retained but they are characterized antithetically. Lautréamont applies this process in consistently contradicting, in the *Chants*, certain passages of the Apocalypse,[21] for example the fall of Babylon (Revelation, 17–19), many elements of which can be found in the strophe concerning the Pact with Prostitution (*Chants*, 1,7). In Revelation, John, an apostle of God, is guided by an angel (a winged, holy being) who shows him a woman described as 'the great whore', sitting 'upon a scarlet coloured beast', 'arrayed in purple and scarlet colour, and decked with gold and precious stones and pearls'. In the *Chants*, Maldoror, a creature of Satan, is guided by a glow-worm (a grotesque, crawling version of the angel), while whoredom appears to him in the guise of a 'belle femme *nue*' (beautiful, naked woman), who comes to *lie down* at his feet. But these are not the only effects of the text-transforming mechanism here.

Inversion of the dramatic situation: the direction of action in the borrowed text is modified by negative or passive transformation. Let us continue with our reading of Revelation. The angel symbolically crushes Harlotry:

And a mighty angel took up a stone like a great millstone, and cast it into the sea, saying, Thus with violence shall that great city Babylon be thrown down, and shall be found no more at all. (Revelation, 18:21)

The punishment, while symbolic, is no less effective, as is shown by what follows:

Salvation, and glory, and honour, and power, unto the Lord our God: For true and righteous are his judgments: for he hath judged the great whore, which did corrupt the earth with her fornication, and hath avenged the blood of his servants at her hand. (Revelation, 19:1–2)

As for the glow-worm, he asks Maldoror to inflict the identical punishment

57

on the beautiful nude in question, but Maldoror unexpectedly reverses the roles:

I took a large stone . . . I climbed a mountain to the top: from there I crushed the glow-worm. Its head was driven into the ground to the height of a man, the stone bounced up to the height of six churches. It then fell into a lake . . .

In response to the frightened cries of Prostitution herself, Maldoror gives his own conception of charity, which is given in opposition to the Creator and refuses to recognize Him as just:

I prefer you to it (the glow-worm); because I feel pity for the unfortunate. It is not your fault if eternal justice created you.

Inversion of symbolic values: the symbols created by a text are borrowed with opposite meanings in the new context. Lautréamont does not hesitate to doctor the most familiar Christian symbols, in his rewriting of Revelation. While the serpent and the dragon are explicitly designated as creatures of the devil in the Bible (Revelation, 20), they are shamelessly used by Lautréamont, the first to represent the Creator himself (strophe v, 4), the second to symbolize hope in the great battle between it and Maldoror the Eagle.

Change in the level of meaning: a semantic configuration is taken over but at a new level of meaning. Thus, the famous vision of the man-eating god in the *Chants* (ii, 8) arises quite naturally out of a literal reading of the angel's invocation in Revelation, 19:17–18:

Come and gather yourselves together unto the supper of the great God; That ye may eat the flesh of kings, and the flesh of captains, and the flesh of mighty men, and the flesh of horses, and of them that sit on them, and the flesh of all men, both free and bond, both small and great.

All that Lautréamont has done is visualize the scene as carnally as possible, disregarding its meaning of spiritual communion. Of the generalized metaphor, he retains only the vehicle, dropping all connotations attached to the tenor. The banquet ceases to be an occasion for all to gather together, and becomes the solitary feast of an ogre.

It can thus be seen that the figures of intertextuality provide a vast territory for exploration whose limits cannot be fixed in advance. It is quite rare for a literary text to be borrowed and quoted as it is. In general, the new context seeks to subdue the borrowed text to its own requirements. Either this intention remains hidden, and then the intertextual reworking amounts to a 'paint job' whose effectiveness depends on how skilfully the borrowed text is adapted, or else the new context proclaims its critical rewriting, and gives a demonstration of how a text is reworked. In either case, the deformation is explained by the desire to avoid a merely tautological undertaking, and one in which, furthermore, there would be a risk that the presupposed text might reconstitute itself, set up its own boundaries, and by its presence even threaten to supplant the context.

IV

Intertextual ideologies

Intertextuality as cultural misappropriation

There are ideological effects which involve the functioning of texts. Analysis of intertextual processing shows rather clearly that pure repetition does not exist, or, in other words, that this processing has a critical function with respect to form. This is true whether there is an explicitly critical intention – as in Menippean satire – or not. If intertextual avant-gardism is often erudite, that is because it is aware both of the object on which it operates and the cultural memories it is haunted by. Its role is to re-utter definitively discourse whose presence has become tyrannical, tinselly discourse, fossilized discourse. There is Petronius, mocking the new epic, Rabelais, shaking off the chains of medieval erudition, Lautréamont, inflicting needed 'corrections' upon romanticism, Joyce, battling with Irish literary traditions or the new journalese. The author repeats in order to encircle, to enclose within another discourse, thus rendered more powerful. He speaks in order to obliterate, to cancel. Or else, patiently, he gainsays in order to go beyond: as Lautréamont derides the great Soft Heads of his age in order to pass on to the assertive discourse of the *Poésies*. Since it is impossible to forget or neutralize the discourse, one might as well subvert its ideological poles; or reify it, make it the object of a metalanguage. Then the possibility of a new *parole* will open up, growing out of the cracks of the old discourse, rooted in them. In spite of themselves these old discourses will drive all the force they have gained as stereotypes into the *parole* which contradicts them, they will energize it. Intertextuality thus forces them to finance their own subversion.

Intertextuality as a reactivating of meaning

Intertextuality is thus a mechanism of perturbation. Its function is to prevent meaning from becoming lethargic – to avert the triumph of the cliché by a process of transformation. Cultural persistence indeed provides nourishment for all texts, but it also poses a constant threat of stagnation, if the text yields to automatism of association, does not resist the paralysing pressure of increasingly cumbersome stereotypes. We have seen how, in *La Bataille de Pharsale*, the jealousy of the hero quite naturally evoked *Un Amour de Swann*. But in this 'quite naturally' there is an inertia which, in the long run, would block any production of new meaning. Literary expression would be confined to the stutterings of a stock of commonplaces indefinitely repeated. This

59

explains the anger of the author expressed in his massacre of Proust's text. Far from being a trivial schoolboy prank, the paronomastic dislocation of this text gives a rather good idea of the significance of the intertextual process: to spotlight the clichés (the 'mythologies') which have become ossified in the sentence, to distance ourselves from their banalities, by overdoing them, and finally to free the signifier from the waste that encrusts it in order to launch it on a new career. Every intertextual citation is, thus, more or less marked by such paronomastic dislocation even if this 'paronomasia' in fact affects the meaning. The semantic relaunching takes place whenever the element is placed in a new context. When systematized, this technique can result in disarticulation of the system of syntactic and semantic combinations of a text and a mixing with other discourses. This is the work done by Butor on a famous page from Chateaubriand in *6,810,000 litres d'eau par seconde*. Trying out a variety of ways of cutting up the text, he tries to blend the words of Chateaubriand and the voices of his protagonists. One can thus explore the semantic potential of a text, bringing out both the key points of its structure and the openness of that structure, its potential infinity (Kristeva), which is also that of the infinite number of possible contexts.[22] In this limiting case, as in others which are less extreme, intertextuality is a way of spelling out the functioning of a text, a 'verifying' of reading through writing. It is a definitive rejection of the full stop which would close the meaning and freeze the form.[23]

Intertextuality as a mirror of subjects

We write 'subjects' in the plural because we understand here the subjects defined in linguistics: the subject of the discourse (*énonciation*), i.e., the speaker or writer, and the subject of the utterance (*énoncé*). They share a common lot, in that contemporary literary consciousness conceives of them both as saturated with fictions. We no longer believe in the subject who perceived himself as the matter of his book, now it is conversely felt to be books which are the matter of the subject, the subject who writes, or is written. Hence there can be no odyssey now without a 'journey through the written word'. Literary truth, like historical truth, can be constituted only in a multiplicity of texts and writings – in intertextuality. This is, in fact, the meaning of Simon's novel: in spite of the erratic quest of the hero through recollections of his translated 'versions' from the Latin and a few books by historians, the *site* of *la bataille* remains undiscoverable. The point is precisely that, in writing, the event cannot be situated; it eludes our grasp; all we can produce are 'versions'. All that can be said is that something is constituted through this cluster of forms, and that thing is the text itself. In a more playful register, Queneau demonstrates the same thing in his *Exercices de style*: what strikes us is not so much the profusion of rhetorical forms that can be used to narrate an anecdote, but something we progressively discover – that the book is merely a system of variants without our ever being able to rely on an 'authentic' version of the anecdote being related. To constitute an event is to juxtapose all possible forms, to work out an exhaustive catalogue. Once the secret of the adequacy to a subject of its language has been lost, only intertextuality will allow the complex truth to be found. But it must be recognized that this use of intertextuality remains profoundly 'intransitive'; discourse, forced to re-state ceaselessly in order to define itself, is obsessed by the process of meaningfulness, or by the constitution of its subject, which amounts to the same thing. Form becomes both erudite and narcissistic. It untiringly remains its own object, on the pretext that its action engenders all the rest.

Beyond the mirror?

Alongside the intertextual productions of literary authors, William Burroughs occupies a place all his own, in that his faith in the transitivity of discourse knows no bounds. He shows scant interest in the language functions which have so far been exploited in literature: representation or exploration of the subject in and through his own statements. For Burroughs, it is necessary to get outside of this language, constructing one in which certain falsifications inherent to all the languages existing in the Occident cannot be formulated. If the subject is really this mummified creature who lives by the social codes which hem in his everyday existence, what better tool than intertextuality to break the mould of old discourses? Intertextuality is no longer just refurbished borrowings, or citations from the Great Books, it is a strategy for scrambling the message, and extends beyond books to all of social discourse. It involves hastily knocking together 'techniques' of destruction to counter the omnipresence of transmitters bombarding us with their lifeless discourse (the mass media, advertising, etc.). It is the codes that we must derange, not the users, and something will give, will be liberated: the words behind the words, our personal obsessions. Another *parole* is born which escapes the totalitarianism of the media but retains their power, and turns against its former masters.

Obsessive intertextuality is not always so radical a project – far from it. But with the help of this extreme example it can be surmised that intertextuality is never anodyne. Whatever its avowed ideological underpinnings, the intertextual use of discourses always has a critical, playful, and exploratory function. This makes it the most fitting instrument of expression in times of cultural breakdown and renaissance.

Notes

1. *The Anxiety of Influence* (Oxford, University Press, 1973).

L. Jenny

2. Marshall McLuhan, *Du cliché à l'archétype* (Paris, Mame, 1973), p. 195; *From Cliché to Archetype* (Viking Press, 1970), p. 189.
3. J. Tynianov, *Théorie de la litérature* (Paris, Seuil, 1965), p. 124.
4. J. Kristeva, *La Révolution du langage poétique* (Paris, Seuil, 1974), p. 60.
5. Y. Lotman, *Structure du texte artistique* (Paris, Gallimard, 1973), p. 47.
6. S. Freud, *The Interpretation of Dreams* (Harmondsworth, Penguin, 1976), p. 404.
7. Ibid., p. 643.
8. C. Lévi-Strauss, *La Pensée sauvage* (Paris, Plon, 1962), p. 31.
9. J. Starobinski, *Les Mots sous les mots* (Paris, Gallimard, 1971), p. 50.
10. Rabelais, *Oeuvres* (Paris, Garnier, 1962), Introduction, p. xvi.
11. L. Jenny, 'La Surréalité et ses signes narratifs', *Poétique* 16 (1973).
12. W. Burroughs. *Le Génération invisible; La Révolution électronique* (Paris, Champ Libre, 1974) [French translation of English original].
13. Ibid. p. 84 in French edn.
14. M. Arrivé, 'Pour une théorie des textes poly-isotopiques', *Langages* 31 (Sept. 1973).
15. Cf. the synthesis of Browne in 'Typologie des signes littéraires', *Poétique* 7 (1971).
16. J. L. Schefer, *Scénographie d'un tableau* (Paris, Seuil, 1969).
17. G. Genette, *Figures III* (Paris, Seuil, 1972), p. 242.
18. C. Simon, *La Bataille de Pharsale* (Paris, Editions de Minuit), 1969, p. 168.
19. Cf. J. Kristeva, *Sémiotike, recherches pour une sémanalyse* (Paris, Seuil, 1969), p. 258: 'Poetic meaning, far from being fixable in immutable units, is considered here as being the result of (a) a grammatical combination of lexical *units*, considered as sememes (word combinations); (b) a complex and multivocal interaction between the semes of these lexemes and the numerous effects of meaning which these lexemes produce when they are reinserted in intertextual space (re-placed in different possible contexts).'
20. Op. cit., p. 178.
21. Cf. P. Sellier, 'Lautréamont et la Bible', *Revue d'histoire littéraire de la France* (May–June, 1974). Sellier notes these borrowings without undertaking any systematic analysis.
22. Cf. F. Van Rossum 'Aventures de la citation chez Butor', in *Colloque Butor* (Paris, Union Générale d'Editions '10/18').
23. 'Intertextual activity' ('pratique intertextuelle') takes on a wider sense for contemporary avant-gardists who attempt to construct a more total theory of the text, embracing its relations with the subject, the unconscious, ideology. *Transposition*, in the sense of Kristeva (*La Révolution du langage poétique*, p. 60) makes a fusion conceivable between heterogeneous systems. H. Meschonnic shares this desire to solve the problem of the relations between 'a language as system', 'an unconscious as system', and 'an ideology as system'. He even sees this as 'the fundamental epistemological problem of poetics' (*Pour la poétique II*, p. 117). What we have called 'intertextual processing', but which would now have a quite different meaning, would be part of what Meschonnic calls 'le vivre', with all the vagueness attaching to that notion: 'the *vivre* is twofold: work in ideology and the social, work in the *je* – both inseparable. (1) It is in the impulse considered as a producer of a language, the language linked by a structural connection with the libido. Thus the *text* is that which tends towards linguistic reification of what psychoanalysts call 'the partial object' . . . (2) It is the transformer of ideology in and by a dialecticalization of the opposition individual/society, personal style/impersonal style in the signifiers as much as in the signs . . .' (ibid., pp. 66–7). As for Kristeva,

she identifies completely subject and process of signification (op. cit., p. 188). Resolving the problem of the relations between a text and the semiotic processes which are deployed within it then becomes the problem of explaining how the 'subject', or its absence, is constituted. What Kristeva designates as the 'géno-texte' becomes the theoretical locus of a sort of fusion between heterogeneous semiotic processes – the occasion for their articulation and for their passage to symbolic status. This operation is described as 'a *process* which tends to articulate, in ephemeral and non-signifying structures (a) impulsional dyads; (b) the corporal and ecological continuum; (c) the social organism and family structures which reflect constraints of the mode of production; (d) the moulds of discourse which give rise to discourse 'genres' (according to the history of literature), to 'psychic structures' (according to psychiatry and psychoanalysis), or to different distributions of the protagonists of discourse (according to the linguistics of discourse in the sense of Jakobson)' (op. cit., p. 83). The way so heterogeneous a group of semiotic phenomena are to be interrelated remains unclear for us, but we did not want to fail to indicate what the notion of intertextuality covers and what is being aimed at by the critical avant-garde who originally introduced the term.

Part III

5. A theory of the figure

JEAN COHEN

In a work that was considered in its time as authoritative, the philosopher Charles Serrus stated: 'There is no justification for assuming that logic parallels grammar. The lawfulness of language is not the lawfulness of thought, and it is futile to establish any kind of correspondence between them.'[1]

Dogmatic pronouncements are dangerous. Since this one was uttered it has been repeatedly disproved, as the trench it dug between logic and linguistics has continued to be filled by an effort from both sides.

From the linguistic side first, where the decisive step was taken when the profound insight of the Port-Royal grammarians, distinguishing two levels of language, a manifest or surface level, and a deep or underlying level, was rediscovered. Transformational grammar attempted to reduce apparently diverse syntactic forms to a single deep structure; American componential analysis and French structural analysis applied the same reduction to meaning. While it might seem hopeless to undertake to relate logical systems and the superficial forms of discourse, the enterprise seems much more promising when it involves deep structure, especially taking into account recent developments in logic itself.

As is well known, there have been two main stages in the development of the relation of logic to language. The first was that of Aristotle in the *Analytics*, where the parallelism between logic and grammar is established *a priori* and, as it were, by definition, since logic is nothing but an analysis of the *logos*. The parallelism was destroyed in the second stage, when Boole and DeMorgan constituted logic as an artificial language, intended to compensate for the defects of natural language: ambiguity, inconsistency and redundancy. But as such, this new logic or linguistics, made entirely for mathematics and by mathematicians, turned its back on what has been called 'natural operational logic'. Governed only by the requirements of formalization and axiomatization, symbolic logic lost sight of what was the original goal of logic: to construct an ideal language which would be the norm for all coherent discourse. Thus implication, which is the key to our intellectual operations, is defined in truth-functional logic so that the false implies the true, which is unacceptable in the eyes of those for whom logic

64

remains 'art of thinking', a guide to the intellect in its search for truth. It is therefore natural that today, with the work of Piaget and his followers, and, more recently, of Robert Blanché, there has begun a kind of return to first principles, through the framing of a 'reflexive logic' which is aimed at making explicit the rules of the mind at work. Furthermore, between these operational rules on the one hand, and linguistic deep structures on the other, a certain degree of isomorphism is beginning to appear.[2] Already, from a semantic point of view, which is all we are concerned with here, a remarkable convergence is to be seen between independent research conducted by the logician Blanché and the linguist Greimas, centring on the same hexadic organization of what the former calls 'intellectual structure' and the latter the 'elementary structure of signification'.[3] This convergence is due to a double movement, towards logic on the part of semantics and towards semantics on the part of logic, whereby both disciplines approach a virtual point at which logic will be the form of content and semantics the content of form for a single reality which is the intellect in action: the intellect being itself the final stage of that long process of equilibration described by Piaget which takes human thought from its intellectual infancy to maturity.

In consequence, the notion of a linguistic norm, so controversial at present, can be put on a solid basis. The norm is no longer to be based on usage, which is infinitely variable at the level of *parole*. It is to be based on a limited and invariant set of operational rules. It then follows that the notion of a deviation as a systematic transgression of the norm, which I have claimed to be the distinguishing feature of poetic language, itself takes on a logical cast. Linguistic deviation and logical deviation tend to merge, and it then becomes theoretically possible to construct a logical model of the figures of poetic language, an algorithm which will be able, perhaps, with further development, to serve as the basis for a calculus of figures.

The present analysis offers a preliminary attempt to realize this possibility. As a first stage, it will obviously have to remain elementary and oversimplified, but that itself should encourage further refinement of the analysis. It will indeed be the case that all the figures examined here are on the semantic level, but this level is the most relevant one in poetry. As for phonic or syntactic figures, rhyme, inversion, etc., it is not impossible that they will be able to be integrated into a more comprehensive model of logic that is also 'reflexive', and which would reflect not only the formation but also the communication of thought.

The basic logical principle, the norm which governs both language and metalanguage, is the principle of contradiction, that prohibits the conjoining of a proposition and its negation: $P \cdot \bar{P}$.[4]

J. Cohen

If we give the proposition its canonical linguistic form, subject–copula–attribute ('S is P'), the principle then forbids the assertion of a molecular proposition formed from two coordinated 'homonymous' atomic propositions, one affirmative, the other negative: 'S is P and S is not P'.

We are reminded of the problems that are posed with respect to this principle by the theories of Lévy-Bruhl concerning 'primitive' thinking, a thought which is 'prelogical' because it is governed by a law of participation not containing the notion of contradiction. In fact, the Bororo who asserts that 'the Bororos are araras' (parrots) would not admit that they are not araras. Thus he, too, is sensitive to contradiction. However, as Piaget remarks: 'For the actual thinking done by a real subject, the difficulties start when he wonders if he has the right to affirm simultaneously both A and B, for logic never directly stipulates whether B implies or does not imply not-A. Can one, for example, speak of a mountain which is only 100 metres high, or is this a contradiction? Can one be at once both a communist and a patriot?'[5] Thus, there is actual contradiction only in relation to the definitions of the terms involved in the proposition, definitions in the broad sense where the contextual implications of these terms are included. The principle is thus at work in practice only in its linguistic applications. What I will try to demonstrate in the present analysis is that the set of semantic figures in rhetoric consists of violations of the basic principle, and that they differ from one another, with all the diversity of their syntactic forms and lexematic contents, only in the force or degree of such violations. This variation in degree will be introduced by a refinement of the notion of contradiction, through the workings of the relevant oppositions: neutrality versus polarity, assertion versus implication, qualitative versus quantitative.

Here there emerges a new and paradoxical notion: that of the 'degree of logicality', replacing the simplistic alternative of all or nothing by a scale of degrees of deviation with respect to the principle of non-contradiction. This notion, parallel to that of 'degrees of grammaticality' proposed by Chomsky, allows us to differentiate the figures according to the amount of their 'alogicality', without, it should be emphasized at this preliminary stage, making it possible to rank them all in a single linear order. At the highest degree we find those figures whose obviously paralogical character was recognized in classical rhetoric. At the lowest degree, we find figures whose abnormality is disguised by the weakness of their alogicality. This explains why Todorov was led to divide tropes into two classes: 'those which exhibit a linguistic anomaly and those which do not',[6] with the second group including such figures as comparison, gradation, and antithesis.

A mistake is not really corrected unless one can explain how, while false, it could have been thought true. Distinguishing different degrees of alogicality will allow us to do this, by showing that while gradation and antithesis are in fact abnormal they are so to a sufficiently weak degree to appear innocent to an analysis that is not fine enough.[7]

There are, in language, two kinds of negation: grammatical negation, the only kind recognized by the logician, and lexical negation. If we restrict ourselves to the surface forms, 'that is improbable' is as much an affirmative proposition as 'that is probable'. But in this example the negation is manifested by a prefix, which is not the case with the opposition between the words 'true' and 'false', although they are in the same relation of contradiction, since 'false' is defined by the dictionary as 'that which is not true'. This is equally the case with all binary paradigms, in which each term can be taken to be simply the negation of the other: 'beautiful/ugly', 'good/bad', etc.

But there ceases to be equivalence between these two types of negation when we have ternary paradigms such as 'prior/simultaneous/posterior', 'black/grey/white', or 'large/medium/small'. In this case, the grammatical negation 'X is not large' is equivalent to the disjunction 'X is small or medium'. We recall also that classical logic had already distinguished two degrees of negation, according to whether the negative element was before or after the quantifier: *omnis non* and *non omnis*. The first is stronger than the second because the first universally negates the predicate while the second denies only its universality. We thus have two degrees of negation and, concomitantly, two degrees of contradiction. Thus 'small' is the strong negation of 'large' while 'medium' is the weak negation of the two other terms. 'Small' and 'large' are the two extreme or contrary terms, which we will call 'polar' terms, while 'medium' will be called the 'neutral' (*ne-uter*) term. It should be emphasized that, while the neutral term is often lacking in our lexical paradigms, the grammatical double negation 'neither . . . nor' always provides a way to express it. By negating this term, we obtain the disjunctive term (AvZ) called a 'complex' term, and this gives us Blanché's hexagon (where A and Z represent the polar terms, N the neutral term, and T the complex term) which can be constructed as follows:

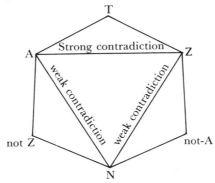

J. Cohen

From this model, which represents the weak and strong forms of contradiction, it will be seen that it is possible to derive and formalize the logical structure of a number of important rhetorical figures. They will turn out to be composed of the conjunction of two of these terms, which, by definition, allow only disjunctions.

Let us begin with pure contradiction: S is $A \cdot \bar{A}$. In this form, the figure was not catalogued in classical rhetoric, and it is hardly attested in classical poetry, at least not to my knowledge. We can however cite as an example the usual exordium of Majorcan folktales: 'This was and was not' (Aixo era y no era) – and it would doubtless not be difficult to find other examples in modern poetry.

Contradiction $(A \cdot \bar{A})$ is in a relation of inclusion with the two negations: strong $(A \cdot Z)$ and weak $(A \cdot N)$. We can thus, a priori, deduce the existence of two figures represented by these two formulas.

The first figure, the high degree of contradiction, conjoining the polar terms A and Z, is the logical formula for a figure well known to rhetoricians and largely attested in the poetry of all periods: oxymoron, a famous example of which is 'l'obscure clarté' of Corneille. Morier defines it as 'a sort of antithesis in which two contradictory words are joined, one of which seems logically to exclude the other'.[8] Under the label of 'paradoxisme' Fontanier gives it a similar definition: 'an artifice of language by which ideas or words which are ordinarily opposed and contradictory are brought together and combined'.[9] The term 'oxymoron' is, however, preferable, being derived from two Greek words, oxus and moros, 'pointed' and 'blunt', so that it is itself a realization of the figure, and thus provides an example of a motivated sign which we can mention in passing, as we begin to look for a more rigorous definition than those just cited.

Note to begin with that both authors use the term 'contradictory', although 'contrary' is more appropriate. It is true that the standard example from Corneille involves a binary paradigm (light/dark) in which the notions of contradiction and contrariety are equivalent, but this is not the case with Nerval's double oxymoron 'La nuit sera noire et blanche' (the night will be black and white), where, with a ternary opposition, only contrariety is relevant. In addition, the words 'joined' and 'brought together and combined' used in these definitions are both confused and inadequate. We have seen that it is logical conjunction that produces oxymoron, while, as we will see below, proximity produces antithesis.

The formula $A \cdot Z$ constitutes the logical deep structure of oxymoron, whose syntactic and lexical realizations may vary indefinitely. Nevertheless, it is possible to connect logic and syntax by refining the analysis. If we compare the following two expressions:

(a) 'Cette obscure clarté qui tombe des étoiles' (Corneille: this dark brightness which falls from the stars)

68

(b) 'Your eyes . . . are brighter than the day, blacker than the night' (Pushkin)

we observe that the contradiction is stronger in *a*, since in *b* it affects only the predicate, while in *a* it involves the subject itself. If we wanted to refine still further, we could also distinguish subtypes of figures according to the kind of coordination involved. It seems in fact to be the case that the use of adversative conjunctions in 'Je suis comme le roi d'un pays pluvieux, riche mais impuissant, jeune et pourtant très vieux' (I am like the king of a rain-soaked land, rich but powerless, young and yet very old), weakens the contradiction by making it explicit. Note furthermore that the same logic-syntactic formula occurs in 'l'obscure clarté' and in *el silencio sonoroso de los rios* (the sonorous silence of the rivers) of Juan de la Cruz.

The content of the two expressions is different, one using visual imagery, the other acoustic, and in a sense they are even converses, since the positive and negative terms are distributed in opposite ways between noun and adjective. Their structural identity remains, however, and this identity of two expressions of authors differing in language and period proves in and of itself that the figure exists as a formal possibility hidden behind its linguistic manifestations.

This abstract 'form' must not be confused with its usual realizations or figures in common use ('figures d'usage') where certain creative manipulations of structure have been transformed into stereotyped expressions. Thus, looking ahead, examples of such realizations would be:

oxymoron: 'aigre-doux' (bitter-sweet)

antithesis: 'mi-figue, mi-raisin' (i.e. half one thing and half another, literally 'half fig, half grape')

hyperbole: as strong as a bull

litotes: not bad!

Speaking of such 'figures d'usage' Dumarsais said that more are created 'in one day at the market at les Halles than are made in many days of academic meetings'. As for the creative figures ('figures d'invention'), on the other hand, while their formal models are in a sense predetermined in the deep structure of language, their linguistic realizations, with the particular content they possess, are created by the poet, who thus has a sort of copyright in them, and only this can preserve their uniqueness and hence their poetic efficacity.

Let us turn now to weak contradiction $(A \cdot N)$. Although the notion of a half-contradiction may at first seem paradoxical, clearly it is akin to familiar beliefs of common sense. If one speaker states that 'S' is white and another that 'S' is grey, it is clear that their assertions will appear less contradictory than if they had stated respectively that 'S' is white and that 'S' is black. Likewise, in politics, if one accepts the relevance of the bipolar axis left/right, one will conclude that the centre is less opposed to either of these two terms than they are opposed to each other. Instead of this, one might admit that the two terms are alike in their extremism. In that case, one would be adopting the ethical conception of Aristotle, whose originality is precisely this reversal of viewpoint, which takes the 'mean' as such as the point of maximum difference within the paradigm. This is a deep insight, and it can be transposed into aesthetic terms, as we will show. But first we must return from politics to poetics, and point out that although the weak form of contradiction is much rarer than oxymoron, examples can still be found: 'les crépuscules blancs' of Mallarmé (white twilights, as opposed to 'nuits blanches', white, or sleepless nights), or 'la lumière blafarde' of Baudelaire (wan light), as opposed to 'la lumière noire', the archetype of which 'obscure clarté' (dark light), 'le soleil noir' (the black sun), 'pâle comme la nuit' (pale as the night) (Nerval) are variants, and which is found as such in the last line of *Ténèbres* by Baudelaire:

> Par instants brille, s'allonge et s'étale
> Un spectre fait de grâce et de splendeur.
> A sa rêveuse allure orientale,
>
> Quand il atteint sa totale grandeur,
> Je reconnais ma belle visiteuse:
> C'est elle! noire et pourtant lumineuse.
>
> (At times shines, stretches, spreads,
> A spectre all of grace and splendour.
> From her dreamy oriental air,
>
> When she attains her full dimensions
> I recognize my lovely visitor:
> It is her! black and yet luminous.)

But the most frequent figure in modern poetry is that which, in *Structure du langage poétique*,[10] I called 'predicative irrelevance'. To account for it, we must consider a second variable from our logical model, that representing the difference in the way the anomaly is realized, according to whether it is part of what is 'posed' by the utterance or of what is 'presupposed'.

For instance, in Mallarmé's *Le Ciel est mort* (The sky/heaven is dead), there is clearly an anomaly, but at first glance it does not seem at all to involve contradiction. Death is the negation of life, not of the sky or heaven. This is why I have stated that it is up to our linguistic sense to perceive the distinction. But in fact it is possible to appeal here to the distinction introduced by Greimas between 'nuclear semes' and 'contextual semes' or classemes.[11] Each lexeme can be analysed into semes, which it presents when it occurs in discourse. But there also exists a system of syntagmatic compatibilities and incompatibilities that functions when the lexeme is introduced. Thus 'dead' requires an 'animate' subject, while 'sky' implies the attribute 'inanimate', the opposition animate/inanimate functioning as a sort of seme larger than the lexeme, since it applies to the whole syntagm. Thus 'mort' and 'ciel' can be stated to be contradictory not because of what they present but because of what they presuppose. Symbolizing presupposition with an arrow, the figure 'irrelevance' can then be represented as follows, with the sentence, as before, reduced to canonical form:

$$S \text{ is } P \atop {\downarrow \quad \downarrow} \atop {A \quad \bar{A}} \quad \text{(or, simplifying, } S \rightarrow A \cdot \text{not } A\text{)}$$

This recalls the first figure, except that this time the incompatibility is somewhat oblique or marginal, so that the anomaly is weakened, and located one degree lower in the scale of logicality.

However, within this figure of oblique contradiction itself we can distinguish two degrees, according to the nature of the irrelevant seme as qualitative or quantitative. Thus we must use a new kind of structure, which can be called 'gradated structure', and distinguish it from the oppositional structure which has figured in our analysis so far.

Most of our adjectives, and the abstract nouns related to them, have as their function the expression of qualities. That is why predication and qualification are often treated as the same thing in grammars, the essential function of all propositions being to attribute a quality to a subject.

Qualities are usually realized lexically as binary oppositions consisting of the extreme terms, which are contraries in the strong sense, and we know that dictionaries habitually mention, for each of these terms, its 'antonym', or contrary term. But within this maximal opposition there is room for more nuanced qualification, and our introduction of the neutral term has already refined the possibilities for predication. However, the neutral term can be interpreted either as a median or tempered qualification or as the absence of any qualification at all. This is why it is often lacking in the lexicon, silence functioning as a neutral term, since saying of someone that he is neither good nor bad is equivalent to saying nothing about him at all from the point of view of ethics.

Now most qualities do not vary according to the principle of all or nothing, but rather admit a whole series of intermediaries between the extremes. Thus, between 'hot' and 'cold', 'temperate' can be inserted as a neutral term; but the operation can be repeated: between 'temperate' and 'cold', 'cool' can be inserted, and between 'temperate' and 'hot', 'warm'; and this can be continued down to the mathematical temperature scale. Furthermore, the polar terms themselves can be exceeded by terms more extreme, such as 'torrid' and 'icy', just as the political paradigm has acquired 'extreme left' and 'extreme right' as supplements to the traditional terms. We know also that everyday language tends to overuse these over-extreme terms, and recent research has shown that the choice of these terms as contraries of a given polar term is characteristic of schizophrenia.[12] The use of such terms is sometimes called 'hyperbole', but this is a mistake when the term is being appropriately applied. An object or substance may really be 'torrid' or 'icy', and hyperbole as a figure exists only if the extreme term does not apply to the subject it qualifies. Thus, in the example given by Dumarsais: 'He went faster than the wind', there is hyperbole because the speed of a man's natural movement is much less than that of the wind. But there would be no hyperbole if the expression was applied to an aeroplane, for instance. In the sentence in question, the real subject, 'the movement of the man', implies a certain speed which is incompatible with that of the wind, but this incompatibility operates between different degrees of the same quality. We can represent this as follows, with A being the speed of the man, and A+ a higher speed:

$$
\begin{array}{ccc}
\text{S} & \text{is} & \text{P} \\
\downarrow & & \downarrow \quad\quad (\text{or } S \rightarrow A \cdot A+) \\
\text{A} & & \text{A}+
\end{array}
$$

If we now represent by A− a speed inferior to A, the formula $A \cdot A-$ symbolizes the inverse figure, i.e., litotes.

This figure is particularly interesting in that it is not always symmetrical with hyperbole. The examples given by Dumarsais, in fact, are not to be represented with a minus instead of a plus, but with a grammatical negation instead of a lexical affirmation. Thus in 'Va, je ne te hais point' the negation 'do not hate' replaces the term 'love' which would be appropriate here. This can be represented as follows:

$$
\begin{array}{ccc}
\text{S} & \text{is} & \bar{\text{Z}} \\
\downarrow & & \downarrow \\
\text{A} & & \text{AvN}
\end{array}
$$

The incompatibility is between one of the presupposed propositions: A, and half of the other: N. 'Not to hate' = to love (A) or to be indifferent (N). Since the context indicates that love is involved, the contradiction holds only between the context (A) and part of the text (N). We thus have here a weaker degree of contradiction than that involved in hyperbole or in gradated litotes.

On the contrary, we move up in the scale of anomaly with irony or antiphrasis where the predicate is constructed with the polar term opposite to that required by the context. Thus we have:

$$
\begin{array}{ccc}
\text{S} & \text{is} & \text{P} \\
\downarrow & & \downarrow \\
\text{A} & & \text{Z}
\end{array}
$$

This is the same structure as that of oxymoron, except that a presupposition replaces an assertion, which weakens the anomaly.

With respect to irony, we note that Fontanier defines it as the act of saying 'the contrary of what one thinks'. Taken literally, this definition would class irony with the 'figures of thought', although Fontanier in fact lists it as a figure of language. In reality, reference to the thought of the speaker is always linguistically irrelevant, and the class of 'figures of thought' should be definitively eliminated, as Bally desired,[13] from the domain of rhetoric. Thus irony, as a figure, consists in saying the opposite not of what one thinks, but of what one says, either in the context, or in what Martinet calls the 'supersegmental' text, intonational or gestural. One can only tell that the utterance 'X is a genius' is ironic if the speaker expresses the opposite in some other way, for example with a smile, whose semiotic function here is to convey the negation of the textual assertion, thus indicating the structure: S is A· not A.

We can now take up 'gradation', defined as an 'order such that what follows always says a little more or a little less than what precedes' (Fontanier). For example: 'Va, cours, vole et nous venge' (Corneille: Go, run, fly and avenge us), which can be found almost identically in: 'Marchez, courez, volez, où l'honneur vous appelle' (Boileau: Walk, run, fly, where honour calls you), where the three verbs can be considered as three increasing degrees of speed. The coordination must still be interpreted. There are two possibilities: succession or simultaneity. The first is normal. 'Go, then run, then fly' is not at all illogical. On the other hand, with simultaneity, 'walk and at the same time run and fly' is an incompatibility of the quantitative type. Each reader must then choose between these two interpretations, and to my mind there is no doubt which answer is better, in this as for all occurrences of this structure to be found in literary texts. Of course normal gradation is very widespread: one example is a curve of economic growth. But in that case succession in time is involved. Abnormal gradation can only be found in poetry, because anomaly is the specific feature of its poetic use.

Let us turn now to the most complex and hence most interesting of the figures, because of the refinements in analysis it requires: antithesis. We shall discuss this figure in more detail and at greater length, but we will not embark on the philosophico-metaphysical discussions to which the problem of the union of contraries seems irresistibly to lead.

For the French reader, antithesis is connected with the name of Hugo, because of the intensive use he made of it in his work and also in his life, if we are to believe his last words: 'Always the combat between day and night.' But it can be found in all poets, even in Racine, whom Laharpe praised for his sobriety in that respect. It is commonly defined in rhetoric, as in the dictionary, as 'the bringing together of opposed terms', and Morier gives as an example this line from Gautier: 'Le ciel est noir, la terre est blanche.' (The sky is black, the earth is white). Here there is no contradiction, however weak, since the two contrasting predicates go with two different subjects, i.e.: S1 is A and S2 is Z.

Nevertheless, in the example cited by Dumarsais, there already appears a kind of surprise or shock, marking an anomaly: 'being reviled, we bless; being persecuted, we suffer it; being defamed, we intreat' (I Corinthians 4:12). This is clearer still in the example given by Fontanier: 'Quand je suis tout de feu, d'où vous vient cette glace.' (lit.: When I am all fire, whence comes to you this ice.) It is true that two different subjects are involved, Hippolytus and Aricia, but they are lovers, and reciprocity is, or should be, the rule. The psychological contradiction represented by this opposition within a loving couple is marked here by the utterance itself.

In reality, from a logico-semantic viewpoint, the only relevant one, antithesis is indeed a contradiction, albeit a weak one. To make this clearer, we must consider not the predicate but the copula, and subject it in turn to the three-term opposition model.

In logic only one copula is recognized: the verb *be*, by which the attribute is designated as predicate of the subject as a whole. One might say that the copula 'be' does not go into details. It takes the subject globally, as an indivisible whole. S is P or is not P, with no intermediate possibility. 'To be or not to be' really *is* the question, or at least it is within the binary opposition involving the verb 'to be' that forms that ancient dyad of the same and the other which split up philosophy at its dawning.

But in language there is, along with 'be', another copula, namely 'have'. In its most common current sense, 'have' designates the relation of possession, of property, but this sense is itself derived from a deeper one where to have is to be partially. 'The thing possessed', says Aristotle in the *Politics*, 'is like the part with respect to the whole.' 'Have' does indeed impose an analysis of the subject into parts, of which only one is affected by the predicate. To say that Joan has a beautiful face is to say that she is at least partially beautiful. No doubt, 'have' does not function syntactically as does 'be', but rather as a transitive verb which requires a noun phrase complement. The sentence is thus to be analysed as:

Joan has a face.
This face is beautiful.

where 'have' seems to designate only the relation of the whole to the part. But with this intermediate step, the proposition does indeed involve a partial predication. We can thus consider the verb 'have' as a weak copula, as opposed to *be*, the strong copula, and we will symbolize these by C and c:

$$S \text{ is } P = SCP$$
$$S \text{ has } P = ScP$$

It is this intermediate position which makes it so easy to pass from one copula to the other. Thus in French we say either 'avoir un rhume' or 'être enrhumé' for 'to have a cold', and what is expressed in French as 'avoir faim' is expressed in English as 'to be hungry'. Similarly, jumping from one copula to the other, the poet can go without a transition from antithesis to oxymoron, as Hugo does in *Contemplations*:

> Oui, mon malheur irréparable
> C'est de prendre aux deux éléments
> C'est d'avoir en moi, misérable,
> De la fange et du firmament,
> . . .
> D'être un ciel et un tombeau.

(Yes, my irreparable misfortune is to partake of both elements, is to have in me, miserable one, something of mud and something of the firmament . . . to be a sky (heaven) and a grave.)

This example corroborates the relatedness of two figures that are distinct only by the degree of the copula, the opposition 'good/bad' being attributed to the subject the first time by the use of 'avoir', the second time by the use of 'être'.

Distinguishing two copulas may help resolve the problem raised by Chomsky apropos of utterances like 'this flag is black and white', from which it cannot be inferred 'this flag is white', although from 'this man is tall and thin' we can infer 'this man is tall'.[14] In his discussion of this problem, Osvald Ducrot suggests three solutions: 'Is this homonymy, and are there two "ands" in French? Or do the two utterances have different grammatical constructions describable at the level of syntactic analysis? Or should one appeal to the fact that "white" and "blue" are colour adjectives, and thus admit that there is in French a category of colour adjectives.'[15] In fact, the problem seems better solved by distinguishing two copulas. If one cannot say of the black and white flag that it *is* black, this is because this sentence implies that the flag is entirely black while it is only partially black. The use of 'is' thus constitutes a figure here, a sort of catachresis for a weak copula which does not exist in English or French and which 'have' can replace in a construction of the type: this flag has a black part. The expression thus has the form of an oxymoron while in reality it is an antithesis, since it attributes two opposed predicates to two different parts of a single subject. Antithesis is to be represented by the formula:

$$S \text{ c } A \cdot Z$$

which makes it a weak form of oxymoron:

S C A·Z

Are we to say that a black and white flag implies no contradiction, of no matter what degree? The question is far-reaching. To answer it, we must make a digression to consider non-linguistic experience, and in this context to distinguish two points of view, the ontological and the phenomenological. From the ontological point of view, first of all, there is an opposition between additive or mechanical totalities, which are pseudo-unities, and organic wholes, which are true unities. The flag belongs to the first category, and that is why there is nothing abnormal about qualifying it in terms of an opposition. Going further, one might even say that a flag, as such, does not exist, if we accept, following Leibniz, that what makes something an *entity* is that it is *one* entity. Consider now the other end of the chain of being, the domain of true organic wholes, such as, for instance, a human being. It is hard to deny the abnormality we perceive in those living contradictions, whether comic or tragic in nature, such as, for example, a woman with the head of a goddess and the body of a monster, or a being with the soul of an angel in the body of a beast, like the 'beast' in the folktale of *Beauty and the Beast*, used by Cocteau with this same antithetical title, and transposed by Hugo into the character of Quasimodo. Let us now take the phenomeno-logical viewpoint, which is the only relevant one for linguistics, if Martinet is right in saying that 'to speak is to communicate experience'. The experience which is analysed in language and is expressed in ordinary discourse is that of the network of appearances, at once stable and collective, which we call *the world*, and on this level the opposition 'true unity/false unity' retires in favour of the phenomenological dualism 'strong form/weak form' discovered by Gestalt Theory.

The strong forms or 'good forms' are created by the convergence of different factors governing the organization of the perceptual field, the two principal ones being proximity and resemblance. Elements in the perceptual field which are relatively close and similar are organized into strong units. Conversely, when proximity and resemblance diminish, the form is frag-mented into distinct units. Consider the case of maximal proximity and minimal resemblance: this is the phenomenal equivalent of antithesis: a form which is at once one and many, half-contradictory, where the organizing factors are in conflict. This is the case with an antithetical pair, such as the tall fat man and the short thin man whose comic resources were so widely exploited in early films, and this is the case with Gautier's black sky and white earth.

It is true, as Morier remarks, that there is exaggeration in this case. No doubt the sky was really grey, and this line of verse contains a double hyperbole whose conjunction produces the antithesis. Pascal criticized such exaggeration as contrived, artificial, for the nature that discourse describes is rarely antithetical. Not that it ignores contraries – we have seen that every quality is organized as an antonymous pair – but, and this is the point, nature is careful to keep such contraries separate. It provides for transitions, in the spatial as well as the temporal order. Between youth and old age there is adulthood, between cold regions and hot regions there are temperate zones. Better yet, if we consider those units formed by the assembling of the relatively homogeneous units which we know as social groups, we see that not only is there a middle term between the extremes, but that, furthermore, in most cases it comprises the largest percentage of the population. This is the meaning of the Gaussian distribution, which tells us that nature, in general, tends to be 'centrist', to be neutral i.e. prosaic. For poetry is intensity, it is what language produces by polarizing the signified through elimination of the neutral term. Here we find the root of the antinomy which Kierkegaard established between ethics and aesthetics. Reason avoids extremities, poetry seeks them out. Poetry is a quest for intensity, and the different figures which we have analysed are all means which language makes available to achieve it.

In opposition to antithesis, we can consider as normal an utterance of the type Sc A·N which uses a weak copula to join a polar term and the neutral term. It is normal in that it expresses unity in diversity, which is the only type of unity we know by experience, all absolute unity being the fruit of abstraction. We have, thus, two normal forms of utterances, applicable to two different domains of the expressible – on the one hand the abstract and notional: S C A; on the other the concrete and empirical: Sc A·N. Belonging to the second type are utterances – which are not at all usual – such as 'a woman with a lovely face and an average body', or 'with a beautiful body and a common soul'. These are softened forms of contradiction, which approach the limit, if we want to establish gradations, of simple non-contradiction. The golden mediocrity which Aristotle considered a virtue is the anti-value to poetry, and this is why Hugo was right to base drama on antithesis, if by drama we are to understand the poeticity of narrative.

But the antithesis is only present at the origin of the drama, at the beginning of the narrative. At the end is the polar term all by itself, in its absoluteness. Drama is not the union of contraries but the elimination of contrariety, by the transformation or singling out of one of the antithetical terms. Thus, in *Beauty and the Beast*, the antinomy is resolved into a happy ending by a (magical) transformation of the negative term: because Beauty loves him anyway, the Beast becomes beautiful too. In *Notre-Dame de Paris* we find the opposite: the positive term is destroyed and the final image of two skeletons embracing symbolizes the attained unity in love of the couple,

77

J. Cohen

by the death of the beautiful body of one and the beautiful soul of the other.

We can now list all our formalizations of the figures examined here in the following table:

FORMULA	TYPE
S C A · not A	contradiction
S C A · Z	oxymoron
S c A · Z	antithesis
S → A · not A	irrelevance
S → A · Z	antiphrasis
S → A · A+	hyperbole
S → A · A−	litotes

These figures are only a small subset of the inventory of figures in classical rhetoric. However it is reasonable to think that many others, recorded under different names, are only variants of the above. We have shown here that 'gradation' is just a form of hyperbole. Quite a few other figures can be reduced to irrelevance. Paradoxically, this is in fact the case with a retort cited by Dumarsais as an example of a 'thought expressed without a figure' (p. 12). The sentence involved is the 'Qu'il mourût' (that he should die) spoken by the aged Horace. Fontanier objects that this is an ellipsis for 'J'aurais voulu qu'il mourût', but this is not sufficient. The utterance is an answer to the question: 'Que vouliez-vous qu'il fît contre trois' (what would you have wanted him to do against three), and this is where the irrelevance appears, for to *die* is not to *do* something. The two terms belong to two classemes that are in opposition – activity and passivity – and thus exhibit that contradiction by implication which defines irrelevance; the only difference between them is grammatical, and concerns the relation between the verb and its complement. A regularized form would be 'Qu'il se fît tuer' (that he get himself killed), an utterance whose content is essentially the same but whose form is different. It is at this formal semantic level, in this 'forme du sens', (form of meaning) to use Valéry's expression, that poeticity finds its relevance.

Dumarsais gives another example of an expression with no figure: 'In another tragedy by Corneille, Prusias says that on a certain occasion in question he wants to behave as a father, as a husband. "Do not be either one or the other", says Nicomède.

Prusias: And what should I be?
Nicomède: A king.

There is no figure here, and nevertheless there is much of the sublime in this single word' (ibid.).

Sublime, granted. But no figure? Was Dumarsais blind? How could he fail to see that the answer of Nicomède presupposes an incompatibility between

78

the word 'roi' (king) on the one hand, and 'mari' (husband) and 'père' (father) on the other, an incompatibility which, and this is the point, does not exist? What we have here is a sort of converse of contradiction which is still contradiction. Instead of combining disjunctive terms, this figure treats conjunctive terms as though they were disjunctive. As such, it constitutes an original figure, which would deserve its own name, but which remains, in its deep structure, faithful to the model of alogicality proposed here.

All the deviations examined here are formed from relations between terms of discourse. They constitute the class of utterance figures, a class which is far from exhausting the totality of actual or possible figures. We spoke earlier of a logic of communication which it will one day be necessary to construct, but which cannot be embarked upon here. I would like just to provide some indication of the richness of a domain of rhetoric which is still unexplored.

Let us consider the 'figure d'usage' which consists in saying 'Pierre, pour ne pas le nommer' (lit.: Pierre, to not name him). Here the contradiction is obvious: the speaker names the one whom he says he is not naming. But it operates on two different levels: on the one hand the object-language, 'Pierre', on the other hand the metalanguage 'pour ne pas le nommer', which points from the utterance to the act of uttering. An identical, although more subtle, mechanism accounts for an apparently innocent procedure: 'correction', defined as 'a figure by which one intentionally retracts what one has just said' (Fontanier, p. 367). An example from J. B. Rousseau: 'Ose applaudir, que dis-je? ose appuyer l'erreur' (dare to applaud, what am I saying? dare to support error).

If correction is not an anomaly in spoken discourse, it is one in written discourse. In the former case, terms which are substituted come at their normal place in the speech chain after the terms they replace; but in writing, on the contrary, the term which is corrected is normally absent or crossed out. There is still contradiction here between the speech act which affirms that one term is being substituted for another and the utterance which in fact presents both terms without any substitution.

The paradox with Fontanier is that he sometimes mentions a deviation, but sometimes leaves one unmentioned. He does not say that 'correction' is abnormal, but he explicitly and specifically discusses the anomaly of 'interrogation'. 'It must not be confused', he tells us, 'with real interrogation . . . where one seeks information or confirmation' (p. 368). The former is a figure, because the speaker asks a question whose answer he is supposed to know, and which in fact he asserts in asking the question. This is thus indeed a 'false interrogation', as Gérard Genette says in his preface to *Figures du discours*. But if that is so, then why not state and formalize the rule of communication which governs interrogative discourse? Let us call knowledge

J. Cohen

'K', the absence of knowledge 'not K', the emitter 'E', the receiver 'R'. The rule of interrogation is that the emitter does not know while the receiver knows. On the contrary, assertion presupposes that the emitter knows and that the receiver does not know. Thus we have:

$$\text{Assertion} \qquad : E(K) + R(\textit{not } K)$$
$$\text{Interrogation} \qquad : E(\textit{not } K) + R(K)$$

We can then calculate that there are two possible interrogative figures: the first, if 'E' is assumed to know, the second if 'E' is assumed not to know. Assertion, symmetrically, will give us two figures, of which the second, where the receiver is assumed to know, covers all figures involving redundancy: repetition, pleonasm, etc. But these are merely suggestions for a code of communication which has not yet been worked out.

Such a model itself presupposes that communication is in some sense functional, in that it allows the circulation of 'information', as defined by information theory. It is with respect to this kind of model that poetic communication is seen as deviant. Because it does not have the same function, and because every function implies a certain structure, poetry has the appearance of being unstructured only with respect to a given structure connected with a specific function. But from the point of view of the poetic function, poetry is no longer abnormal. It has its own norms, its own logic, so to speak, whose rules, if they exist, remain to be discovered. It is the task of a second, positive kind of poetics to recover the intelligibility which is lost to discourse.

This task was undertaken by classical rhetoric under the name of tropology. But it was based on an old and fundamental error concerning the nature of tropes. It was not realized that the dichotomy which was established between tropes and non-tropes was not homogeneous, because it rested on the distinction between the two opposing axes of language, the syntagmatic and the paradigmatic. I attempted, in the last chapter of my *Structure du langage poétique* to correct this error of vision, but I related my proposed correction to a dualist theory of the signified, which, in fact, is completely independent of it. Hence the study of tropology must be taken up again on its own behalf, in order to guarantee complete internal coherence to the theory of the figure proposed here. This is the task whose basic principles we are now going to try to outline.

The great French rhetorical tradition of the classic period, that illumined in particular by the names of Dumarsais and Fontanier, was centred on elocution. By *elocutio* was understood what Saussure later called 'parole', but nowadays tends to be called 'discours'. In fact it was under the title *Figures du*

80

discours that Fontanier hoped to see united one day his two great works *Le Manuel classique pour l'étude des tropes* (1821) and *Le Traité général des figures du discours autres que les tropes* (1827).[16]

This distinction – as fundamental as it was traditional – of the figures of rhetoric into 'tropes' and 'non-tropes' is what the present analysis would like to reconsider. Not that rhetoric was wrong to make the distinction. On the contrary, we will criticize it here for not having understood that what was involved was a distinction in nature. There was an error of perspective which has been carried down from the origins of the science of figures to our own day, and which is perhaps partly responsible for the eclipse of rhetoric for almost two centuries.

Many of the theoretical problems which have been raised are solved by preterition, i.e. simply by our ceasing to worry about them. But this does not at all mean that these problems have ceased to exist. We know that it took two thousand years for modern logicians to discover the depth and relevance of the problems of ancient logic. Rhetoric, similarly, in its effort to uncover the structures of literary discourse as a set of empty forms, started out on the route to formalism, as this is being explored by current research. Nor is rhetoric to blame if the sudden invasion of substantialism and historicism, that is, of the twofold priority accorded to content and linear causality, for two centuries closed the royal road which it had opened. But rhetoric is guilty, after the admirable analytic and taxonomic work it accomplished, of not having been able to discover the structure – by this I mean the internal organization – of what it called the figure. It is true that rhetoric did not have available the tools of linguistic analysis which we possess today. In particular, the distinction of the two axes of language, syntagmatic and paradigmatic, was unknown. That is why, no doubt, as we will attempt to show, it was not able to discern the place and the function of the trope within the rhetorical mechanism.

The figure is traditionally defined by rhetoric as a deviation with respect to usage. Dumarsais recalls that the beginning of his famous treatise *Des Tropes:* 'It is commonly said that figures are ways of speaking distant from those which are natural and ordinary; that they are certain turns of phrase and certain ways of expressing oneself which differ in some way from the common and simple manner of speaking' (p. 2). Among these 'manières de parler' there are some which involve meaning, and which are the tropes. All the rest, which do not concern meaning, will be called, for want of any other common feature beside this negative one, 'non-tropes'. Tropology is thus the strictly semantic part of the theory of figures, and, for Dumarsais, it is nothing other than a study of phenomena of polysemy, that is, of the types of relations which exist among the various signifieds of a given signifier. Here the doctrine is more or less constant and varies little from one author to another. The inventory of relations and corresponding figures is approximately as follows:

FIGURE	RELATION
Metaphor	= Resemblance
Metonymy	= Contiguity
Synecdoche	= Part-Whole
Irony	= Contrariety
Hyperbole	= More for Less
Litotes	= Less for More

We will not discuss here this traditional classification, though there is much that could be said about it. For instance, if metaphor is to be defined as a relation of resemblance between the two signifieds, then the most commonly cited examples are illegitimate. Thus the example of 'renard' (fox) for 'clever fellow' is questionable, for the relation is Part-Whole, cleverness being part of the comprehension of the term 'fox', one of the semes composing its meaning. This involves, then, a synecdoche – which we might distinguish as 'abstract', as opposed to concrete synecdoches ('sail' for 'boat') where the part is material – but not a metaphor, that term being reserved for cases like French 'queue', whose basic meaning 'tail' is extended to a line of people, for here there does exist a relation of partial identity, since tails and queues possess a common feature (linear extension) as well as differential features.

But this is secondary. What is fundamental is that there exists between the two signifieds in question a hierarchical opposition, expressed in traditional terminology as 'sens propre' (literal meaning) and 'sens figuré' (figurative meaning). For Dumarsais, in fact, this opposition only makes sense diachronically, the true meaning being the 'primitive' or 'etymological' signified, that is, the one given to the term by those who created and first used it. Thus 'leaf' in 'leaf of paper' is figurative, since the term originally designated 'the leaf of a tree'. Dumarsais thus absolutely rejects common use as a criterion, as can be seen from this example, where the sense called figurative is, in French, as usual as the other. It is thus clear that tropology is for him no longer part of rhetoric but of 'Grammar', and we understand how he could write his famous 'I am persuaded that more figures are created in one day . . .'. We would still like to ask Dumarsais why, given his position, he assigns a particular effect to tropes. They render language, he tells us, 'more vivid, or more noble, or more pleasing' (p. 13). Is this true of 'feuille de papier'? Certainly not. We have to conclude that in this case there really is no trope and that the definition given by Dumarsais is not correct. In fact, Fontanier does make that objection: 'How can such usage be reconciled with that force, that beauty, which distinguish them, that happy effect they produce . . .?' (p. 65).

It is for this reason that Fontanier adopts a criterion which is resolutely synchronic. A 'Saussurien' before his time, he knows that the historical point of view is linguistically irrelevant, and that it matters little to the user whether the meaning he gives to a word is the original one or a derived one. 'Either words are used in some genuine sense, that is, in one of their habitual and ordinary meanings, primitive or not, or else they are used in a deviant sense, that is, in a meaning which is given to them for the moment and which is no more than an artificial borrowing' (p. 66). Only in the second case is there a trope. The criterion is thus usage, i.e., the frequency of use in a given state of the language. Once a sense becomes usual, it loses by that very fact its status as a figure. Fontanier is quite clear on this point. In his commentary on Dumarsais' *Tropes*, he writes: 'One can prove with a thousand examples that what are initially the boldest figures cease to be regarded as figures when they have become wholly common and usual' (p. 6).

Genette has nevertheless contested this criterion.[17] Fontanier is accused of inconsistency in that he in fact substituted, for the opposition 'usual/ non-usual', another, more relevant one, namely 'necessity/freedom'. In support of this interpretation it is supposed to be possible to cite certain of his texts. For example: 'It follows from our definition that figures, *no matter how common and familiar they have been rendered by habit,* only merit and conserve this label to the extent that they can be used freely, and are not as it were imposed by the language' (p. 64). The words we have italicized do seem to prove that the figure can remain a figure, even when it is, in the author's own words, 'common and familiar'. Moreover, Fontanier adopts the distinction introduced by the Abbé de Radonvilliers between 'figures d'usage ou de la langue' and 'figures d'invention ou de l'écrivain'. How is it possible to define the figure as what is not usual and at the same time admit the existence of 'figures d'usage'? Is this not a contradiction in terms? But in fact, as a good linguist should, Fontanier knows that there are degrees in usage. Frequency of use is a variable that can assume different values. Among synonyms there exist some terms which are less usual than others, which are only used by subgroups or in certain situations. Among these are the words of 'jargons' or 'argots'. Likewise, for the same signifier some signifieds will be less usual than others. Among these are the 'tropes d'usage'. 'Renard' stands for the fox itself in the large majority of its occurrences in utterances. That is its proper meaning. 'Clever fellow' is a *less* usual meaning for 'renard', but is still usual. It is therefore a 'figure d'usage', and is listed in the dictionary as a 'figurative sense'. On the other hand, the 'tropes d'invention' 'are still a sort of private property, the private property of the author: thus one cannot use them as one's own or as if they were common property, but only as something borrowed or quoted' (p. 188).

As for the opposition of what is free and what is necessary, the author applies it only to 'catachresis', that is, to terms whose figurative sense is the only available sense in a given context, as for example the 'wings' (*ailes*) of a windmill. The user is indeed conscious of a twisting of the meaning, but one which here is not only usual but the only usable sense. In such a case the figure ceases to be a true figure: this is the zero degree of deviation. (These are the 'dead images' which Bally spoke of.) 'Figures d'usage', on the other hand, are deviations of the first degree. They form a sort of sub-language within the language, and from this point of view the speaker has a choice between two signifiers to express the same signified, one of which, not having this meaning as its 'proper sense', will thus appear as a deviation. We propose to give the name 'stylistics' to the study of this subcode constituted by the 'figures d'usage', reserving the term 'poetics' for the 'figures d'invention', which are the ones that have the highest degree of deviation, since, by definition, they are only used once, with the term 'rhetoric' covering all the figures.

Finally, within the 'figures d'invention' Fontanier makes another distinction which this time does not involve deviation from usage, but rather deviation with respect to what he calls 'certain rules strongly prescribed by reason'. Barry had already made a distinction between 'close' metaphors and 'distant' metaphors, according to a criterion based on the distance between the two senses which is still usable. Thus the relation of similarity between two signifieds can vary in terms of various criteria; for instance according to the number of semes they have in common, or the position – dominant or not, extrinsic or intrinsic – of the differentiating seme. A whole typology of tropes could be established on the basis of such criteria, but this is not our concern here. We note only that a third degree of deviance is introduced according to the distance separating the two *signifieds* in a relation of substitution. While Fontanier, as a good classicist, condemns tropes which are 'distant', modern poetry has adopted them as the norm. It was Reverdy who said: 'The characteristic of the strong image is that it is produced by a spontaneous confronting of two very separate realities'; and Breton reaches the limit: 'For me, the strongest image is that which has the highest degree of arbitrariness.'

But we retain from Fontanier this notion – which is fundamental – of the degree of deviation, of the gradated variation of 'figurality': a notion which is contained in its entirety in his introductory definition of figures as forms by which 'the discourse is deflected *more or less* far from what would have been its simple and usual expression' (p. 64).

One can thus assign a rank to each type of figure, a degree in the scale of deviation, and the whole tropology of Fontanier can be summarized in the table on p. 85.

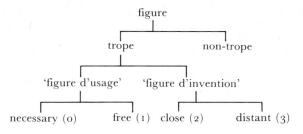

The numbers on the bottom line represent the degree of deviance of each figure, starting with degree zero, where the figure does not function as such, and going up to degree 3, where the figures of modern poetry would be entered.

It can be seen how much more complex this tropology is than that of Dumarsais, who was satisfied with a simple dichotomy between 'sens propre' and 'sens figuré', itself based on an etymological criterion whose relevance we can no longer admit. In spite of its deficiencies and lacunae, this table is still usable, with, however, one reservation, but an important one, since it involves its primary distinction: the opposition between tropes and non-tropes.

Between the two types of figures, Fontanier, along with all other ancient and modern rhetoricians, establishes a horizontal distinction. For him, all figures are deviations, of which some affect the meaning, others the syntax, others the sound. Inversion, which puts the predicate before the subject, violates a syntactic rule, just as the trope which gives a word a signified which does not belong to it violates a semantic rule. Thus, the figures are all isomorphic, and the distinction between them is established only on the basis of whether the level on which the deviation is found is semantic, syntactic, or phonetic. In adopting this viewpoint, Fontanier is not aware that he is involved in a contradiction.

Consider the two tropes which Fontanier records under the labels of 'paradoxism' and 'metaphor'.

He defines paradoxism as 'an artifice of language in which ideas or words which are ordinarily opposed and contradictory are brought together and combined with one another', and he gives as an example this line from *Athalie:* 'Pour réparer des ans l'irréparable outrage' (to repair the irreparable ravages of time). As for metaphor, it consists in 'presenting an idea in the guise of another idea . . . which is connected with the first by nothing but a certain conformity or analogy'. His example is: 'Gourmander sans relâche un terrain paresseux' (to scold unceasingly an idle field), where *gourmander* does not mean 'reprimand' but 'cultivate'. It is true that there is deviation in both cases, but how could Fontanier fail to see that these two deviations, as he defines them, are radically different? They are not situated on the same linguistic axis.

Paradoxism is a kind of contradiction. It violates a rule of combinatory incompatibility which exists solely on the syntagmatic level, between terms present in the utterance: for example, 'réparer' and 'irréparable'. The deviation exists *in praesentia*, to use Saussure's terminology. On the other hand, the difference between 'reprimand' and 'cultivate' which constitutes the metaphor in the second example is *in absentia*. It exists only on the paradigmatic level, between potential signifieds of which only one, by definition, is realizable. If by 'trope' we are to understand a deviation of the paradigmatic type, then paradoxism is not a trope. Contradiction is not a change of meaning, but an incompatibility of meaning. How are we to explain this confusion?

In fact, a minute's reflection will reveal that both axes are present in all figures, that all are composed of two anomalies, of which one, however, functions to correct the other. What shows this is that, when he discusses his paradoxism, Fontanier actually superimposes the two types of anomaly: ' "Repair" stands for "try to repair" or "apparently repair": that is what one immediately understands, and what brings it about that "repair" and "irreparable" not only do not clash at all but fit together perfectly.' What is described here is a two-stage mechanism:

(1) a contradiction occurs between 'repair' and 'irreparable';

(2) 'apparently repair' is substituted for 'repair', which removes the contradiction.

Only this mechanism can provide the answer to a question that is very simple, but is never asked by Fontanier: why is there a trope, why is there a change of meaning? If *repair* is the proper meaning of 'repair', why does the receiver reject it and substitute another sense which does not belong to the word? In the case of paradoxism, the answer is clear: because, with the proper meaning, the utterance is contradictory, since the two terms 'repair' and 'irreparable' 'clash', while, on the contrary, with the meaning change, the terms 'fit together perfectly'.

Let us now turn to metaphor. How can the complete isomorphism of the two figures be missed? The same question asked above arises here. Fontanier assumes a hierarchy between proper and figurative meaning. The 'sens propre' is the usual meaning, which is recorded as such in dictionaries, the one which should normally come first into the receiver's mind. Why, then, does he reject it, why does he replace it by another meaning? There is not much of a problem for the 'figures d'usage', where the figurative meaning, although secondary, is usual and thus available. But in the present case, which belongs to the 'figures d'invention', 'cultivate' is not and has never been the meaning of 'gourmander'. Why then is a signified assigned to this signifier which has never belonged to it? Obviously because with the regular meaning there is a contextual incompatibility. Exactly as in the case of paradoxism: 'reprimand' and 'field' produce a meaning clash, like 'repair' and 'irreparable'. The difference is that in this case there is no manifest contradiction. The semantic anomaly still exists, however, and it can be shown that it involves a contradiction, although now at a deeper level. 'Reprimand' requires an animate object, while 'field' implies inanimateness.[18] The contradiction obtains between semes that the terms do not pose but imply. The contradiction is less strong, but it is not any less real. Speaking of 'réparer l'irréparable', Fontanier tells us that such a sentence 'cannot without absurdity be taken literally'; but is not the same true of 'gourmander un terrain'? Could one without absurdity take this expression literally? The relative weakness of the contradiction explains why it was not perceived. The attention of the analyst in this case was directed to the second stage of the process, the change of meaning, while in the case of paradoxism the contradiction is so flagrant that it could not escape the observer, who thereby defined the figure in terms of it. But since the two figures are isomorphic and both exhibit in their first stage a syntagmatic anomaly of the same type (a combinatory incompatibility), they should not on any grounds be included in the category of tropes. The term 'trope' singles out, in the figure, the second stage, which is essential, since it is the goal of the figure, but which is still a *second* – dependent – stage, since it would not exist without the first. Every figure involves a two-stage process of decoding, the first stage being the perception of the anomaly, and the second its correction, through exploration of the paradigmatic field which contains the network of relations of resemblance, contiguity, etc., with whose help a signified will be discovered that can provide the utterance with an acceptable semantic interpretation. If an interpretation is impossible, then the utterance will be considered absurd. That is the case with the utterances constructed as examples of absurdity by logicians, such as 'Napoleon is a prime number'.

In short, the figure exhibits a bi-axial organization, consisting of two perpendicular axes, the syntagmatic axis where the deviation is established, and the paradigmatic axis where it is cancelled out by a change of meaning. This can be represented by the following diagram:

$$\text{Trope} \quad \left| \quad \begin{array}{c} \text{apparently repair} \\ \uparrow \\ \text{repair/irreparable} \end{array} \right.$$

Paradoxism

We see emerging from this a classificatory scheme with two entries, according to the type of anomaly and the type of meaning change. There are paradoxisms which are metonymic, others which are metaphorical, as there are metonymic or metaphorical irrelevances, depending on the type of change which corrects the anomaly. To sum up, it looks as if each of the two axes of language has been hiding the other. On the semantic level, the paradigmatic axis of *meaning change* has covered up the syntagmatic axis of *meaning incompatibility*. The result is that rhetoric has left untouched the study of the area of 'semantic anomalies'.[19] One of the essential tasks of the new rhetoric must therefore be to fill this gap, by finding, naming, and classifying the kinds of violations of combinatory constraints, inherent to the semantic level of language, which constitute what are known as 'figures'.

As far as non-tropes are concerned, what has happened is the reverse. The syntagm has concealed the paradigm. Rhetoric has analysed syntagmatic deviance as such, but it has missed its paradigmatic correction. In short, every figure involves two stages: the theory of tropes has neglected the first, the theory of non-tropes has forgotten the second. It has not seen that every non-trope implies a trope, because every deviation requires its own correction by a change of meaning, and that it is this converse and compensatory interaction of the two anomalies which constitutes the internal dynamics of any figure.

Consider, for example, 'interrogation', which is a figure when an interrogative form in fact refers to an affirmative signified: 'Who does not know?' for 'everybody knows'. There is in fact a change of meaning; thus this is indeed a trope. When then is it called a non-trope? Or what about inversion? It is, we are told, a 'figure de construction' because it represents a syntactic deviation, which is true, and a non-trope because it does not affect the sense, which is false. All French grammarians admit that a preposed adjective takes on a 'generic' meaning, although when postposed it has only a 'specific' sense. '"Une blanche colombe" is a dove whose doveness is white: from this come the metaphoric values attributed to the dove (chastity) and to whiteness (candour)', according to P. Guiraud.[20] Is this not a change of meaning? Do we not have here – as the author explicitly says – a metaphor? And can it not be the same mechanism that is at work in the 'Figures de diction', such as rhyme, where the anomaly, constituted in the first stage by the homophony of semantically different terms, is corrected, in the second stage, through the substitution of 'metaphorical values' which confer on the homophones the semantic closeness required by the principle of parallelism?[21] Thus 'soeur' rhyming with 'douceur' produces a connotation of sweetness absent from 'Jeanne est la soeur de Pierre'.

In every case, thus, we find the same structure in the figure, the same orthogonal syntagmatic-paradigmatic organization, the same mechanism with the same function, the only one capable of accounting for the purposive organization of the figure.

For this is the ultimate question. Why does the figure exist, why does anomaly exist? To this question, the unanimous answer of the rhetoricians, which they in fact made part of the definition of the figure, was that the function of 'figurative language' was aesthetic. The figure contributes to the 'grace', 'vivacity', 'nobility', etc., of discourse, equally vague and more or less synonymous terms which all refer to the important aesthetic function, which, with 'instruction' and 'persuasion', constituted the functional multiplicity of language according to traditional rhetoric.

There remains then the problem of explaining the effect in terms of the structure. Deviation of itself is not enough to account for the aesthetic value it creates in discourse. But this problem has a ready-made solution, coming from the aesthetics of the image. There is a principle which is not questioned by any rhetorician, namely the parallelism of the oppositions 'figuré/propre' and concrete/abstract. The figurative meaning is 'concrete', i.e., it creates an 'image'. It lets us 'see', while the proper, literal meaning lets us 'think'. This led to the terminological confusion which gradually arose between 'trope' and 'image', and which has continued down to the present day. Underlying this, there is an implicit theory of the history of language. Words which originally refer to what is perceptible normally evolve towards abstraction. Rhetorical language is a return to the basics of language. Every figure brings us back from intelligibility to sensibility, and rhetoric thus represents the opposite of the ascending dialectic movement which goes from the percept to the concept, which has defined philosophy since Socrates. Philosophy and rhetoric are thus in symmetrical opposition, and together describe a great linguistic circle which starts from and returns to the original imagination.

This conception is based on a profound truth which modern intellectualist poetics seems to have forgotten. The fundamental specificity of poetic language escapes it. It generally interprets this as a specificity of the signifier, which is taken to refer in its own particular way to a signified which remains the same, and which could be expressed as well – if not better – in the nonpoetic metalanguage of the exegete or critic. This attitude commits the fallacy of 'ignoratio elenchi'. If in fact the same signified can be expressed in a different way, why does poetry exist? Why is there metre, rhyme, inversion, paradoxism, repetition, why all the figures? The currently fashionable theory of ambiguity gives a quite thin answer to this question. Plurality of meaning satisfies at most the principle of economy. If the only function of poetry is to compact into a single sentence what prose could say in more than one sentence, its advantage is minor. We are not so miserly about words as to feel a shudder of pleasure whenever we encounter an abbreviation. Perhaps one should see in the theory which equates poeticity with semantic 'richness' a distant echo of bourgeois economics. A small number of signifiers for a large number – or even an infinite number – of signifieds, now there's a good linguistic investment if there ever was one.

Qualitative transformation of the signified is indeed the goal of all poetry – and of all literature. Rhetoric was right on this score. But we must ask whether what is involved is really a return to the image. This conception faces two objections:

(1) figurative meaning is not always more 'concrete' than proper meaning. There are numerous examples that show the contrary to be true. 'Apparently repair' is no more concrete than 'repair', 'boat' is no less abstract than 'sail'.

(2) even if the meaning was really concrete it would not necessarily induce an 'image'. We do not want to reopen here the old debate about whether thinking involves images, only to point out and criticize the confusion which seems to prevail here between the signified and the referent. Just because the referent of 'fox' is concrete, that is, tangible and perceptible, while that of 'clever' is not, must we conclude that one cannot understand the sentence 'that man is a fox' without really imagining the animal? This is not at all certain. Furthermore, in the case of figures like 'solitude bleue' or 'blanche agonie' (Mallarmé), how could anyone imagine what is unimaginable?

The question is thus still open. I have elsewhere adopted the so-called 'emotional' theory of meaning. This label, borrowed from traditional terminology, tends to give a misleading idea of the theory, and it would be desirable to find a better one. But whatever answer is given to the fundamental question of the nature of poetic meaning, it was still important to show that the very structure of the figure forces us to ask that question.

Valéry has written: 'The poet, without knowing it, lives and moves in a world of *possible* relations and transformations, of which he only perceives or explores the momentary and particular aspects which matter to him in a given state of his interior functioning.'[22]

To discover and understand this 'world of relations and transformations' is indeed the object of the rhetorics of discourse, and the task of modern poetics is to continue this work, whose majestic course was, unfortunately, interrupted in the 19th century. Hugo declared 'War on rhetoric'. It was the curious fate of romanticism to produce poetry which was so beautiful! and poetics which was so bad. Not until Mallarmé and Valéry do we find authentic poets who have rediscovered the relevance of rhetoric as the science of the possible forms of literary discourse. But even so the prejudice has survived to our own day. The theory of figures violates the two sacred principles of the currently reigning literary aesthetic: the uniqueness of the work of art, and its unity or totality. By conceiving figures as a sort of linguistic universal which can be transposed from one poem or one poet to another, the theory denies what constitutes the specificity of the literary art, its unique character, its essential individuality. 'Every diamond is unique and resembles nothing but itself', says a Hindu proverb, ignorant of chemistry. Furthermore, by isolating segments of the discourse, analysing it into forms which, while no doubt connected and interacting, are still separable, one denies that total unity, that unfissured compactness which makes the work a self-enclosed whole. And on the horizon of structural poetics looms the frightful bulk of the machine, the threat of poetry automatically produced from a stock of figures on punched cards. But we need not worry. It remains for genius and inspiration to make good use of these merely possible forms and give them content which is both original and poetically genuine. This is by no means an easy task – let those who doubt that try it themselves.

Notes

1. *Le Parallélisme logico-grammatical* (Paris, Alcan, 1933).
2. For experimental corroboration of these correlations, cf. H. Sinclair de Swaart, *Acquisition de la pensée et développement du langage* (Paris, Dunod, 1967).
3. Robert Blanché, *Structures intellectuelles* (Paris, Vrin, 1966). A. J. Greimas, *Sémantique structurale* (Larousse, 1966).
4. Negation will be symbolized either by 'P̄' or by 'not P'.
5. *Psychologie de l'intelligence* (Paris, A. Colin, 1956), p. 41.
6. *Littérature et Signification* (Paris, Larousse, 1967), p. 108.
7. I have already discussed comparative anomaly in 'Poétique de la comparaison: essai de systématique', *Langages* 8 (1968).
8. *Dictionnaire de poétique et de rhétorique* (Paris, P.U.F., 1961).
9. *Les Figures du discours*, collection 'Science' (Paris, Flammarion, 1968).
10. Paris, Flammarion, 1966.
11. op. cit. p. 50.
12. Cf. Luce Irigaray, 'Négation et transformation négative dans le langage des schizophrènes', *Langages* 5 (1967), pp. 84–98.
13. *Traité de stylistique française* 1, p. 186.
14. 'Logical syntax and semantics', *Langages* 2 (1966).
15. *La Linguistique*, ed. André Martinet (Paris, Denoël, 1969), p. 239.
16. With Gérard Genette, I have been able to contribute to the realization of this hope by publishing the writings of Fontanier under this title (in the collection 'Science' (Paris, Flammarion, 1968)).
17. In the preface to *Figures du discours*, pp. 10–11.
18. 'Gourmander' can be characterized as: transitive verb + object, as the interrogative form 'Qui' (and not 'que') 'Pierre gourmande-t-il?' shows.
19. Cf. T. Todorov, *Langages* 1 (1966).
20. *Syntaxe du Français* (Paris, P.U.F., 1962), p. 112.
21. See *Structure du langage poétique* (Paris, Flammarion), p. 224.
22. *Questions de Poésie, Oeuvres* (Pléiade), vol. 1, p. 1290.

6. Parallelism and deviation in poetry*

NICOLAS RUWET

According to the celebrated formula with which Roman Jakobson sums up what, for him, constitutes the distinguishing feature of poetic texts as opposed to other types of discourse, 'the poetic function projects the principle of equivalence from the axis of selection into the axis of combination' (Jakobson, 1960, 358). In other words, poetic texts are characterized by the superimposing, over the different types of relations – phonetic, phonological, morphological, syntactic, semantic – which organize the discourse sequence, of relations of another type, based on the equivalence – on various levels of linguistic structure – of elements located at different points of that sequence.

The most obvious merit of Jakobson's formulation is its suggestion that a single principle underlies the multitude of processes – rhyme, metre, stanzaic forms, syntactic parallelisms – which have, alone or in combination, been considered at different periods, for different languages or cultures, as characteristic of poetry. These procedures may vary greatly from one language, culture, epoch, genre, or poet, to another; none of them, taken in isolation, can be held to be universally typical of poetry. But, if Jakobson is right, they are all particular manifestations of a principle which *is* universal and forms part of the definition of poetic language.

However, Jakobson's proposal is not without problems, and I have elsewhere indicated several (cf. Ruwet, 1972b, ch. 9). I would like here to return to one of them, and perhaps the most important. The notion of equivalence between various elements of a text is so general – as long as it has not been specified more precisely in what respects these elements are to be taken as equivalent – that it is not obvious that it will allow us to account for the specificity of poetic texts. Jakobson's formula brings out strikingly a feature which is common to rhyme, metre, syntactic parallelism, etc., but nothing tells us, for example, that one could not equally well subsume under this formulation principles of the organization of discourse, which are applicable to texts not regarded as poetic. In fact, as I pointed out in the article cited below (Ruwet, 1972b, 215), if we take seriously the discourse analysis studies of Zellig Harris (cf. Harris, 1952, and especially 1963), the

* This is an abridged and slightly modified translation of 'Parallélismes et déviations en poésie'.

92

specificity of poetic texts seems to disappear completely. For Harris, it is possible to describe the structure of any connected text – short story, scientific article, newspaper article, conversation, etc. – using systems of equivalences, which can be represented by two-dimensional matrices.[1]

After a brief discussion of a few of the principles which govern the organization of discourse in general, beginning with a critique of Harris' proposals, I will attempt to show that it is possible to preserve Jakobson's principle, by giving it more specific content (content which is in fact implicit in his work). I will then proceed to the main point of this article, and will show that the results obtained allow us to consider in an at least partially new light the old question of the role of deviations in poetry, as well as that of poetic 'creativity'.

1

Harris does not propose a theory of discourse, strictly speaking (that would specify, in particular, the notion of 'possible connected text in a language L'), but rather a set of analytical procedures which allow a certain structure in a text to be uncovered. These procedures are essentially an extension of procedures for distributional analysis. His starting point is the text considered as a sequence of sentences, and distributional methods give him a representation of these sentences as sequences of morphemes with constituent structure. The approach is based entirely on the notion of equivalence – Harris extracts equivalence relations between elements of the successive sentences which constitute the text. Two sequences in the text are considered to be equivalent (a) if they are identical (i.e., if they consist of different occurrences of the same morphemes or the same sequences of morphemes), or (b) if, while different, they occur in equivalent environments. Through intensive recourse to the notion of environment, as well as by the 'normalization' of the text through the technique of transformations,[2] Harris manages to establish a series of equivalence classes, and to represent the structure of the text in the form of a table with two kinds of entries, each row corresponding to a sentence given in 'normalized' form, and each column to an equivalence class.

The problem is clearly whether it is possible to reformulate the analytic procedures of Harris as a theory of discourse (as Chomsky reformulated the methods of distributional analysis as a grammatical theory, namely the phrase structure model). To put it differently, does representing a text in the form of a table of equivalences help clarify the notion of 'possible connected text in a language L'; does it allow us to distinguish what is perceived by a speaker of the language as a coherent text from what appears to him to be only an incoherent sequence of unrelated sentences? I will not pursue this question since, in an excellent but too little known (at least in France) review of Harris (1963), Manfred Bierwisch (1965) has answered this question in the negative, in what seems to me to be conclusive fashion. In particular, Bierwisch showed that Harris' procedures allow quite straightforward description, in the form of a table, of perfectly incoherent sequences of sentences, and, conversely, that they fail to provide representations of this kind for texts which are immediately perceived as coherent.[3] Thus the theory which can be constructed on the basis of Harris' procedures is at once too strong and too weak. If there exist principles governing text coherence, we need to look for them elsewhere than in the kind of representation Harris sought to provide.

Obviously, this negative finding does not help us much with the problem we are concerned with here – the lack of specificity of Jakobson's principle of equivalence. We may note, however, that the inadequacy seems to be related to the fact that Harris was looking for principles governing the structure of texts at a level which, to simplify somewhat, is that of surface structure (in that these procedures operate almost entirely on the level of morphemes, sequences of morphemes, and their superficial constituent structure). In particular, Harris intentionally put aside any semantic[4] or pragmatic considerations. This should be kept in mind, since it plays an important role in what follows. As a matter of fact, although there does not exist, at present, a serious and comprehensive theory of discourse, the few interesting attempts that have been made indicate that the factors accounting for the coherence of a text are to be looked for on levels quite different from that of surface structure. Without entering into the details of this extremely complex matter, I will briefly discuss a few of the principles which seem relevant, as they have been sketched in an interesting article by Irina Bellert (1970).

Bellert defines a discourse (or a connected text) in the following way: 'A discourse is a sequence of utterances $S_1, S_2, \ldots S_n$, such that the semantic interpretation of each utterance S_i (for $2 \leqslant i \leqslant n$) is dependent on the interpretation of the sequence $S_1, \ldots S_{i-1}$' (1970, 335). She also characterizes 'the semantic interpretation of any utterance' as 'the set of consequences or conclusions that can be drawn from that utterance' (ibid.). It can be seen that she focusses from the start on the logico-semantic form of utterances; the analysis of discourse – and the determining of the principles governing its coherence – presupposes that one has established a logico-semantic representation of the utterances which compose it.[5]

Without going into any detail, and simplifying greatly, I will mention as illustration two of the kinds of mechanisms which, according to Bellert, play a crucial role in the organization of a connected text. It will be observed, in any event, that these mechanisms are intuitively familiar.

The most obvious connectors of utterances in a discourse are linguistic indices . . . proper names, English personal, demonstrative, or relative pronouns, certain adverbs ('here', 'there'), nouns or noun phrases preceded by definite determiners, which we may call definite descriptions . . . [their] function is to point to extralinguistic 'objects' or particulars that the hearer is supposed to identify in accordance with the instruction contained in the index and the situational or linguistic context . . . linguistic indices either point directly to extralinguistic 'objects' or refer to certain other indices in the preceding utterances and through the latter fulfil their indexical function of pointing to extralinguistic 'objects'. What is common to all linguistic indices is their identifying (referring) function and lack of predicating function. (ibid., p. 346)

Roughly, for an utterance to say something about the world, it must at least contain certain indexical elements (in traditional terms, deictic elements), and for a sequence of utterances to constitute a connected text, there must exist certain systematic relations between indexical elements which occur in different utterances of that sequence (in traditional terms, anaphoric relations). The problem, clearly, is to formulate precisely the constraints obeyed by these relations,[6] but the general idea is rather clear, and it is easy to see how the elimination of such relations, or certain violations, for example in the order of certain indexical elements, would suffice to convert a connected text into an incoherent sequence of utterances. Let us consider a simple example taken, slightly modified, from Bellert (ibid., p. 350):

(1) (a) Picasso has left Paris.
    (b) The great painter went to HIS STUDIO ON THE MEDITERRANEAN COAST.
    (c) He likes that PLACE a lot.

(1)(a)–(c) is obviously a coherent discourse, and it is clear that one of the reasons for the coherence is the existence of anaphoric relations between various indexical elements occurring in (a), (b), and (c). Thus, 'the great painter' and 'he' are anaphoric with 'Picasso', and 'that place' with 'his studio on the Mediterranean Coast'. These relations are subject to various constraints, some of which are specific to the grammar of a certain language,[7] while others are linguistically universal.[8] It would be sufficient to eliminate certain of these relations (e.g. to replace the definite description 'the great painter' in (b) by an indefinite noun phrase, such as 'a great painter'), or to modify the order of certain indices (e.g., to exchange 'Picasso' and 'he'), to convert (1) into a sequence of utterances which no longer forms a totally coherent whole.[9]

As Bellert observes, the constraints operating here are not just linguistic, but also pragmatic; they constantly appeal to the speaker's knowledge of the world. Suppose we replace (1) by (2):

(2) (a) Stravinsky has left Hollywood.
    (b) The great painter has gone to his house in California.
    (c) He likes that place a lot.

If I know nothing about music, geography, or the biography of Stravinsky, insofar as all the linguistic constraints on anaphor are respected in (2), this will seem coherent to me, but I will be inclined to conclude that Stravinsky is a great painter, and perhaps that Hollywood is not in California, or at least that Stravinsky's house is not in Hollywood. If, on the other hand, I know geography and Stravinsky's biography, this text will appear completely aberrant.

Bellert then discusses the role played in the coherence of a text by a class of lexical items, which can belong to quite different grammatical categories, but which have in common that their use implies certain beliefs on the part of the speaker. She calls these 'implicative terms'. If I utter (3):

(3) Pierre stopped smoking last Monday.

this implies that I believe, or in any case that the listener has the right to believe that I believe, that (4) is true:

(4) Before some moment last Monday, Pierre used to smoke.

and that is due, in the last analysis, to the semantic content of the verb 'stop'. Similarly, if I say 'I regret that Pierre has already left', that implies that I believe that Pierre has already left. Again, in (1)(a), the use of the verb 'leave' implies that Picasso was in Paris at a certain moment before the moment of the action described in (1)(a), etc. In general, uttering a sentence has a certain number of consequences, some of which are related to the use of lexical items (such as 'stop', 'regret', 'leave',[10] in these examples), consequences which are themselves expressible by sentences of the language. All this is well known and rather obvious.

The important point, emphasized by Bellert, is that, for a sequence of sentences to constitute a coherent discourse, there must be some overlap among the consequences that can be deduced from the sentences on the basis of the implicative terms they contain, and in general there should not be any contradiction between the consequences of the sentences. Let us consider a simple example:

(5) (a) Pierre bought flowers at noon.
    (b) He will give them to Marie this evening.

Among the implications of (5)(a) is the one statable as 'after noon, Pierre had some flowers'; this implication is directly related to the semantic content of the verb 'buy'. Furthermore, one of the consequences of (5)(b) (linked to the semantic content of 'give') is 'before this evening, Pierre will have some flowers'. Assuming various constraints on anaphor and tense, we observe that (5)(a) and (5)(b) have an implication in common: for a certain time, Pierre has flowers. It is clear that – assuming the same constraints on tenses and anaphors – all we need do is substitute 'sell' for 'buy' in (5)(a), or 'steal' from' for 'give to' in (5)(b), to create different implications which are not overlapping, and are in fact contradictory. If we do this, then (5) ceases to be a coherent discourse, or at least it requires a special interpretation, with, for example, the assumption that there has been ellipsis. (Observe that the substitution of 'buy from' for 'give to' in (5)(b) will also make the discourse incoherent, and will also produce a simple counter-example to Harris' theory.)

The existence of partially shared implications in successive sentences of a text is not determined solely by the presence in these sentences of 'implicative' lexical items. Other factors are also involved which were not studied by Bellert. Consider, for example, the case of a discourse consisting of a question and its answer. It is evident that not any declarative sentence is a possible natural answer to any question. The relation between the *focus* and the *presupposition* in each of the sentences must be taken into consideration (on these notions, see especially Chomsky, 1972, 89ff.; also Jackendoff, 1972; Katz, 1972, etc.). Briefly, for a declarative sentence to be a possible answer to a question, the two sentences must have the same presupposition. Consider the following examples:

(6) (a) Was it Pierre that hit Paul?
    (b) No, it was Jules that hit Paul.
    (c) No, it was Jacques that Pierre hit.
    (d) No, it was Emile that kissed Marie.

Clearly, only the pair (6)(a)–(6)(b) forms a natural discourse. This is because (6)(a) and (6)(b) share the same presupposition (someone hit Paul) and differ only in their focus (Pierre in (6)(a), Jules in (6)(b)); on the other hand, the presuppositions of (6)(c) (Pierre hit someone) and of (6)(d) (someone kissed Marie) differ from those of (6)(a).

All this is extremely summary, and certainly does not exhaust the conditions determining the coherence of a text. Furthermore, it is frequently the case that apparent violations of the conditions mentioned above do not affect the comprehension of a text, because of the operation of special conditions, such as, for example, the 'conversational implicatures' of Grice (1967).[11] But these brief remarks will give a general idea of the kinds of principles which are to account for the coherence of a text. The main point is that these principles cannot be defined directly in terms of the distribution of morphemes in surface structure, but crucially appeal to the logico-semantic representation of the sentences of the text, as well as to pragmatic considerations.

Let us return now to Jakobson's principle. It should first be noted that, if one understands the notion of equivalence in the most general sense, one is again faced, although not in the same fashion, with the problem that was raised earlier, in our discussion of Harris. Bellert's principles may appear to involve particular cases of equivalence. The indexical elements 'Picasso', 'the great painter', 'he' in (1) are all equivalent, in that they are all coreferential; the verbs 'buy' and 'give', in (5), are equivalent in that both are implicative elements of the same type, and have certain consequences in common, etc. Apparently we have not made much progress.

But in fact we have taken a big step forward. The types of equivalence we have been dealing with all involve essentially the semantic, referential, pragmatic aspects of utterances; they apply at the interpretative level, and are related only indirectly to the syntax of utterances.[12] Furthermore, they are practically independent of the morphological, phonological, and phonetic aspects. Now let us run through the rich catalogue of poetic procedures given in Jakobson, 1960. Whether we consider rhyme, the various types of metrical systems, syntactic parallelism, or the rest, these processes involve exclusively[13] just those 'superficial' levels whose role is negligible or secondary in the usual structuring of discourse. One syllable is placed in an equivalence relation with another, one group of phonemes with another, one word stress with another, one syntactic pause with another, one surface syntactic structure with another, and all this independently of the semantic and pragmatic rules that operate in the discourse segment in question. Whenever a codified system is involved, the rules by which it can be represented are situated on other levels than, and are independent of, rules of discourse organization of the Bellert type; a sonnet, for instance, is governed by two distinct types of organization, located on different levels.

Thus it is now possible to reformulate Jakobson's principle, giving it more specific content: *poetic texts are characterized by their setting up of equivalence relations, whether codified or not, between different points of the discourse, relations which are defined on superficial levels* – where, by 'superficial', we mean phonetic, phonological, morphological, and/or surface syntax.[14] Note that this reformulation has certain empirical consequences – for example, that there should exist no known or possible type or style of poetry which is based exclusively on equivalence relations defined on the level of deep syntactic structure (e.g. in the sense of the standard theory of Chomsky, 1965).[15] Note also that, whereas the repetition of particular lexical items may play a role in certain poems (or in the work of certain poets, cf. the notion of 'key words'), there do not seem ever to have been developed or codified poetic forms based on the repetition of certain lexical items, to the exclusion of constraints involving matters like rhyme, metre, syntactic parallelism, etc.

2

Once Jakobson's principle of equivalence[16] has been delimited more precisely (I will speak henceforth of parallelisms rather than equivalences), and once it is accepted that a poetic text is simultaneously governed by two different kinds of organizing principles, one type involving semantic and pragmatic principles, the other parallelism, the problem arises of the interaction, in a given style or poem, of these two types. Jakobson has laid much stress on the semantic effects of parallelisms, and in various analyses he has provided striking examples of these.[17] One can ask about the nature of these semantic effects – which doubtless do not belong to semantics in the narrow sense of the word (e.g. that dealt with in Katz, 1972), but rather are 'symbolic' in nature.[18] I will not here approach this question directly, but in a roundabout way, by asking a rather different question: given that the principle of 'superficial' parallelism is superimposed in poetry on the semantic and pragmatic principles of discourse organization, cannot the use of parallelisms allow these other principles to be dispensed with to some extent? In other words, does it ever happen that parallelisms, instead of only being superimposed over the 'ordinary' principles, are substituted for them? We will see that this is indeed the case, and that in such substitutions can be found the key to numerous deviations that have been observed in poetic texts.

2.1

I will consider first a very well-known example, the *Ballade des dames du temps jadis* by François Villon. Let us leave aside the role of rhyme, prosody, and the ballad form. From a syntactic point of view, the poem is almost wholly built on the alternation of two questions, one of which is varied in diverse ways, and the other repeated identically four times, in the last line of each stanza:

(7) (a) Dites-moi où, n'en quel pays,
           Est Flora, la belle Romaine,

       . . .
     (b) Mais où sont les neiges d'antan?

We have here a violation of some of the principles sketched above, those concerning the relations between a question and its answer. Normally, a question like (7)(a), whose presupposition is 'Flora, the beautiful Roman, is somewhere, in some country', calls for an answer in the form of a (perhaps elliptical) declarative sentence which has the same presupposition, and which specifies the element left indeterminate in the question ('où, n'en quel pays'); a natural answer might be '(She is) in Italy', '(She is) in the land of Shadows', etc.[19] However, instead of a declarative answer, we find another question, (7)(b), whose presupposition ('Yesterday's snows are somewhere') has only its predicate, indeterminate ('is/are somewhere'), in common with that of (7)(a). In a precise sense, then, (7)(a) and (7)(b) lack a common

99

implication. However, far from creating an effect of incongruity, this violation seems to work very well, and is in fact one factor in the charm and lasting renown of this ballad. How is this to be explained?

One might claim that the violation is more apparent than real, since both (7)(a) and (7)(b) are rhetorical questions, that is, questions for which one does not really expect an answer; and in fact, given our knowledge of the world, in each case the answer is obvious: 'Flora . . . is not anywhere', 'The snows of yesteryear are not anywhere' (in other words, the presuppositions of (7)(a) and (7)(b) are false). But this observation would only make the matter more puzzling: if the answer to (7)(a) is known in advance, why uselessly double (7)(a) with (7)(b), whose answer is also known in advance? It is clear that a purely semantic or pragmatic analysis is insufficient.

However, (7)(a) and (7)(b) have something else in common. Reduced to essentials, the two sentences have the same surface structure: the interrogative element 'où', followed by the present tense of the verb 'être' and a subject noun phrase which is definite and feminine. It is worth emphasizing this parallelism in surface structure; the two sentences have common semantic elements, but they could have been phrased, given the possibilities of French syntax, using different surface forms ('Dites-moi où . . . Flora . . . est', 'Où les neiges d'antan sont-elles?', 'Où est-ce que les neiges d'antan sont?', 'Où est-ce que sont les neiges d'antan?'). The parallelism is accentuated by metrical and stanzaic elements, by the repetition, four times, of (7)(b), and by the variations on (7)(a), in which the same surface form appears ('Où est la très sage Héloïs . . .', '. . . où est la reine . . .?'). Only at the very end of the poem, when the parallelism is firmly established, do we find other interrogative forms ('Où sont-ils, où, Vierge souvraine?', 'Prince, n'enquerrez de semaine//Où elles sont . . .').

The mechanism which accounts for the effect produced by the poem can, I believe, be described as follows. With the failure of the conditions which normally determine the progress of a discourse, the reader is left with the most visible aspect of textual organization: the structures of syntactic parallelism, accompanied by the concomitant semantic elements, and re-inforced by the whole apparatus of rhymes, metre, stanza forms. In other words, he is led to seek a semantic connection between elements which in fact are semantically unrelated, but are syntactically parallel: 'Flora . . .' and 'les neiges d'antan'. One aspect of this projection of the syntactic parallelism onto the semantics can also be expressed in more logical form. The fact that two sentences, which have partially similar presuppositions ('she is/they are somewhere') which we know by experience to be false, are placed in parallel invites us to regard them as two examples of a generalization: what is past no longer exists, there is no point to transposing into spatial terms what belongs to the temporal.[20] But I think it would be a mistake to stop there. 'Flora' and, in general, the 'belles dames du temps jadis', are equated with 'les neiges d'antan'. In our common experience, a whole range of things, ideas, perceptions, memories, are associated, more or less directly, more or less precisely, with snow: whiteness, cold, immaculateness, fleetingness, the sadness or sterility of winter (plus here, with 'd'antan', memories of last year), etc. Similarly, all sorts of things are associated with the 'belles dames du temps jadis': femininity and beauty, of course, tragic or happy love, the pomp and splendour of bygone courts and festivities, the costumes of the past, etc. These two fuzzy sets of associations, which vary from reader to reader – and which contain notions which are not in any case part of a definition of the concept of 'snow' or of these 'belles dames' – are placed in a direct relation. One is projected on the other, and more or less clear analogies are evoked between them: the spotless morning snow, so quickly soiled, changed to slush, becomes the 'symbol' of the evanescence of beauty, virginity, love . . .; reciprocally, beauty, splendour, pomp, the more or less mythological character of the 'belles dames', blend with the idea of snow, calling up glittering images of the snow, its brilliance, etc. (note the role of morphology: 'les neiges d'antan', is feminine plural, like 'les belles dames . . .'). In short, a whole series of ideas is evoked or suggested – and there would be no point (and no doubt this would be impossible) in formulating these phenomena of evocation as consequences in the logical sense.

2.2

A simple and exemplary case of the working of the mechanisms we are trying to describe is provided by the *Quelques écrits de Clarisse Juranville* of the Belgian surrealist Paul Nougé.[21] The way in which these texts were composed is itself significant. One day Nougé discovered in an attic a forgotten grammar textbook, *La Conjugaison enseignée par la pratique*, by Clarisse Juranville (Paris, Larousse, no date). Basing himself only on examples in the exercises, he derived brief poems from it, using the technique of collage, and occasionally substituting certain words for others. Here is the simplest one:[22]

> (8) Vous dépouillez nos arbres
> Vous prodiguez les méfaits
> Vous conjurez les sorts
> Vous divulguez nos secrets
> Vous ramenez au jour les vieilles écritures
> Vous fatiguez la terre de votre bruit
> Vous distinguez les bons d'entre les mauvais

(You strip our trees You lavish misdeeds You ward off spells You reveal our secrets You bring to light old writing You tire the earth with your noise You distinguish the good from the bad)

If a certain semantic unity is immediately apparent (all the sentences have a second person plural subject, all the verbs are in the present tense . . .) it is none the less clear that this poem does not fit Bellert's definition of a connected text. Although the meaning of each sentence in isolation is easy to understand (in spite of certain indeterminacies to be discussed below) it is not at all clear that the 'semantic interpretation of each utterance S_i (for $2 \leqslant i \leqslant n$) is dependent on the interpretation of the sequence $S_1, \ldots, S_{i-1}$'. This is because the use of various implicative terms ('dépouiller', 'conjurer', 'ramener au jour', etc.) does not create any visible connection between the successive sentences, in terms of common implications; moreover, besides the repetition of 'vous' (which is not, strictly speaking, an anaphoric element), there is no anaphoric relation from one sentence to another.

On the other hand, the structure of the text, in terms of parallelisms, is obvious. Each sentence has a declarative form, composed of the subject 'vous', a transitive verb in the present which belongs to the first conjugation (resulting in the total uniformity of the suffixes in '-ez'), and which is always trisyllabic, and a direct object which is a definite noun phrase in the plural (except in line 6), is inanimate (except, perhaps, in the last line), has the form determiner + noun (except in line 5, where there is an adjective, 'vieilles', and in line 7, where 'bons' and 'mauvais' are substantivized adjectives), plus, in final position in the last three lines, another complement which is different in each line ('au jour', 'de votre bruit', 'd'entre les mauvais').

This description enables us to divide the poem into two sections, a 'quatrain' with very uniform internal structure, and a 'tercet' with a structure that is more complex and varied. The quatrain has other elements proper to its internal organization: an 'enclosed' structure owing to the arrangement of the determiners of the direct objects ('nos'–'les'–'les'–'nos'), and an alternating structure due to the succession of monosyllables and disyllables at the ends of the lines ('arbres'–'méfaits'–'sorts'–'secrets') with rhymes of a sort. The tercet contrasts with the quatrain in having a second person singular possessive ('votre bruit') instead of the first person plural possessive ('nos'). Finally, in the first, fourth, and seventh lines there is alliteration in the first syllable of the verb: *dé*pouillez, *di*vulguez, *di*stinguez (the last two are even closer phonetically: *di*vulguez–*di*stinguez).

If any semantic unity emerges, it is essentially due to these parallels. In particular, it is not covered by the principle of linear order which follows from Bellert's definition.[23] Only if we consider the poem in its entirety, as a simultaneous whole – where each sentence is viewed from the same perspective as every other, in large measure independently of the order in which they appear – do we observe such unity. The interpretation of each sentence, owing to the influence of the parallelisms, acts indirectly on that of the others, whether they precede or follow it. This interpretation remains basically equivocal. Thus, some of the sentences would normally have negative moral connotations ('vous prodiguez les méfaits', 'vous divulguez nos secrets'), others are neutral, or could in other contexts have positive connotations ('vous conjurez les sorts', 'vous distinguez les bons d'entre les mauvais'); the result of their being placed in parallel is that what would otherwise be judged as good is viewed in the same way as what would otherwise be judged to be bad, and vice versa. With all the verbs being of agency,[24] we also feel that a certain responsibility and a certain power are attributed to 'vous'. This power consists either in the ability to reveal what is hidden ('vous divulguez nos secrets', 'vous ramenez au jour les vieilles écritures'), or to create disorder ('vous prodiguez les méfaits', 'vous divulguez nos secrets', 'vous fatiguez la terre de votre bruit'), or to create or restore order ('vous conjurez les sorts', 'vous distinguez les bons d'entre les mauvais'). The 'vous' has the power to create or to change situations; this power is described in observational terms, without any value judgement (despite the opposition between 'vous' and 'nous' in lines 1 and 4; all that is suggested is that the 'nous', obliquely presented, is distinct from 'vous'). This power remains totally ambiguous (which produces a certain irony in the last sentence),[25] and all the more so because some of the sentences, in isolation, are partially indeterminate: 'vous dépouillez nos arbres' can be judged positively or negatively (according to whether one interprets it as 'You strip our trees of the insects covering them/of their dead branches . . .', or 'You strip our trees of their leaves/of their fruit'), as can 'vous ramenez au jour les vieilles écritures' (does this refer to the deciphering of ancient alphabets, or to the bringing to light, wanted or not, of forgotten documents?). Even 'vous prodiguez les méfaits' is somewhat equivocal, in that, clearly, 'méfaits' has been substituted for 'bienfaits' (cf. the cliché 'prodiguer des bienfaits').

2.3

It would not be difficult to multiply examples, taken from quite diverse kinds of poetry, from popular verse to surrealism,[26] to illustrate the point I am making. Very often the rarity, sometimes the total absence, of anaphors, the relaxing of logical connections due to implicative terms and presuppositions, as well as ellipses of all kinds, are compensated for by various sorts of parallelisms, which create, between the elements they connect, 'symbolic' relations of equivalence, opposition, or contiguity, which cannot in general be treated in terms of logico-semantic representations in the strict sense. One could study, from this point of view, for example the sonnets of Nerval, in particular 'El Desdichado' and 'Delfica', many of Rimbaud's poems, such as

'Solde' and 'Départ' in the *Illuminations en prose*, quite a few poems by Baudelaire,[27] Tzara, Breton, etc. To be convincing, the demonstration would often require extended explication. I will limit myself here to a very brief discussion of a single example, but one that is very different from the poem of Nougé.

One of the most beautiful of the late poems of Yeats, 'Long-legged Fly',[28] is a striking example of a quite common phenomenon: it consists of three stanzas each of which, taken separately, aside from certain subtleties, forms a coherent discourse, but between which there is no logical connection, at least at first glance. The unity of the whole is established by parallelisms:

a. An identical two-line refrain at the end of each stanza, which introduces an explicit comparison, and exhibits internal parallelism: 'Like a long-legged fly upon the stream/His(Her) mind moves upon silence.' Richard Ellman (1968, 202) notes that the relevance of the refrain is not immediately apparent, if one considers only the first stanza. The full richness of the comparison only appears when one considers the poem in its entirety; it is an excellent example of the non-linear nature of poetry: the relation of the refrain to each one of the stanzas echoes its relation to the others and enriches it.

b. The stanza structure, which is rather distinctive: each stanza has eight lines (plus the refrain). The rather complex stress pattern is roughly the same from stanza to stanza; only the even lines rhyme, two by two (2 and 4, 6 and 8), thus dividing each stanza into two quatrains.

c. Syntactic parallelisms: each stanza is syntactically divided into two parts, corresponding exactly to the two quatrains. Although the second, declarative, half sometimes consists of a complex sentence, sometimes of juxtaposed sentences, the first has essentially the same internal structure: a subordinate clause of purpose ('That civilization may not sink . . .'/'That the topless towers be burnt . . .'/'That girls at puberty may find . . .'), followed by an imperative ('Quiet the dog . . .'/'Move most gently . . .'/'Shut the door . . .'). In the second quatrain, the parallelisms are less evident, but each time there is a division into two sections: the first presents an individual directly ('Our master Caesar . . .'/'She . . .'/'. . . Michael Angelo . . .'), and the second is focussed in each case on a body part (an inalienable property) of the individual in question, a different part each time ('His eyes . . .'/'. . . her feet. . . .'/'His hand . . .').[29]

These mechanisms of parallelism allow an overall interpretation to emerge: Caesar, 'She' (Helen of Troy?), Michelangelo, appear as three prime examples of genius, of whom 'actions which individually ought to seem silent, slow, and trivial . . . turn out finally to be of the highest consequence' (Ellman, 1968, p. 202).

3

In the examples which we have just discussed, the parallelisms functioned in the place of semantic and pragmatic constraints on discourse. We can now ask another question: can phenomena involving parallelism account for other kinds of deviance that are to be found in poetry, but which are more directly grammatical in nature – violations of syntactic rules, of selection restrictions, of subcategorization, etc.?

3.1

I will treat just two examples, one very simple, the other much more complex. First, consider the beginning of the famous poem by Verlaine (from *Romances sans paroles*, 'Ariettes oubliées' III):

> (9) Il pleure dans mon coeur
>   Comme il pleut sur la ville

(It weeps in my heart as it rains on the town)

We find here, in the first line, a very clear example of a purely syntactic violation: 'pleurer' normally requires as subject a lexically full noun phrase, and here it has an 'empty' subject, the impersonal pronoun 'il'. This constraint is syntactic, and not semantic, in that it would be conceivable to have in French a verb 'pleurer' taking an impersonal pronoun as subject and assigning the semantic function of location,[30] or support, of the process expressed by the verb to a verbal complement, for example an indirect object. We would then have, instead of or alongside 'je pleure', the form 'il me pleure', which does not exist, although there exist verbs of this type in French, as in 'il me souvient de' (I recall) alongside 'je me souviens de', or 'il me faut faire cela' (it behoves me to do that) alongside 'je dois faire cela' (I must do that).[31] The grammar of French thus specifies, by a selectional feature, that 'pleurer' requires a lexically full subject; this is the rule that is violated in Verlaine's poem. What is the reason that this violation is so easily accepted?[32]

Once again, the answer is rather simple. The violation is enmeshed in a whole network of parallelisms. There is syntactic parallelism, between 'il pleure dans mon coeur' and 'il pleut sur la ville'; in both cases, we have an impersonal clitic subject pronoun, a verb in the present, and a locative complement of identical internal structure: preposition + definite determiner + noun.[33] There is also sound parallelism, most obviously between [il plœrə] and [il plö], but also with the internal rhyme 'pleur'/'coeur', with the echo of the two 'il's in 'la ville', and even the partially similar phonetic structure of 'coeur' and 'ville' at the ends of the lines (two monosyllabic nouns ending in a liquid). The parallelisms have an obvious semantic effect (which is, of course, reinforced by the explicit comparison using 'comme'): the semantic analogy between 'pleurer' and 'pleuvoir', is underlined, and weeping becomes, like raining, an impersonal process no longer directly attributed to the speaker of the poem.[34]

3.2

I will now examine in greater detail one of the best-known poems of e. e. cummings, in which grammatical violations are numerous and particularly clear: the poem numbered 29 in *Fifty Poems* (1939):[35]

(10) anyone lived in a pretty how town
(with up so floating many bells down)
spring summer autumn winter
he sang his didn't he danced his did.

Women and men (both little and small)
cared for anyone not at all
they sowed their isn't they reaped their same
sun moon stars rain

children guessed (but only a few
and down they forgot as up they grew
autumn winter spring summer)
that noone loved him more by more

when by now and tree by leaf
she laughed his joy she cried his grief
bird by snow and stir by still
anyone's any was all to her

someones married their everyones
laughed their cryings and did their dance
(sleep wake hope and then) they
said their nevers they slept their dream

stars rain sun moon
(and only the snow can begin to explain
how children are apt to forget to remember
with up so floating many bells down)

one day anyone died i guess
(and noone stooped to kiss his face)
busy folk buried them side by side
little by little and was by was

all by all and deep by deep
and more by more they dream their sleep
noone and anyone earth by april
wish by spirit and if by yes.

> Women and men (both dong and ding)
> summer autumn winter spring
> reaped their sowing and went their came
> sun moon stars rain

This poem has already been the object of many commentaries, and one of its most violently ungrammatical sentences, 'he danced his did', has become almost as famous among linguists and writers on stylistics as Chomsky's 'colourless green ideas sleep furiously'. It seems to me, however, that most of these discussions fail to reach the heart of the matter.[36]

There is no doubt at all that the poem contains a large number of clear syntactic violations. Let us note a few. In line 1, 'anyone' occurs in subject position in an affirmative declarative sentence, although normally this indefinite pronoun is only allowed in negatives ('I didn't meet anyone at the party') and interrogatives ('did anyone get drunk at the party?').[37] In the same sentence 'how' occurs in the position of an adjective, although it is an adverb, and furthermore, an interrogative adverb. In line 3, there is a succession of nouns ('spring summer autumn winter') having no apparent connection to the rest of the discourse. In line 4, we find finite verb forms in the position of a noun ('he sang his didn't he danced his did').[38] In line 10, there are two occurrences of a PP–NP–V construction ('down they forgot as up they grew'). This construction exists in English, and has often been described in terms of a transformation which moves to the beginning of a sentence a prepositional phrase which often consists of a preposition alone (cf. 'they went down the hill' → 'down the hill they went'; 'they went up' → 'up they went').[39] The problem is that, on the one hand, 'forget' does not accept this kind of prepositional phrase, and on the other hand, 'grow,' which does (cf. 'they grew up') has idiomatic status in this construction and does not allow the pre-position of the PP. Thus, in one case there is violation of a subcategorization restriction, and in the other application of a transformation which would normally be blocked by the verb. In line 12, an adverbial construction occurs which, while highly idiomatic, does exist in English: X by X (where X stands for a grammatical category which can vary from case to case: cf. 'they arrived one by one'; 'they did it little by little'), but it is realized with lexical items that do not allow it ('more by more'). Recall also the rarity of punctuation marks: there are only two sentence final periods (at the ends of stanzas 1 and 8). In each case the following sentence begins with a capital, and in both cases the word is the same: 'Women'. Moreover, there are many parentheses one of which, at least (in line 19: '(sleep wake hope and then) they'), seems misplaced; and sometimes the absence of punctuation produces ambiguity, for example in the passage between stanzas 3 and 4.

I will discuss only briefly the way in which linguists have approached the problem posed by these deviations. Levin (1962b) asks how one could modify and/or enrich the grammar of English so that it could generate, for example, 'he danced his did'. Thorne (1965) has indicated the difficulties and the arbitrariness in such an undertaking, but the solution which he proposes – assuming that the poem is written in a dialect other than Standard English and trying to write the rules of that dialect[40] – is hardly satisfying (even if Thorne does make some penetrating comments, which I have found helpful). In addition to the fact that it is based on a confusion between the level of grammar and that of the analysis of a particular text, this solution is purely descriptive, and avoids rather than solves the problem of the nature of deviations and of their function in a text. It seems to me necessary to adopt the principle that this poem is written in Standard English (after all, it is addressed to readers who speak Standard English), with clear grammatical deviations, which are indeed perceived as deviations, but which evidently create particular and systematic effects.

The first thing to be noted is the localized character of the deviations – localized, that is, with respect to the grammar of English, not with respect to the text as a whole. As some of the examples we have already discussed suggest, it is quite often possible to determine what rule has been violated at a given point in the text, and certain minimal changes at particular points will often result in perfectly normal English sentences. For example, substituting 'someone' for 'anyone', and 'big' for 'how'[41] in line 1 gives a grammatically perfect sentence: 'someone lived in a pretty big town'. Similarly, the elimination of 'down', and the permutation of 'up' and 'they grew', in line 10, produce a grammatical sentence: 'and they forgot as they grew up'. Again, in line 12, two changes ('noone' replaced by 'someone' and 'more by more' by 'more and more') give a normal sentence. Other deviations are relatively superficial: in line 3, the sequence of nouns (which, semantically, follows the order of the seasons), 'spring summer autumn winter', can rather easily be interpreted as an elliptical version either of a series of time adverbials modifying 'anyone lived . . .' or 'he sang . . .' (in spring, in summer, in autumn, (and) in winter),[42] or of a series of independent or coordinated sentences forming, with 'anyone lived . . .' and 'he sang . . .', a coherent discourse (it was spring, (and then) it was summer, etc.); this sort of ellipsis is, after all, rather common in language in general. In other words, it is clear that many of the rules of English have remained valid, and that we are certainly not confronted with a simple sequence of *mots en liberté* – to use Jakobson's expression (see Boas' view of grammatical meaning in Jakobson, 1971, p. 495).

Our second observation – and here we find a curious reversal of the situation in some of the examples discussed above (Villon, Nougé, etc.) which conformed syntactically while taking liberty with logico-semantic organization – in spite of some ambiguities, the principles which usually govern discourse coherence are on the whole respected to a remarkable extent. Once we have understood the nature of the deviations (and have observed the role, to be considered below, of parallelism), we see that this text tells a story which, with some lacunae and ambiguities, proceeds logically. It has a beginning ('anyone lived . . .'), various incidents are described ('children guessed . . . that noone loved him more by more . . .'; 'one day anyone died . . .'; 'busy folk buried them . . .'), and it has an ending, which in a sense closes the loop leading back to the beginning ('Women and men . . . reaped their sowing and went their came . . .'). This logical order is due to the abundant and correct use of anaphors (*'anyone . . . he* sang *his* didn't . . .'; *'Women and men . . . they* sowed *their* isn't'; *'children* guessed . . . and down *they* forgot as up *they* grew . . .'; *'anyone . . .* that noone loved *him . . .'*; *'noone . . . she* laughed *his* joy . . .' etc.),[43] to the uniform use of the past tense, the narrative tense (with a few exceptions that can be explained in a natural manner: the parenthetical use of the generic present in 'and only the snow can begin to explain . . .', the interpolated 'i guess', and the present reference of 'and more by more they dream their sleep'), accompanied by appropriate temporal indications ('spring summer . . .'; 'one day . . .'), and to the presence of a certain number of implicative terms which provide succeeding sentences with consequences in common (for example: 'anyone *lived* . . . one day anyone *died* . . . noone *stooped* to *kiss* his face . . . busy folk *buried* them').[44]

Our third observation is that this poem is written in a regular and traditional form: it comprises nine four-line stanzas, each line obeying the same dactylic pattern with four beats. This gives it a homely flavour, somewhat reminiscent of a children's song, not without similarity, for instance, to 'Humpty Dumpty'. It also contains rhymes, distributed in a rather particular manner: while there are no full rhymes in stanzas 5, 6, and 7, the first four and the last two stanzas each have their first two lines rhyming ('town/down', 'small/all', 'few/grew', 'leaf/grief', 'deep/sleep', 'ding/spring'); furthermore, stanzas 2 and 9 have, in their last two lines, the same imperfect rhyme, and with a word in common ('same/rain', 'came/rain'). This rather special distribution of the rhymes suggests a division of the poem into three sections, with the last tying up with the first – which is not without its counterpart in the semantics. There is also a certain number of internal assonances and alliterations ('how/town', '*d*id his *d*ance', '*b*usy folk *b*uried them'), about which nothing further will be said, and the same is true of the refrain-like role of 'spring summer autumn winter' and 'sun moon stars rain'.

These observations show that, on various levels – grammatical, semantico-logical, 'conventional'[45] – this poem has many normal or traditional features. However, this tells us nothing about the question of the syntactic deviations.

In addition, the reader has no doubt been tempted to object to my treating, for example, as normal cases of anaphora, the coreference of 'he' with 'anyone' in stanza 1, or of 'she' with 'noone' in stanzas 4 and 3; it is in fact obvious that, in (11) - taken independently of a context, and contrasted with (12) – 'she' is not a possible anaphor of 'no one':

(11) No one came; she kissed me.
(12) Juliet came; she kissed me.

For the reference to be possible, one must assign a special, deviant interpretation to 'anyone' and 'noone', and we have not yet given any indication that such an interpretation is possible.

Once again, the answer is to be sought in the fact that the various deviations are involved in a tight network of parallelisms,[46] in particular syntactic ones. Let us review the principal cases.

Consider the first deviation, that which consists in the use of the indefinite pronoun 'anyone' as the subject of a declarative sentence. This sentence would be difficult to interpret in isolation; at best, one might view it as a mistake, with 'anyone' being substituted for 'someone'. But we find in the text ten occurrences of human indefinite pronouns ('anyone', 'noone', 'someones', 'everyones') all having the same internal structure (quantifier + one(s)),[47] with six in subject position,[48] two others coordinated and functioning as 'dislocated' subjects ('they dream their sleep', 'noone and anyone . . .') and two in object position, one indirect ('cared for anyone . . .') one direct ('married their everyones'). Sometimes, even outside a context, the resulting sentence could be a normal English sentence (for example, 'noone stooped to kiss his face'), but most often the deviations are obvious, although of diverse types (compare that of line 1 to that due to the non-existent plurals 'someones' and 'everyones' in line 17). Given these facts, a consistent pattern emerges: everything suggests that 'anyone', etc., are being treated as definite noun phrases;[49] and if we take them as such, the deviations disappear, and furthermore the anaphoric uses involving these words (cf. (11) above) become regular. We can go even further: since one of the characteristics of indefinite pronouns is the absence of any particular lexical content, it is quite reasonable to assimilate them here to another category of definite noun phrases which also have this property, namely proper nouns. 'Anyone', 'noone', etc., are thus easily taken as proper nouns designating insubstantial individuals, and this places us on familiar ground, that, for example, of 'my name is Nobody' in the Odyssey.[50] Note also that in everyday language indefinites are sometimes used as proper names, as in the French 'j'ai rencontré Untel', 'Monsieur Tout-le-Monde', 'Machin m'a dit que . . .', the English 'I spoke to so-and-so/whoever', etc. Thus, the content of the poem is becoming clearer: it tells the story, the life, loves, and death, of a 'man without qualities' – 'anyone'.

Other human, indefinite, or generic noun phrases appear in the poem: 'Women and men', 'children', 'busy folk'; they are all in subject position.[51] Although they have more precise lexical content, they all designate very general human categories, and this maintains the general and indeterminate character of the story being narrated. Note the almost total syntactic parallelism of stanzas 2 and 9, those which begin with 'Women and men'.

Let us consider now another example of deviance, that of 'he danced his did'. I have admitted, as have all other commentators, that this sentence has the structure $NP-V$ $[_{NP}Det-N]$, and that the anomaly consists in the occurrence of a finite verb form in the position of a noun. However, *a priori*, at least one other analysis is possible, according to which (recall the rather general absence of punctuation) we would have here, not a single sentence, but two juxtaposed sentences, both of the form $NP-V$: 'He danced', 'His did'. The anomaly would then consist only in the substitution of a possessive for the nominative ('his' instead of 'he'); and this analysis is not implausible in itself, since there exist brief dialogues of the type 'He danced – Yes he did', or 'Did he dance? – He did'. In fact, in certain contexts 'his did' is perfectly grammatical, for example, 'My sister didn't dance. His did.' If such an analysis has never been envisaged, that is because 'he danced his did' is not isolated, but belongs to a veritable paradigm, constituted by thirteen occurrences of the same construction, spread over six stanzas of the poem, with twelve of these occurrences being in pairs:

> (13) he sang his didn't
> he danced his did
>
> they sowed their isn't
> they reaped their same
>
> she laughed his joy
> she cried his grief
>
> laughed their cryings (and)
> did their dance
>
> (they) said their nevers
> they slept their dream
>
> they dream their sleep
>
> reaped their sowing (and)
> went their came

It is clear that it is the totality of this paradigm which forces us to reject the second analysis and adopt the first. I will not go into detail concerning the divergences and convergences among the various occurrences of the construction (there is a whole system of binary relations here which should be looked at more closely), but it seems to me that we find here, if on a much larger scale and in a much more daring fashion, something comparable to what we noted in our discussion of the two lines from Verlaine. The fact that 'he danced his did' is placed in parallel with a series of occurrences of the same construction, of which some can be natural ('did their dance') and others are easily interpretable – in which, in any case, the object of the verb does have a noun ('they slept their dream', 'reaped their sowing') – is what forces the reader to regard 'did' as a noun, and at the same time helps him to find an interpretation.

The parallelism does not only focus on the $NP-V$ [$_{NP}Det-N$] construction; it also provides a series of more specific clues. Most of the (real) nouns which occur are 'derived nominals' related to verbs ('grief', 'cryings', 'dance', 'dream', 'sleep', 'sowing'), and this makes them closer to 'did'. We seem to have a sort of musical chairs of verbs and nouns; an item which appears at one moment in the position of a verb appears later in the position of the noun object, and vice versa: 'they sowed their isn't/they reaped their same/reaped their sowing', 'she laughed his joy/she cried his grief/laughed their cryings', 'they slept their dream/they dream their sleep'; 'he danced his did' then looks like a variant (syntactic if not semantic) of 'he did his dance'. Most of the occurrences can be interpreted as cases of one or the other of two constructions involving a verb and its object, both very common, and related to one another. One of these is the construction consisting of a verbal operator (a verb with no semantic content) followed by an object noun which is a derived nominal (see Chomsky, 1972; also Giry, 1972), with the construction being approximately equivalent to a simple intransitive verb (cf. 'walk'/'take a walk' in English, 'sourire'/'faire des sourires' in French); this is the construction found in 'he did his dance' (cf. 'he danced'). The other is the so-called 'cognate object' construction ('to dream a dream', 'sing a song', 'dance a dance'). These two constructions have in common the absence of semantic (thematic) independence of the object with respect to the verb: a semantic function which could have been fulfilled by the verb alone is distributed, in two different ways, over the verb and its object. It is rather common, with these two constructions, to have, in the determiner of the object, a possessive referring to the subject ('to live one's life', 'to take one's bath', etc.). In general, many verb–object constructions, and not just these two types, allow or require an (inalienable) possessive in the object which refers to the subject, and these constructions are often of a more or less pronouncedly idiomatic character (cf. 'to lose one's mind/way/temper', 'to get one's way/kicks', in French 'prendre son pied', 'prendre sa source', 'faire ses dents', etc.); this facilitates our taking 'he danced his did', 'they reaped their same', etc., as rather peculiar idiomatic constructions. Finally, many transitive verbs, including some of those present here, allow, alongside or

112

instead of ordinary objects, sentential complements ('they dreamed that they slept') or headless relatives ('they said what they did'; 'they did what they said', 'they sang what they didn't'; compare also 'they reaped their sowing' – which is odd in that normally 'sowing' designates the action rather than its object or result – to 'they will reap what they have sowed'). In other cases, when the verb–object construction seems bizarre, one can often substitute for it a construction with another type of complement (compare 'she laughed his joy' with 'she laughed at his joy' or 'she laughed with joy', or '(they) went their came' with 'they went as they came' – cf. French 'Jean s'en alla comme il était venu'). Everything looks as if cummings, starting with a normal construction of English – one which is firmly anchored in the poem because of the parallelisms – is extending it in various directions: by exchanging the cognate objects of different verbs ('they slept their dream'/'they dream their sleep'), by using, instead of frozen possessives, true anaphors referring to other referents than the subject ('she laughed his joy'), and by creating 'portmanteau constructions' (in the sense in which Lewis Carroll spoke of portmanteau words), resulting from the telescoping of different possible constructions into one: 'he danced his did' is thus the portmanteau version of 'he did his dance'/'he danced his dance'/'he danced what he did . . .', 'they went their came' that of 'they went as they came' and 'they went their way', etc.

I will deal with the other types of deviations more quickly, since, on the whole, they have the same characteristics. Consider 'more by more'. Again, we find what amounts to a paradigm: thirteen occurrences of *X* by *X*, concentrated at two locations in the poem, confirming the tripartite division already noted:

(14)   more by more

        when by now and   tree by leaf
        bird by snow and   stir by still

                                    side by side
        little by little   and was by was
        all by all and   deep by deep
        and more by more

        wish by spirit and   if by yes

As we have noted, this is a rather idiomatic construction; it is not possible to determine in any general way which lexical items can occur. Certain of these examples are grammatical ('side by side', and 'little by little', although the latter, modifying 'busy folk buried them', produces a rather droll effect). It is clear that the construction is adverbial, but there is a systematic ambiguity in its use here: while 'more by more' seems to modify 'noone loved him', and 'side by side' seems to unambiguously modify 'busy folk buried them', the fact that most of the occurrences of this construction are situated at the boundary between two stanzas or two sentences, or both, prevents us from being sure which of the two sentences is modified; for example, 'when by now' and 'tree by leaf' could as easily modify 'noone loved him' as 'she laughed his joy she cried his grief' (in this case, the ambiguity is not really important, and it is conceivable that these adverbials go with the preceding as well as with the following sentence). The problem arises also with lines 28–9: 'little by little . . . deep by deep' could go with 'busy folk buried them' or with 'they dream their sleep', or partly with one and partly with the other. Here there would be an important semantic difference depending on the choice made.

On the whole the deviations have striking analogies with those we spoke of in relation to 'he danced his did'. Again we find portmanteau constructions: 'more by more' (and perhaps 'deep by deep') results from the telescoping of X by X and X and X (cf. 'more and more', 'deeper and deeper'), 'all by all' from that of X by X and X in X (cf. 'all in all'), etc. In many of the cases the two X terms are lexically different, but even if there is not always a construction of the form X particle X available (where particle = conjunction or preposition) it is always rather easy to reconstitute a fairly simple semantic or pragmatic relation between the two terms connected by 'by' ('when/now', 'tree/leaf', 'stir/still' – note the alliteration – 'bird/snow', 'wish/spirit', 'if/yes'). This variant, which introduces different terms on either side of 'by', recalls that involving permutation of cognitive objects in 'they dream their sleep', etc. Another common feature is the systematic playing with simple binary relations (between verb and object in one case, X and X in the other), with the alteration being different in practically every case. We find the same effect in 'Women and men' ('both little and small'/'both dong and ding').

The last deviations that I will deal with are those of 'and down they forgot as up they grew'. I have already mentioned their localized, circumscribed character. In addition to the fact that the 'up'/'down' opposition occurs elsewhere twice in 'with up so floating many bells down', and that it is another instance of the role of simple binary oppositions in the poem, the essential point is the internal parallelism of the two constructions: 'down they forgot/up they grew' (note also the alliteration 'forgot'/'grew'). In isolation, each of the sentences would simply be deviant, and, in the case of 'down they forgot', difficult to interpret; placed in parallel, they suggest a striking 'semantic' interpretation which is both clear and amusing: the notion of upward movement is given new life in 'grew up', and that of downward movement, which is certainly not logically connected in any way with the idea of forgetting, appears to be associated with it in a quite natural manner.

It is thus evident that the deviations in this poem do not occur randomly, but remain within limits that are established by the grammar of English and the parallelisms created, and that they produce all sorts of comic or allusive effects.[52] 'Anyone lived . . .' tells us the story of the life, at once simple, exemplary, and tragi-comic, and lived against a background where nature and society are reduced to their most elementary aspects, of two anonymous protagonists, Anyone and Noone. A kind of implicit moral emerges: 'Life should be taken as I take language, with a blend of seriousness, attention, irony, and freedom.' The poem is, in a sense, and in the same spirit, a development of a sentence from *Finnegans Wake*: 'They lived and loved ant laughed end left'.[53]

4

A few brief remarks by way of conclusion. First of all, the matters considered above can, no doubt, help to clarify, and also receive clarification from, the problems posed by the translation of poetry. This is not at all novel, but it seems to me that one of the difficulties, perhaps the central difficulty, of translating poetry is due to the fact that the poem always exhibits the two-fold kind of organization we have been speaking of. A good translation is always a compromise which aims at retaining as much as possible both of the logico-semantic representation and of the effects arising from parallelism; and any good poetic translation is also, necessarily, an invention, a creation, in that the translator is led to seek, in the target language – whose resources may be very different from those of the language of the original – syntactic, morphological, and phonological equivalents for the materials which in the original served as the building blocks for parallelisms. One could thus engage in genuine experiments consisting either in the construction of translations based on the information obtained by analysis (for example, a translation of cummings into French based in part on the comments given above), or else in the examination, in the light of one's analyses, and with data concerning the intuition of monolingual or bilingual readers, of existing translations, which would, no doubt, be an indirect way to verify whether the facts uncovered about parallelism are actually relevant.

Secondly, it will be necessary to investigate the limits on statements of the kind made above, especially with respect to the semantic or symbolic effects of parallelisms. Since these effects are often only indirectly related to the logico-semantic representations of utterances, and may depend on many factors involving belief, experience, and culture, it is doubtless totally illusory to think that we can ever describe them completely. So the traditional disciplines, such as philology, literary history, or criticism, thematic or other, retain their rights. But they can at the same time benefit from grammatical analyses of parallelisms (since such analysis may sometimes suggest, sometimes exclude, certain interpretations), and go beyond them, by giving a richer and more concrete content to the suggested effects. But what seems to me to be excluded is that there will ever be developed a 'generative criticism';[54] such a notion seems totally contradictory. All that one can hope for in this area is to discover certain general constraints – on the types of parallelisms, their interactions, their interactions with logico-semantic form and with 'ordinary' constraints on discourse, or the general types of symbolic effects that they can produce – but it seems to me utopian to imagine that we will ever be able to predict the particular types of effects that are brought about.[55]

On the other hand, one domain where application of the approach suggested here may prove to be fertile is that of the typology of style. We have seen (consider the differences between Nougé and cummings) that the types of equilibrium achieved between grammatical constraints, logico-semantic constraints, and phenomena of parallelism, vary a great deal from one poet (one period, etc.) to another. One might take these types of relations as a basis for establishing a typology of styles (one has already been sketched in Jakobson, 1960). In addition, there no doubt exist rather precise constraints on the kinds of deviation allowed on one level, in the light of what happens on other levels. It is rather difficult to imagine, for instance, poetry that combines the syntactic liberties taken by cummings with the surrealists' freedom with logico-semantic constraints. It seems to me that there is a vast area to be explored in this direction.[56]

One point deserving attention is the following: is the principle of parallelism (the projection of equivalence relations onto the sequence, to paraphrase Jakobson) a specifically linguistic principle? Since, at the time when Jakobson formulated his theory, it was generally thought that paradigmatic and syntagmatic relations played a central role in language, and, in a sense, characterized it exhaustively, it was possible to believe that the principle in question belonged exclusively to the domain of language (and thus was within the competence of the linguist). But transformational grammar has taught us to see much more abstract and complex mechanisms at work in human language, which cannot be reduced to the simple distinction between the paradigmatic and the syntagmatic. On the other hand (and no one has done more than Jakobson to convince us of this) it has become clear that the distinction between paradigm and syntagm – between equivalence and contiguity – is to be found everywhere, and that it is difficult even to imagine any connection at all between two facts or two ideas which cannot be described in terms of (various combinations of) these two types of relation which, by that very fact, are thoroughly trivialized. It is a fact that phenomena of parallelism are to be found elsewhere than in poetry – in music, for instance, to take the most obvious example. This being so, it appears that the only thing that is specifically linguistic in the various types of parallelism is their material. Furthermore, if the role of the linguist is essential in discovering them, describing their workings and their interactions with other levels, it would seem that the last word – when it is time to raise the problem of explaining parallelisms, the problem of the constraints which govern them and the problem of their perception by the reader or hearer – belongs to the psychologist concerned with cognitive processes, in particular with the psychology of perception (parallelisms, which are 'superficial' phenomena, are essentially part of the theory of perception), and with the psychology of the 'association of ideas'.

To conclude, it should be clear from all that has been said so far that poetry, whatever it is, is not an 'anti-language' or counter-language, in spite of what is sometimes claimed. What characterizes poetry, once again, is the interaction of two (or more?) different kinds of articulation. The various types of violations which we have encountered can (almost) always be understood in terms of such interaction. But what remains obscure – and I have no intention of seriously considering this problem here – is the relation between this interplay and the aesthetic aspect – what makes a poem a great poem. I will offer one or two observations. First of all, since a distinction has always been made between 'versified prose' and 'real' poetry (cf. Jakobson, 1960), it would be interesting to ask whether one of the fundamental differences between 'bouts rimés', scientific treatises in verse, etc., on the one hand, and Yeats, Baudelaire, Li Tai Po, etc., on the other, does not reside, at least in part, in the use made of parallelisms. In the *Art poétique* of Boileau, we find many of the mechanisms of parallelism, but, in a sense, these serve no purpose: the rhymes, the prosody, do not have any special symbolic effect. (The only important effect is mnemonic.) No doubt, this difference is essential, but the linguist, as such, cannot resolve this matter alone.[57] A second comment of a different kind can be made. The approach inspired by Jakobson has often been accused of being incapable of accounting for certain types of texts held to be (great) poetry (certain forms of modern poetry, for example), that do not exhibit any of the known varieties of parallelism.[58] I will make two comments about this. First, I would not find it objectionable if a theory of poetry which assigned a central role to parallelisms excluded certain kinds of modern 'poetry' – any more than I would be disturbed by a general theory of music which could account for Mozart, Debussy, Gesualdo, Schönberg, Gagaku, Gregorian chant, etc., but which would exclude as non-music, for example, John Cage's *Radio Music*; I would rather view this as a corroboration of the theory. It must be recognized that, for historical reasons which it is not my business to discuss, we live in a time when it has become possible for anyone at all, with little risk, to apply to anything at all

117

N. Ruwet

such words as 'music', 'poetry', or 'painting'. Second, the term 'poetry' has
come to be applied to quite different things (this has a long history, which
began in the Romantic era, if not earlier; cf. the 'poetry which is in things,
not words', 'a poetic sunset', etc.); it is, often, simply synonymous with
'beauty'. But since the word 'beauty' has become almost obscene (let alone
'taste' and 'sublime'), people look for substitutes, like 'poetic', 'modern', if
not 'valid' and 'revolutionary', this being perhaps particularly true of the
French words. The time may have come to restore their meanings to these
words, and one might then begin to reflect in a more productive way on the
relations between the 'poetic' (defined in terms of the interaction of
parallelisms and of ordinary constraints on discourse) and the 'beautiful'
(which surely depends on many other factors).

References

Bellert, Irina (1970), 'On a condition of the coherence of texts', *Semiotică* 2(4),
pp. 335–63.
Bierwisch, Manfred (1965), review of Z. Harris, *Discourse Analysis Reprints, Linguistics*
13, pp. 61–73. Reprinted in Jens Ihwe, ed., *Literaturwissenschaft und Linguistik* 1
(Frankfurt, Athenäum Verlag, 1971), pp. 141–54.
Chomsky, Noam (1965), *Aspects of the Theory of Syntax* (Cambridge, Mass., MIT
Press).
— (1972), *Studies on Semantics in Generative Grammar* (The Hague, Mouton).
Ellmann, Richard (1968), *The Identity of Yeats* (Oxford, University Press (first edition,
1954)).
Emonds, J. E. (1972), Evidence that indirect object movement is a structure-
preserving rule', *Foundations of Language* 8(4), pp. 546–61.
Fauconnier, Gilles (1974), *La Coréférence: syntaxe ou sémantique?* (Paris, Seuil).
Giry, Jacqueline (1972), *Analyse syntaxique des constructions du verbe faire* (Paris, CNRS,
LADL).
Grice, H. P. (1967), *Logic and Conversation*, The William James Lectures, Harvard
University, unpublished; a partial version can be found in P. Cole and J. L.
Morgan, eds., *Syntax and Semantics* III (New York, Academic Press, 1975), pp. 41–58.
Harris, Zellig (1952), 'Discourse analysis', *Language* 28(1), pp. 1–30.
— (1963) *Discourse Analysis Reprints* (The Hague, Mouton).
Hayek, F. A. (1967), *Studies in Philosophy, Politics and Economics* (New York, Clarion
Books, Simon and Schuster).
Jackendoff, Ray S. (1972), *Semantic Interpretation in Generative Grammar* (Cambridge,
Mass., MIT Press).
— (1973), 'Base rules for prepositional phrases', in S. Anderson and P. Kiparsky,
eds., *Festschrift for Morris Halle* (New York, Holt, Rinehart and Winston),
pp. 345–56.
Jakobson, Roman (1960), 'Linguistics and Poetics' in T. A. Sebeok, ed., *Style in
Language* (Cambridge, Mass., MIT Press), pp. 350–77.
— (1971), *Selected Writings*, II (The Hague, Mouton).
— (1973), *Questions de Poétique* (Paris, Seuil).
Katz, J. J. (1972), *Semantic Theory* (New York, Harper and Row).

Kiparsky, Paul (1968), 'Metrics and morphophonemics in the Kalevala', in *Studies Presented to Professor Roman Jakobson by his Students* (Cambridge, Mass., Slavica Publications), pp. 137–48.

Klima, E. S. (1964), 'Negation in English', in J. A. Fodor and J. J. Katz, eds., *The Structure of Language* (Englewood Cliffs, N.J., Prentice-Hall), pp. 246–323.

Kuroda, S.-Y. (1976), 'Reflections on the foundations of narration theory', in T. A. van Dijk, ed., *Pragmatics of Language and Literature* (Amsterdam, North-Holland), pp. 108–40.

Levin, S. R. (1962a), *Linguistic Structures in Poetry* (The Hague, Mouton).

— (1962b), 'Poetry and grammaticalness', in *Preprints of Papers for the Ninth International Congress of Linguists* (Cambridge, Mass.).

Milner, Jean-Claude (1973), *Arguments linguistiques* (Paris, Mame).

Ruwet, Nicolas (1967), *Introduction à la grammaire générative* (Paris, Plon); English translation, *Introduction to Generative Grammar* (Amsterdam/New York, Elsevier/North-Holland).

— (1972a), *Théorie syntaxique et syntaxe du français* (Paris, Seuil); English translation, *Problems in French Syntax* (London, Longman).

— (1972b), *Langage, Musique, Poésie* (Paris, Seuil).

— (1975a), 'Montée du sujet et Extraposition', *Le Français moderne* 43(2); English version in M. Lujàn and F. Hensey, eds., *Current Studies in Romance Linguistics* (Washington, D.C., Georgetown University Press, 1976).

— (1975b), 'Synecdoques et métonymies', *Poétique* 23.

Sperber, Dan (1974), *Le Symbolisme en général* (Paris, Hermann); English translation, *Rethinking Symbolism* (Cambridge, University Press, 1975).

Thorne, J. P. (1965), 'Stylistics and generative grammars', *Journal of Linguistics* 1(1).

Notes

1. There is a brief summary in Ruwet, 1967, pp. 232ff.
2. In Harris' sense of the term, which is very different from Chomsky's; see Ruwet, 1967, pp. 232ff. and, more recently, Milner, 1973, ch. 4.
3. This is because Harris' procedure depends crucially on the presence in a text of more than one occurrence of the same lexical morpheme. Bierwisch shows, on the one hand, that it is possible to construct totally incoherent texts which satisfy this condition, and, on the other hand, that it is not difficult to find perfectly coherent texts which do not satisfy it (he gives as an example the beginning of a story by Brecht; see also example (1) below). Harris gets out of this difficulty by considering anaphoric pronouns, etc., as equivalents of their antecedents, and by appealing to meaning as a last resort. But this is simply to admit that a discovery procedure based on the distribution of morphemes in surface structure is inadequate; for while it is rather common that texts of some length exhibit repetitions of the same lexical items, that is merely because it is natural, and almost inevitable, when one is speaking of a given subject, to repeat words related to that subject. This does not tell us much about the principles which make a sequence of sentences a coherent text.
4. This is a simplification, but see n. 3 above.
5. For what follows, the precise way the theory represents the articulation of logico-semantic representation with syntactic representation does not matter much. In particular, I will remain neutral with respect to the current debate

between advocates of generative semantics and partisans of the standard or extended standard theory (see Chomsky, 1972).

6. On these constraints, see especially Fauconnier, 1974, and various studies by Kuroda (in particular Kuroda, 1976), by Karttunen, etc.

7. For example, in French the use of 'il' and 'celui-ci', which are both possible anaphors, is governed by different constraints; to see this, it suffices to replace 'il' by 'celui-ci' in the French version of (1): 'Il aime beaucoup cet endroit'. With 'celui-ci', the sentence is anomalous, and seems to mean that 'his house likes that place', since 'celui-ci' is the French equivalent of 'the latter' (moreover, there is a clash in gender agreement).

8. See Fauconnier, 1974.

9. Besides the role of anaphoric relations, we should also mention the basic role that temporal indications play in keeping a discourse coherent, whether these involve verbal tenses or time adverbials, explicitly or implicitly present in the utterances.

10. The examples given are all verbs, but there are implicative terms in most grammatical categories, nouns or adjectives (like 'downfall' and 'sudden' in 'Pierre's sudden downfall surprised me'), prepositions (like 'before' in 'Pierre reached Paris before Paul/before war broke out'), etc.

11. If, for example, to the question 'Where is Pierre working?' I answer 'I met Jacques in Vincennes', this answer, which is not 'natural' in the sense under consideration above, can be acceptable in certain contexts, when, for example, I know (and know that the person I am speaking to knows) that Jacques is Pierre's devoted assistant, and is always to be found where Pierre is.

12. Only indirectly, especially because there will often be different surface structures corresponding to the same underlying logical representation. This does not mean that, in a discourse, the choice between two different surface structures which correspond to the same logical form (a passive sentence and the corresponding active sentence, for instance) cannot have different consequences for the coherence of a text. As for independence with respect to morphology, consider the example of the two forms of the comparative in English (with and without 'more'): this difference has no importance from the viewpoint of logical representation, but it can be crucial in poetry.

13. I leave aside here the role of tropes in poetry. See a brief remark in section 4, n. 56.

14. By superficial syntactic structure, I mean here superficial phrase structure, possibly to the exclusion of particular choices of lexical items. On the other hand, I do not wish to claim that the 'superficial' levels which are involved are exactly those which are defined in present linguistic theory. It is possible that, to describe certain kinds of poetry, it will be necessary to define, for example, levels that are intermediate between the phonetic and the morphophonemic (systematic phonemic); on this matter, see Jakobson, 1960 and Kiparsky, 1968.

15. This would exclude, for instance, a (codified) system of parallelisms which required that all the sentences in a stanza have the same deep structure (or one of two alternating deep structures), while imposing no constraint on the resulting surface structures.

16. See e.g. Jakobson, 1960.

17. See Jakobson, 1973 and Ruwet, 1972b.

18. In the sense, no doubt, of Dan Sperber. Sperber, 1974, was not available to me when this article was written.

19. Cf. Nerval ('Les Cydalises'): 'Où sont nos amoureuses?/Elles sont au tombeau!' (Where are our beloveds?/They are in the tomb!)

20. Still more precisely (and this is connected with the presence of '*Mais* où sont . . .?'), one might say that the two questions in the poem are not exactly parallel. The 'sender' asks the first question of some indeterminate receiver (the reader?), then, thinking better of it and without waiting for the answer, he asks another question, which explains the 'mais'. This may indicate that, while the answer to the first question is not obvious, the answer to the second is.

21. Published, with the title *Quelques écrits et quelques dessins*, and with the author's name given as Clarisse Juranville, at Brussels, by René Henriquez (1927) (illustrated with five drawings by René Magritte). Reissued in Paul Nougé, *L'Expérience continue* (Editions de la Revue les Lèvres Nues, Jane Graverol, Brussels, 1966). André Souris, who was himself an active member of the Belgian surrealists, and a close friend of Paul Nougé, brought these poems to my attention, and informed me of the circumstances of their composition. (André Souris had himself set several of them to music, with the title 'Quelques airs de Clarisse Juranville mis au jour par André Souris' (1928).)

22. From Paul Nougé, *L'Expérience continue*, p. 375, untitled.

23. The idea that poetry – and works of art in general – do not obey a purely linear principle of organization is obviously not at all new. Here we can do no more than merely indicate one of the kinds of mechanisms (no doubt not the only one) that account for this. From the sketchy analyses presented here – which it would be desirable to develop further – it should also be clear that the opposition that certain Parisian critics would like to introduce between those who see a poem as a 'foyer d'éclatement' – a focus of dispersal – and those who try to find in it principles of coherence (an enterprise which is sometimes described as ideological and reactionary – I have been so accused in public) is totally artificial – and all the more so in that, as long as the attempt has not been made to show, with concrete analyses, just in what sense a poem is a 'foyer d'éclatement', the undertaking is devoid of any empirical content.

24. 'Fatiguer' does not require an agent, but that is not the case here (cf. Ruwet, 1972a, ch. 5). The agency appears clearly if one inserts in each of the sentences an adverb like 'délibérément', as is possible in each case.

25. 'Les mauvais' can hardly be interpreted here other than as referring to people. This is because it is impossible to see it as anaphoric, as would be the case, for instance, in 'Voici des fruits. Distinguez (triez) les bons d'entre les mauvais' (Here is some fruit. Pick out the good (ones) from the bad). The reason is that, although in general a noun phrase of the form Article + Adjective can, in French, when used anaphorically, refer indifferently to an animate or inanimate antecedent, there seems to be a constraint which restricts its non-anaphoric use to a 'human' interpretation.

26. Regarding Russian folk poetry, see Jakobson, 1973.

27. See e.g. my analysis of Sonnet 39 from the *Fleurs du mal* (Ruwet, 1972b, ch. 10).

28. See *Collected Poems of W. B. Yeats* (London, Macmillan, 1952), pp. 381–2.

29. In a more complete analysis it would also be necessary to take into account the asymmetries between the stanzas, which are made possible by the parallelisms, and also the correspondences existing only between two stanzas, for example 'to a distant post'/'in this lonely place'. Note as well the symmetry of the two outside stanzas, dealing with two explicitly named and really existing historical figures, both men (Caesar and Michaelangelo), as contrasted with the middle stanza, dealing with a female protagonist who is not named ('She . . .'). It should be kept in mind that parallelisms function as much in creating contrasts and asymmetries

as in creating comparisons or symmetries; what is important, in either case, is that the effects are obtained by mechanisms which are distinct from normal logico-semantic mechanisms.

30. I will not say anything here about the way in which a theory of thematic functions (see Jackendoff, 1972; Ruwet, 1972a, ch. 5) would handle this function: 'location', 'source'? This is irrelevant here. But see n. 34 below.

31. Concerning the arguments against deriving the two members of each of these pairs of sentences from a common deep structure, see Ruwet, 1972a, chs. 2 and 5; Ruwet, 1975a.

32. Outside of any context, the 'il' of 'il pleure dans mon coeur' could be interpreted as a truly referring pronoun with a human referent, cf. expressions like 'to cry on somebody's shoulder', 'elle est venue pleurer dans mon giron'. Note that Verlaine was careful to introduce the poem with a quote from Rimbaud, 'Il pleut doucement sur la ville', which creates a context. But it seems to me that even in the absence of this epigraph the facts of parallelism described below would be sufficient to explain the violation. In any case, the epigraph seems to have played no role in the independent existence which these two lines have had for a very large audience.

33. More exactly (see n. 32), it is the presence of the impersonal construction in the second line which forces the reader to take the 'il' of the first line as an impersonal pronoun.

34. This is the point at which the question of how the theory of thematic relations would handle the 'je' of 'je pleure' becomes interesting (see n. 31). If it turns out that 'je' should be treated as 'source', the theory could explain the effect as due to a shift from the function 'source' to the function 'location' (or 'goal'?); but distinguishing between these functions is not always easy in the present state of the theory (cf. Ruwet, 1972a, p. 186) and I will make no proposal in this matter.

35. Cited from the paperback edition published by Hawthorn Books, New York.

36. Cf. Levin, 1962b, and Thorne, 1965.

37. This is a simplification, but in any case, in cummings's poem, it is clear that there is a violation. For discussions of these phenomena, see Klima, 1964; Jackendoff, 1972.

38. But see the text below.

39. This construction has been studied by Emonds, 1972, and Jackendoff, 1973.

40. The term 'dialect' has been used, and misused, in various ways in certain recent linguistic discussions. If Maurice Gross (personal communication) is right in maintaining that the only reasonable definition of the word is geographical or social, it is clear that it is not applicable here. Furthermore, the kind of rules for this 'dialect' that Thorne is trying to develop would not work for many other poems by cummings; their predictive value is just about zero. This does not mean that it is impossible to characterize, linguistically, constants in the style of e.e. cummings; but such a characterization requires, as a preliminary, the study of a large number of his poems from the point of view we have adopted, which assigns a crucial role to the phenomena of parallelism.

I am forced to admit that the idea, first put forward, I believe, by Levin (1962a, p. 41), and which I took over in Ruwet, 1972b, p. 18, that 'a poem . . . articulates . . . its own code, in which it is the unique message', may be responsible for this confusion. I believe that this sort of metaphorical formulation, which boils down to the platitude that each great work of art is unique, should be abandoned. I plead guilty on this charge.

41. The interpretation of 'pretty how town' is problematic; should 'pretty' be interpreted as an adjective or as an adverb? I am somewhat inclined to favour the adverbial interpretation, for two reasons: (a) the rarity of preposed descriptive adjectives in the poem: the only example is 'busy folk'; (b) interpreting 'pretty' as an adverb would, in a sense, help regularize the construction; as an adverb 'pretty' can modify not only adjectives ('pretty big', 'pretty intelligent') but also adverbs, in particular manner adverbs (and 'how' is a manner adverb), as in 'pretty intelligently', 'he was wounded pretty severely', etc. The adverbial interpretation thus creates a connection between 'pretty' and 'how'; furthermore, this interpretation is more compatible than the other with the quite abstract, indeterminate nature of the poem as a whole (cf. the comments in the text on the use of the indefinites 'anyone', etc.).

42. This is the only analysis considered by Thorne; cf. Thorne, 1965.

43. But see the text below.

44. There is an ellipsis of a rather common type here: it is to be understood that 'noone' has also died.

45. I borrow this term, useful but not very happy, from Levin, 1962a, where it is used to designate such codified regularities as rhyme, metre, etc.

46. Almost all of them are. There remain isolated cases which could perhaps be shown to exhibit some regularity by a study of all of cummings. One example is the use of 'how' in line 1. But even in this case the deviance is not totally idiosyncratic: there is something in common between the two deviations of line 1 ('anyone' and 'how'). In both cases, terms are used in a declarative sentence which do not belong there, and which can occur in interrogatives. In addition, both lack any precise lexical content, even though they occur in positions where one would expect lexically full terms. The semantic effect of indeterminacy is the same in both cases.

47. This obviously creates an internal rhyme. Anyone trying to translate the poem into French should, no doubt, attempt to work with the paradigm 'quelqu'un' ('quelqu'une'), 'chacun', 'aucun'. Line 17 ('someones married their everyones') reminds me of the expression 'à chacun sa chacune'.

48. In one case ('anyone's any was all to her'). More precisely it is a determiner of the subject, with the head noun being itself a quantifier of the same type, 'any', contrasted with 'all'.

49. This imposes a reinterpretation of line 26, 'and noone stooped to kiss his face'. In null context, this is a grammatical sentence meaning the same thing as 'and nobody stooped to kiss his face'; but inserted in the paradigm (note in particular the coordination in line 13 'noone and anyone'), it has to be reinterpreted with 'noone' understood as a proper noun.

50. Similar word play can be found in Lewis Carroll. Note also the 'Everyman' of Ben Jonson, and the 'Jedermann' of Hofmannsthal.

51. The only other subject which occurs (outside of anaphors) is a definite inanimate noun phrase, 'the snow', which is connected rather with adverbials (cf. 'bird by snow' and 'stars rain sun moon' which immediately precede it).

52. For example, 'Women and men (both dong and ding)' (note the inversion in both cases: cf. 'men and women', 'ding dong'), as well as the playing with binary oppositions that are sometimes comic, sometimes poetic or surprising, seems to me a discrete, ironic allusion to the principle of yin and yang, fitting in with the notion of 'eternal recurrence' suggested by the refrains ('spring summer . . .', and 'sun moon . . .') and their variants. In 'he sang his didn't he danced his did' one might also want to see an allusion to *La Cigale et la fourmi*. 123

53. A quick glance at other poems of e.e. cummings (for instance, also from *Fifty Poems*, 3, 'if you can't eat you got to'; 10, 'spoke joe to jack'; 27, 'buy me an ounce and i'll sell you a pound'; 34, 'my father moved through dooms of love') reveals the same general type of mechanism – even if the particular grammatical violations are different from poem to poem. See n. 40.

54. See a recent issue of *Change*, 16–17 (1973).

55. Concerning the difference between two kinds of scientific theories, one kind which (as is the case in physics) can predict or explain particular facts or events, and another kind which can only provide an 'explanation of the principle', see Hayek, 1967. Hayek shows that, if most human sciences can aim only at theories of the second type (this is the case, for example, with economics), there are also cases of this in the natural sciences, such as the theory of the evolution of living things by natural selection.

56. I have intentionally omitted from this article the question of the role of tropes in poetry. (I will take up this matter elsewhere.) It should be clear (a) that a large part of the effects of metaphor or metonymy to be found in a poetic text are due to the role of parallelisms, and (b) that it is impossible to describe metaphors, in particular, solely in terms of semantic representation, in the narrow sense. From this point of view, certain recent attempts of rhetoricians to describe tropes in terms of a 'semic' analysis – and also the reducing of all tropes to synecdoche – seem to me to be misguided (see Ruwet, 1975b).

57. Briefly, I tend to think that the presence of parallelisms is a necessary, but not sufficient, condition for the existence of great poetry.

58. There is also the problem of the prose poem, which I will not deal with here, except to note that some of the most beautiful of the prose poems of Rimbaud (see section 2.3 above) or of Baudelaire (for instance 'Un hémisphère dans une chevelure') exhibit many syntactic parallelisms.

7. A critique of the motif

CLAUDE BREMOND

In a recent communication setting out the 'Semantic principles of a new Index of Motifs and Subjects',[1] Meletinski returns, fifty years after V. Propp, to discussion of the indexes developed by folklorists of the Finnish school for the classification of motifs and subjects in the folktale. The past and present contribution of these catalogues cannot be denied, but that should not be allowed to serve as a pretext for overlooking their glaring weaknesses in methodology. Recent developments in the semiotics of narrative have made us more demanding.

To a greater extent, perhaps, than *The Types of the Folktale*,[2] whose appropriateness to its object is more or less apparent, the *Motif-Index of Folk Literature* by Stith Thompson,[3] now seems vulnerable. The sheer size of these six large volumes poses a problem in the first place: an enormous amount of work, but how was that done, and why? Motifs have been collected on a vast scale, but what is a motif? How is a motif to be recognized, collected, and formally represented? What information would we want to find under a motif heading? What weight are we to give to it when two motifs are said to be related and grouped into a single class, and the classes are ordered in a hierarchy? Finally, what are the goals of the enterprise and what forms of consultation are envisaged?

These are our main questions of the Index and of Thompson's introductory comments, as we leaf through them with the recent rapid progress of semiotics in mind.

The first surprise is how meagre and vague are the answers to these questions. Motifs are characterized allusively and in passing, in the course of one sentence of the Introduction, as 'Those details out of which full-fledged narratives are composed' (p. 10). A brief reference is made to the work of researchers who have tried to sharpen the notion of a motif, or even to classify kinds of motif, but Thompson does not dwell on this at any length: he feels less obliged to discuss the definitions of others for not offering any definition of his own. Since any specification involves a limitation, the notion of a motif, as he conceives it, should remain as broad as possible: 'When the term *motif* is employed, it is always in a very loose sense, and is made to include any of the elements of narrative structure' (p. 19).

This eclecticism is justified by the pragmatic aim of furnishing answers to the most varied questions: 'Sometimes the interest of a student of traditional narrative may be centered on a certain type of character in a tale, sometimes on an action, sometimes on attendant circumstances of the action. Hence I have endeavored to use all the elements of tales that have in the past been objects of special study and similar elements that are likely to serve as such objects in the future' (p. 11).

There is, therefore, no definition of the motif, but rather a criterion of selection: the *Motif-Index* will retain, out of the 'multiform' infinitude of information to be found in a narrative, only what seems to deserve, for one reason or another, the attention of researchers. More precisely: 'Most of the items are found worthy of note because of something out of the ordinary, something of sufficiently striking character to become a part of tradition, oral or literary' (p. 19).

Banal acts of eating or sleeping are not worth recording, but 'Eating on a magic table, food furnished by helpful animals, food that gives magic strength – these become significant and are likely to be handed down by the teller of tales' (p. 19). The folklorist's test of relevance is that of the journalist: 'A dog bites his master' is not a motif worth including in the index, but 'The master bites his dog' is. There is no definition of the *motif*, but there is the notion of an *interesting* motif.

The grouping of the motifs evinces the same blatant rule-of-thumb approach: the classification, Thompson explains, is meant to meet the practical necessity of arranging them according to principles that are simple and easily understandable to users. Each motif is identified by a dominant feature, on which it is assumed folklorists will readily agree, and this feature is used to classify the motif. When a motif contains other important features, or a feature which might be taken to be dominant, a system of cross-references allows it to be mentioned in other chapters than the one where it is treated.

To carry out this guiding principle, 'motifs dealing with one subject are handled together' just as, in a library, all history books are kept in the same room, and all the books on Roman history, or the French Revolution, are shelved together. How did Thompson go about preparing the list of relevant subjects, and arranging them in a hierarchy of chapters, sections, and subsections? This came about, he says, spontaneously, step by step, by trial and error: at some points the need was felt to split up a group of motifs, at others to combine two classes into one. The finished work may give the impression of being organized rationally, the contents having ended up by being arranged in the order dictated by their mutual affinities, but nonetheless 'the classification of materials is the result of a gradual evolution, not of any preconceived plan' (p. 19).

The work is organized into twenty-three chapters, headed by letters of the alphabet, each devoted to a major conceptual or narrative category: A. Mythological motifs; B. Animals; C. Tabu; D. Magic; E. The dead; F. Marvels; G. Ogres; H. Tests; J. The wise and the foolish; K. Deceptions L. Reversal of fortune; M. Ordaining the future; N. Chance and fate; P. Society; Q. Rewards and punishments; R. Captives and fugitives; S. Unnatural cruelty; T. Sex; U. The nature of life; V. Religion; W. Traits of character; X. Humour; Z. Miscellaneous groups of motifs.

Within each chapter, the division into sections and subsections is realized either by headings in bold-face, or by a system of numbers ending in zero. Take chapter Q, 'Rewards and punishments'. There are four major sections: from Q 10 to Q 99, 'Deeds rewarded'; from Q 100 to Q 199, 'Nature of rewards'; from Q 200 to Q 399, 'Deeds punished'; from Q 400 to Q 599, 'Kinds of punishment'. Looking at this last section, we see that it is divided in turn into twelve subsections, each defined by a general heading and assigned a number ending in zero: Q 410: 'Capital punishment'; Q 430: 'Abridgement of freedom as punishment'; Q 450: 'Cruel punishments', etc. This last heading then groups the motifs themselves: Q 450.1: 'Torture as punishment'; Q 450.1.1: 'Torture as punishment for murder'; Q 451: 'Mutilation as punishment', etc.

For each motif so recorded, the *Motif-Index* provides: (1) a formula in italics which is supposed to characterize the motif and allow it to be recognized in the texts (for example, J 225.0.1: 'Angel and hermit'); (2) in some cases, a summary of the narrative context, the preceding, simultaneous, or following events (in the same example: 'Angel takes hermit with him and does many seemingly unjust things'); (3) in some cases, an indication of the number of the tale type which has the motif as a characteristic element (here Type 759); (4) an indication of bibliographic sources concerning the motif – those which refer to studies on the motif and those which publish texts containing the motif (here, among others, DeCock, *Studien en Essays* 178ff.; Crane Vitry 179, No. 109); (5) sometimes, cross-reference to other motifs, related or comparable (for motif J 225.0.1, the *Motif-Index* has two cross-references: F 171.6 'Mysterious punishments in other world'; V 235: 'Mortal visited by angel'). This system of cross-references makes it possible, in particular, to indicate, for a given heading, motifs that might have been placed under that heading, but which have been put elsewhere.

How is the *Motif-Index* to be consulted? Thompson closes his 'Introduction' with 'Some suggestions as to using the index'. He supposes first of all that the user wants to find a motif in the *Motif-Index*. For this, he advises us to look in the general table of contents, then in the table of contents for each chapter, to find the heading most likely to have had that motif assigned to it. It might be the case that the motif has not been classified under the heading which first comes to mind; in such a case, it will no doubt be found in the cross-references given under that heading. However, the search may prove fruitless for, as Thompson says, 'Often the fundamental nature of an item may not seem to be the same to the searcher as it has seemed to me' (p. 24). A detailed alphabetical index, which occupies the sixth volume of the work, is available then to help the reader. If we suppose, for example, that in connection with a text where an angel is accompanied by a hermit, I do not have the time to explore thoroughly chapters J: 'The wise and the foolish', F: 'Marvels', and V: 'Religion', then as a last resort I can consult the alphabetical index under the words 'Angel' and 'Hermit'. I will find nothing under *Angel* (no doubt because of an oversight of the author), but under *Hermit* I will find the reference I am looking for: 'Angel takes hermit with him and does many seemingly unjust things J 225.0.1'.

What is the purpose of such consultation? The motifs and tales have been catalogued in order to facilitate comparative studies: 'If gradually all the tales, myths, ballads, and traditions were catalogued according to the same system, great progress would be made in rendering possible completer comparative studies than can now be undertaken' (p. 24). No details are given concerning the programme of these studies, but this is not Thompson's objective when he envisages the use to be made of it. On the contrary, he insists on what could be called 'close' use of the work: it is to provide a model and a framework for research whose goal is to enlarge the *Motif-Index* itself. In a sense, he conceives of this work, if not as an end in itself, at least as the decisive stage of an enterprise which can and should be indefinitely continued. It would be a mistake to accuse him of a tautology when he writes that 'The principal use of the present index, I hope, will be for cataloguing motifs in various collections of tales and traditions' (p. 24).

No more precise indications can be found in 'Purpose and Importance of an Index of Types and Motifs',[4] the article in which Thompson announced his project, nor in the brief 'Narrative motif: analysis as a folklore method',[5] in which the motif is simply defined as an item important enough to be remembered. It is clear that theoretical speculation did not monopolize the author's attention either before he undertook his labours, or after he finished the work. We can readily believe him when he assures us that the work took shape gradually, day after day, through constant shuffling and reshuffling of the material. This does not prevent him, however, from claiming scientific status for his endeavour, and presenting the *Motif-Index* as an attempt 'made to reduce the traditional narrative material of the whole earth to order (as, for example, the scientists have done with the worldwide phenomena of biology)' (p. 10).

The advantages of the procedure followed by Thompson are those of any rule-of-thumb approach: considerable freedom in the selection of the items to be indexed, since anything at all in a narrative can become a motif; formulations which almost literally reproduce the textual occurrence of the motif; classes of motifs which are created according to the principle that 'things that look alike go together', without having to state, except case by case, what point of resemblance should take precedence over all the points of difference of motifs that are partly similar and partly dissimilar; a hierarchy of motif classes which aims neither at systematization nor to be exhaustive, whose virtue is rather the concreteness of the categories used, and the simplicity of the rubrics. All in all, a catalogue which obeys the quite pragmatic consideration of offering the user only categories that are immediately intelligible to all, and reducing the apparatus to be mastered to a few indispensable rules giving guidance through the mass of information.

But there is a price to be paid. While apparently advantageous, the indeterminacy of the notion of motif in fact leads to: (1) arbitrariness in the identification of textual occurrences elevated to the status of motifs; (2) slackness in the conceptualization and formulation of the motifs extracted from these textual occurrences; (3) anarchy in the categorization and classification of the motifs.

Identification of the motif

It should be mentioned first of all that the indeterminacy of the notion of motif, intended to be as broad as possible, is compensated for by the application of an oddly restrictive criterion of selection. Or rather, there are two criteria, one external and the other internal to the motif. Thompson begins by stating that he records as a motif any element of narrative structure which has been or could be the object of a folklorist's study. This is not very informative. Sensing the fragility of this first criterion, he adds that the majority of the items selected have been chosen because of some unusual or striking detail, which fits them to be remembered by the story-teller. As the tale travels from place to place and undergoes transformations, these details are the marks that preserve its identity. Their role is thus comparable to that of the 'special identifying marks' listed on a passport for purposes of police identification: the folklorist counts on their resistance to erosion in assigning the tale being studied to a family of related stories, in certifying it as one *variant* of a *type*. The goal of the *Motif-Index*, its subordination to the research project of the diffusionist school, surfaces briefly: to ascertain, via the motif, the folktale type; to retrace, via the folktale type, the vicissitudes of a theme.

It is no longer possible to accept these presuppositions without discussion. In the first place, the utility of an index of motifs cannot be restricted to diachronic study of the vagaries of a tale. It is at least as interesting to undertake the synchronic study of the system of motifs characteristic of a tradition at a given point in its development, and in its relation to a given form of culture. For such study, the distinction between 'striking' and 'trivial' details does not have the same relevance, for all details participate in the functioning of the system, and the banal (or apparently banal) detail may turn out to be as significant as the unusual one.

Naturally, the most memorable moments of a story, in folklore and popular literature, correspond to an awareness of the extraordinary, to departures from the predictable course of events. So in this sense, we may admit that the 'full-fledged' narratives are indeed constructed, as Thompson asserts, *out of* such elements, and so as to enhance their effect. We can also admit that the reproduction of a narrative, its transmission from one story-teller to another, and its diffusion across cultural barriers, is facilitated by the details most 'striking' to the imagination. But does this mean that other, less original, elements are not as essential to the structure of the narrative? This is far from evident. Certain formal articulations can be seen as indispensable independently of whether their treatment is striking or banal: the punishment of the villain at the end of a fairy tale, for example, is expected by the audience, and the tale-teller rarely fails to satisfy his listeners' expectations. Does this mean that he must depict a spectacular scene, some especially ingenious or atrocious form of punishment? Not at all. If he hasn't the time, if he forgets the details, if his imagination fails him, he may be content merely to indicate, without going further, that the king ordered the culprit to be put to death. We will continue to insist on this point, which is central for our argument in what follows: there exist, not just other narrative units, but other *essential* narrative units, than those which fulfil the requirement of being unusual or striking.

Furthermore, there is no reason why a researcher should limit his attention to the study of details, whether unusual or trivial, which the story-teller and his audience perceived as essential. Episodes which are inserted to mark time, or as connectors, 'expansions' in which the events presented anchor the story in a reality which is prosaic and familiar for both narrator and audience, but exotic for the researcher, may contain valuable information. In this respect, the criterion of selection applied by the *Motif-Index* carries a risk of distortion. Suppose that a researcher wishes to study 'Death in folklore and popular literature'. Opening the *Motif-Index*, he sees that an entire chapter is entitled *The Dead*. Glancing at the contents of the chapter, he sees that it is divided into four sections, which deal with: (1) E 0 to E 199 – Resuscitation; (2) E 200 to E 599 – Ghosts and other revenants; (3) E 600 to E 699 – Reincarnation; (4) E 700 to E 799 – The soul.

This list already suggests that the real thematic link in the chapter is not death, but survival, or rather, the capacity of the soul to become separated from the body, to appear in various guises, to reinhabit its own body or another. What about death, in all this? It was considered as too banal an event to deserve a place in the inventory. It was only the failure of death to occur when expected that gave this motif its chance to appear in the *Motif-Index*. Of course our researcher will not admit defeat so easily: reading through the work at random, he will gather an ample and varied harvest of examples in chapters such as Q: 'Rewards and punishments', or S: 'Unnatural cruelty'. But even then death will not be recorded as such, but as incidental to something else, because of the particular circumstances that accompany it.

Thompson believed himself to be showing extreme openmindedness in his decision to allow into his index any kind of detail which might hold the attention of a researcher. But his conception of research on folk material limits enquiry to the sphere of problems proper to a single school.

How can the motif be conceived so as to be free from this unconscious arbitrariness? As long as a motif is considered to be potentially any element at all of narrative structure, selecting motifs according to the subjective criterion of their 'interestingness' is inevitably a constraint: anyone who wanted to extract from the narrative text all the details capable of being taken, for one reason or another, as objects of study would be engaged in an infinite task. Suppose, however, that we want, given some narrative corpus, to compile a systematic (though not exhaustive) catalogue of the narrative units of which the stories are composed. This undertaking is conceivable under certain conditions: (1) it must be established that the narrative message involves levels of structure; (2) some of these levels must involve the combination, by coordination or subordination, of a finite number of units, which we can agree to call 'motifs'; (3) it must be possible to isolate and categorize these elements for the purpose of our classification.

Every narrative plot exhibits this kind of organization. Considered at a high level of generality and abstraction, it can be broken down into two, three, or four major developments (its 'movements', in Propp's terminology); at a lower level of generality and abstractness, each development is in turn reducible into a series of events or actions (Propp's 'functions'); and these events themselves are rendered as a combination of more concretely determined events. This hierarchical organization allows systematic tabulation of the units constituting each level: we can determine the largest and least numerous divisions first, then those on the next level down, then the parts of these parts, etc., making an exhaustive list at each level. We will, perhaps, have to stop at a level of concreteness where the detail has become too abundant for our analytic capacity or patience; but at least we will be able to say precisely at what level our analysis has stopped, and to guarantee the exhaustiveness of our cataloguing for the levels analysed.

Whether formulated in general or particular terms, whether abstract or concrete, the motifs should exhibit a certain amount of homogeneity: to do this, they should conform to the same structural model. What might this model be? Post-Proppian narrative semiotics did not take long to develop it, but it is even more significant that Thompson refers to it in passing as if it were intuitively obvious. The researcher's interest, he tells us, may be directed toward the character, or the action, or the attendant circumstances of the action (p. 11). He thus gives us a rough sketch of the characteristic structure of the elementary narrative proposition, as Todorov, in his *Grammar of the Decameron* (The Hague, 1969), would later formulate it: a subject (agent or patient), a verb of state or action, qualitative attributes, and possibly what Tesnière called 'circumstantials' (complements of time, place, manner . . .).

On leafing through the *Motif-Index*, we observe in fact that the majority of the motifs recorded receive, or could receive, a formulation conforming to this model. But we also find many deviations, either through *hypotrophy*, though this is relatively rare, or through *hypertrophy*, which is much more frequent.

Hypotrophy: the verb, which is, in our view, the heart of the motif, has been eliminated, so that the motif is reduced to the mention of a subject and its attribute, or to two subjects, etc. Chapter A, for example, contains long lists of divine attributes (A 123.2.1: 'God with many faces', with its specifications A.123.2.1.1: 'God with two faces', A.123.2.1.2: 'God with three faces', etc.). We agree here with the opinion of E. Meletinski, that such formulations, which do not contain the minimal nucleus, subject + verb, have no place in an index of *narrative* motifs. Of course, we do not deny the interest of a catalogue of the qualitative attributes of various subjects, when these are categorized rigorously, but that is the object of a different work, an index of *descriptive* traits. A god's having several faces would have narrative meaning only if the god, in the course of the story, acquired or lost this attribute, or if it gave him superiority in combat, etc. When it is merely a 'natural epithet' without function in the plot, the trait is outside the relevant domain of interest here.

Hypertrophy: this case is much more frequent than the preceding one. The motif, as proposed in the *Motif-Index*, agglomerates several narrative propositions which should no doubt have been listed separately. Here, for example, is Motif M13: 'Those caught in adultery are to have eyes put out. When king's son is found guilty he insists on the punishment. He finally compromises by having one of his own and one of his son's eyes put out.' With this much hypertrophy, the motif takes on the dimensions of a complete story. A number of short tales are entered in the *Motif-Index* as *motifs*, and, in *The Types of the Folktale* as *story-types*: motif K 741 is also story-type AT 175.

A refusal to elaborate the notion of the motif explains this confusion but does not justify it. In the mini-story M 13, the motif should have exploded into four or five motifs. However, these overstuffed formulations reveal a scruple worth drawing attention to. Thompson has refused to fragment the plot because he wants to preserve, for each narrative proposition, the context which provides its *raison d'être*. The intuition by which he is guided is that of Propp's *function*: the significance of a motif comes only from its relation to one or more other motifs which introduce it or which it introduces, and with which it forms a whole that gives the story its particular meaning. The point is worth keeping in mind: the formulation of a motif should satisfy a twofold organizing principle, both internal and external, and reconcile two imperatives: that of *analysis*, which isolates the motif and decomposes it into its constituent elements (agents, patients, verbs, circumstantials, etc.), and that of *synthesis*, which associates the motif with others, to define its function in the context (an antecedent acting as a *cause*, a consequent functioning as an *effect*, an 'included' acting as a *means*, an 'includer' functioning as an *end* . . .).

Formulation of the motif

The size and formal model of the motif are becoming clearer. How is the substance of the narrative to be poured into this mould? In other words, how is the transfer to be carried out from the text, where the motif has been observed in one of its manifestations, to the index, where the motif will be defined for users?

We should begin from this evident fact: that no two texts ever present the same motif in an identical form. Our decision to recognize that we have the same motif, manifested by two variants in two texts, is possible only if we are willing to assign greater weight to certain analogies which we judge to be essential, giving less weight to differences which we judge to be accidental. Even when the motif is drawn from a single text (as is often the case with the *Motif-Index*), what is extracted is not a mere quotation. When we read, under A 32.3.2, the following motif 'Creator beats his wife while intoxicated from beverage he invents', we strongly suspect that this is not a literal citation. Perhaps the text really reads 'X beats Y' where X and Y are proper names. All the other elements of the motif have been inferred from the context by a series of decisions made by the folklorist. But what the context *allows* us to conclude it does not *force* us to conclude. When someone identifies the individuals X and Y in terms of their roles as 'creator' and 'wife of creator' he reveals his decision to treat as essential details two elements which the text, by itself, does not distinguish from other elements. In complementary fashion, the decision to specify neither the instrument which the creator uses to beat his wife (even though the text may mention that he used a stick) nor the nature of the potion or drug he invented (which the text surely indicates) reveals an intention to omit details judged to be superfluous. This activity of reformulation, undertaken to give the event referred to more generality, and thus to prepare a mould that fits not only the occurrences of the motif already observed but also as yet unobserved ones of the same type, is unavoidable.

The question thus raised for the researcher who has intuitively judged the same motif to be present in a certain number of texts is what level of abstractness may be adequate for statement of the various elements (agents, patients, verbs, circumstantials). His formulations should be neither too general, otherwise what is responsible for the characteristic flavour of this particular motif will be lost, nor too particular, for it must be broad enough to encompass all the realizations of the motif already observed, as well as those not yet recorded. The point, though obvious, is worth emphasizing: formulating a motif consists, in all cases, in substituting, for the words of the original text, words of another text, so as to assign different *weights* to the words of the original. The details judged to be most relevant for characterizing the motif will be assigned starring roles, with the most concrete terms (those that are richest in intension and poorest in extension); for details that are less relevant, playing still necessary though minor roles, there will be labels that are vaguer, or open-ended lists (ending in 'etc.'). Finally, elements viewed as accidental, and thus not relevant to the definition of the motif, will be intentionally omitted from the formulation.

Since this reworking is unavoidable, the researcher should assume full responsibility for it, and be aware of its consequences. The most immediate one seems to us to be the impossibility of giving the motif a rigid, stable definition. Any formulation of a motif should be considered as tentative, and revisable. No doubt, when working with a limited corpus, the researcher will have the legitimate, and comforting, feeling that he is approaching asymptotically the 'right' version of the motif, represented by a core of variants perceived as quite close to one another. But around this core, there will still remain a nebulous cluster of deviant forms that can only be integrated into the definition of the motif if we are willing to generalize its terms; and the nucleus itself will constantly be in danger of splitting – the new versions we encounter will offer novel details, allowing the definition to be made more precise, but at the cost of circumscribing a nucleus within the nucleus. The motif, rather than having a unique definition, involves a pyramid of hierarchical definitions, going from the most general to the most specific, from the most abstract to the most concrete. Each formulation can operate as a reference point to locate the centre of gravity of certain forms of the motif. But this centre is likely to shift as the sphere of investigation is enlarged; and in any case the formulation given will not apply to the nebula of deviant forms, which extend beyond it in all directions, but only to a select subset.

We will examine shortly the classificatory role which this hierarchy of formulations can play in an index. For the present, it will suffice to note that it satisfies the need for a framework within which motifs can be located and described. In a corpus of narratives developing the same theme, a motif may be treated at varying levels of generality and abstractness. The same event can be condensed into the abridged variant '*X* orders *Y* to be killed', receive a more explicit second formulation in the more circumstantial '*X* orders *Y* to be put to death by torture', and have a third form where the tortures are spelled out. It is the same event, but is it the same motif? Perhaps not, according to Thompson, who will accommodate the third variant in his chapter Q: 'Rewards and punishments', or S: 'Unnatural cruelty', but might hesitate about including the first two. Certainly so, in our view, for we consider, following Propp, that the three formulations have the same function in their narrative context, designate the same event, and differ only in the degree of explicitness of the contents of that function.

Each entry of the *Motif-Index* bears traces of this activity of motif-elaboration at variable levels of abstractness, but the endeavour is guided by no explicit rule. Thompson's silence in his introduction is eloquent. Nothing can be found to suggest that the motif is other than a fragment of text having the status of a natural curiosity, like a shell picked up from a beach, or a flower plucked in a meadow, or that the excision of this textual fragment, its expression as a *motif*, something to be found in other texts, its transcription for the benefit of users of the index, require even the slightest manipulation. Thompson speaks (or rather does not speak) as if the motifs detached themselves from texts and fell at the collector's feet like leaves in autumn, as if two variants of the same motif differed no more than two leaves from the same tree.

Like most folklorists, Thompson feels himself to be on solid ground only if he is working close to the level of factual observation. But the abstractness of a motif *is* a fact that is available to concrete observation, as well as an epistemological necessity.

The categorization of motifs

Our attempt to determine the conditions of the formulation of the motif has led us to a hierarchical classification of motif *states*. But now the motif itself no longer looks like a discontinuous entity: as we follow it downwards, it is differentiated into more specific sub-motifs, each with its own sub-motifs; upwards, in the direction of increasing generalization, the motif joins with other motifs into an archi-motif, and this can unite with others into a still more extensive class, and so on. There thus emerges the outline of a solution to the problem of motif classification.

This solution is at the opposite pole from that chosen by Thompson. Not that the double mechanism of generalization into an archi-motif and specification into sub-motifs is unknown to him. On the contrary, the *Motif-Index* makes extensive use of it: on the one hand, the headings in bold-face with a number ending in zero are characterized as *general* motifs that introduce the series of motifs numbered 1, 2, 3, etc.; on the other hand, each of the motifs can be supplemented by a more particular motif specifying it further. For example, under the general formulation D 1550 'Magic object miraculously opens and closes', we find a preliminary specification D 1551: 'Waters magically divide and close', followed by a series of sub-motifs D 1551.1, D 1551.2, D 1551.3, etc., all concerning the magical dividing of the waters, but specifying this operation according to the magical object used to bring it about (salt, a branch, a root, powder, a stick, a diamond . . .).

This effort to articulate a hierarchy is especially noticeable in the downward direction: it is always possible to subdivide a motif that is already quite concrete by adding some small detail (this supplementary labour is the main task reserved by Thompson for his successors). As for the opposite direction, that of increasing generalization, the effort does not go far: we arrive almost immediately at a juxtaposition of categories held together only by a more or less loose thematic bond. These fruits of empirical induction do not pretend to cover systematically the terrain they delimit: in places the categories overlap, elsewhere they leave yawning gaps. Thus they are all the more impossible to stratify.

To explain such anarchy, it is not sufficient to blame the negligence of the authors of the *Motif-Index* in carrying out their programme. If the tendency to subsume the particular under the general, which is normal in any activity of classification, peters out so quickly here, this is because it is counteracted by a prevailing tendency to multiply categories indiscriminately. Thompson began by selecting as motifs certain details which seemed striking to him, unusual, worth recording because of some singular feature; he gave these motifs a formulation chosen so as to bring out that feature. Then the time came when the motifs developed in that way had to be arranged in a classification: again, the odd characteristic, the striking, interesting one, seemed to offer itself naturally as a means of distinguishing the motifs dealing with a single theme, grouping them together under the same entry, the same section, the same chapter. The headings of each of these divisions were then deduced from this constantly highlighted feature: behind the motif 'The creator beats his wife' we can see taking shape the heading 'Creator's companions', the section 'Creator', and the chapter 'Mythological motifs'. But this classificatory principle, an entirely artificial one, does not at all overcome the heterogeneity of the elements it groups together. Just as the motif is not an immediately given datum ('donnée') of the folktale, so the organizational schema of the *Motif-Index* does not arise from a spontaneous

136

arrangement of the motifs, under the pressure of some would-be immanent logic. No doubt Thompson feels differently, when he observes, with guileless, delighted surprise, comparable to that of the creator on the seventh day, that the final ordering of the work, like a mirror, presents him with the reflection of the main themes of his investigation: all he is doing is finding in it the order, or rather, on our view, the disorder, which he has put there.

To clarify the mechanism behind this illusion, we will take an imaginary example. Consider the three narrative propositions:

(a) The dragon carries off the king's daughter;

(b) The devil casts a spell on the king's daughter;

(c) The devil carries off a peasant's daughter.

Drawn from a given number of variants, these formulations might, at a given stage of analysis of the corpus, be taken to be three distinct motifs; but the folklorist might equally well, at a later stage, have good reasons for grouping them into overlapping pairs, as variants of the supermotifs:

(a + b) An evil being harms the king's daughter;

(a + c) An evil being carries off someone's daughter;

(b + c) The devil harms someone's daughter.

At a third stage, an even more general formulation might cover the three initial propositions:

(a + b + c) An evil being harms someone's daughter.

The legitimacy of each of these groupings will depend on the corpus, and its ramifications, being studied, but there is no doubt concerning their orientation: the most abstract formulations gradually tend to become general classificatory categories.

Now let us see what happens when we try to apply the principles for selection and classification of the *Motif-Index* to the three initial motifs. In (a), (b), and (c), taken in isolation, we can discern no overriding detail: each of the elements of the motif seems to have as much right to be chosen as any other. Suppose, however, that our first generalization, whether intuitive or reasoned, has led us to single out the formulations (a + b), or (b + c), or (a + c). The procedure advocated by Thompson is now applicable: option (a + b) favours the patient (the king's daughter); option (a + c) favours the action (carrying off); option (b + c) favours the agent (the devil). It is possible to list the first option under a heading 'Princesses' (which in fact exists in chapter P: 'Society'); the second, under a heading 'abduction' (which has its equivalent in chapter R: 'Captives and fugitives'); the third, under the heading 'The devil' (which figures in chapter G: 'Ogres', at number G 303).

It can be seen how the normal movement to generalization (evident from the successive elaboration of the categories (a + b), (a + c), (b + c), then (a + b + c), from the basic motifs (a), (b), and (c)), is suddenly deflected because of the improperly privileged status accorded to a particular detail that allows it to be elevated to the rank of a general classificatory category. The outcome of this will be, for example, that a certain initial motif (a), which has been associated with (b) by a researcher working on a given corpus, will be included in the chapter 'Society', while the same motif (a), associated this time with (c) by another researcher working with a different corpus, will be listed in the chapter 'Captives and fugitives'.

But this is only the first stage of a continual diaspora: if applied rigorously, the guiding principle of the *Motif-Index* should lead to the indefinite proliferation of entries, with chapter-titles that get more and more artificial in the attempt to subsume these entries.

Consider, for example, a motif (a'), which enriches and particularizes the initial motif (a) as follows:

(a') The dragon carries off the king's daughter on her wedding night.

The logic of the system would force us to class this form of the motif not with the others in which a dragon carries off a princess (by creating a sub-motif) but in an entry titled 'Wedding night', to be included in a section 'Wedding ceremony' of chapter T: 'Sex'. This is because it can be argued that in this new metamorphosis the unusual, striking, noteworthy detail is not the carrying off of the princess by a dragon, a banal news item in the world of faërie, but rather, as a tabloid might front-page it, PRINCESS CARRIED OFF ON WEDDING NIGHT!!!

The ultimate consequences of the principle of selection for striking detail are now clear: the categories serving to classify motifs tend to proliferate indefinitely, unsystematically, and, above all, without any possibility of being arranged in a hierarchy. To return to our earlier comparison, the motif's passport is made out exclusively in terms of its 'special identifying marks', with little attention given, as primary 'entries', to those general characteristics which are common to all (nose, forehead, eyes, mouth, hair), or to their most common aspects (blue or brown eyes, brown or blond hair, etc.). Thompson has started off from the false idea that the *essence* of the motif, as much for the story-teller and his audience as for the researcher, is indistinguishable from the *accident*, the detail which is responsible for its popularity. This is not at all true. The importance of the motif is determined by its *function* in the narrative; its originality is a different matter: it is not demanded of every functionary that he fulfil his function with brio, strikingly, but he *is* expected to fulfil it. It might be objected that it was not Thompson's intention to list all motifs, in the sense which we give to this word, but only the interesting ones. But even if this were the case, the only economical principle for doing so would be to categorize the motifs in terms of their most general functions, which are limited in number, before characterizing them by the details which make them exceptional, since such details can vary *ad infinitum*.

Motif and function

The term 'function' is not used here by chance. Some years before the project of the *Motif-Index* was begun, Propp had already subjected the notion of the motif to careful scrutiny, and had urged that it was necessary to replace it, as the constituent unit of the folk narrative, by a formal element which he termed the 'function' (*Morfologija Skazki* (Leningrad, 1928)).

When Propp attacked the conception of Veselovski, who described the tale as a mosaic of invariable motifs, the accusation with which he charged his compatriot was analogous to that we have been arguing against Thompson. What was Propp's objection? He claimed in effect that a 'motif' such as 'The dragon carries off the king's daughter' disintegrates upon analysis, because each of its elements allows an endless chain of substitutions, attested by a host of variants: 'The devil carries off the king's daughter', 'The devil causes the harvest to rot', etc. Behind this unstable cloud of changing formulations there is, however, a constant: the function 'Villainy', for which the various actions (carrying off, causing to rot, casting a spell over, etc.) act as support in the chain of events of the folktale.

The brilliance of Propp's intuition lies in understanding that the instability of the motif need not prevent the narrative being based on the combination of a certain number of invariants: at a given level of abstraction, the tale is analysable into a sequence of actions that are always identical and always disposed in the same order. These actions contrast with the motif by their abstractness (for example, the 'villainy'), by their subordination to a syntactic rule that specifies their position in the sequence of actions, and by their restricted number (there are thirty-two in the fairy tale). Finally, these are true structural units, not arbitrary creations of the analyst.

We are beginning to see how, by taking as a basis these narrational invariants, we could rethink the plan of an *Index*. Each of Propp's functions (or similar ones) provides a chapter heading; in sequence they will articulate the work according to a systematic and homogeneous order which has nothing in common with the heterogeneous alignment of Thompson's chapters. The task that remains is: (a) to complete the list of functions needed to account for narrative genres other than the fairy tale; (b) to determine a hierarchy for the material included under each function; (c) if necessary, to determine the hierarchy of the functions with respect to one another.

Unfortunately, when Propp proceeds to carry out his project, our disappointment is as great as were our expectations. The functions, as he proposes them, turn out to be impossible to range among themselves in a hierarchy, and unable really to come to grips with the anecdotal variety of the folktale. Between these *forms* and their *contents* there are no mediating

C. Bremond

agencies. When Propp gets down to the task of describing and assigning an order to this material, his purely rule-of-thumb approach is as flagrant as Thompson's. Through its successive broadenings, each function ends up as no more than a label covering a permanently open-ended list of items: in the function 'Marriage', marriage can be replaced by a sum of money; in the function 'Villainy', the concept can be diluted to apply to any kind of 'lack'. His formal rigour allows considerable laxity of content.

What is lacking in Propp's attempt? (1) He has failed to recognize that functions are not merely coordinated along a linear axis, but can also be subordinated to other functions, and be organized, according to the level of generality which each represents, into a hierarchical system of concepts (where, for example, the 'Punishment' of the villain and the 'Reward' of the hero are two specifications of the archifunction 'Recompense'). (2) He has failed to understand that the functional invariant does not reduce to the single concept of an action 'envisaged from the point of view of its role in the development of the plot', but rather embraces a model of the narrative proposition which needs to be made explicit and codified. Thus the functional invariant hidden behind 'The dragon carries off the king's daughter' cannot be reduced to the action of perpetrating a misdeed. This is just an ellipsis, a label, the abridged version of a narrative proposition which in a more developed model would be: X causes harm to Y by performing action Z. All of the elements of this proposition, taken at the level of generality or specificity required by the corpus, contribute to its definition. By operating with the principle that 'it does not matter much who performs the action or why he does so', Propp has so to speak amputated the function of its arms and legs: no matter how undeniable the primacy of the verb in the narrative proposition may be, it is not possible to maintain that the addition of individualized actors (agents and patients), of qualifying attributes of these actors, and of various circumstantials (specifications of time and place, goals and means, etc.) is irrelevant to the function of this proposition in the development of the plot.

The atheoretical empiricism of Thompson and the formalism of Propp are both shackled, the first on the level of intuitive generalization of the individual concrete fact, the second on the abstract level of a mutilated model of the narrative proposition, and thus each is as unfit as the other to provide a genuine classification of the events in a narration. They are able to grasp the constituent unit, the motif or function, by one of its edges only. But this unit is a hybrid: it does not exist merely as form or merely as matter, but as a composite of both in varying proportions, rising and falling like a balloon between abstract formulations which make it approach the Proppian function and concrete expressions which make it resemble the Thompsonian motif. We can only approximate its statistically most frequent positions by

140

means of a tree whose trunk corresponds to the most abstract form and whose branches correspond to those manifestations which are the most richly and diversely circumstantial. It is indispensable, as Thompson recognized, to leave open, at the tips of the branches, the list of formulations which, by the addition of new details, or by mutations of existing ones, force us to recognize new genera, species, sub-species, and varieties of the same motif. But it is no less necessary – and this is where the most serious deficiency of Thompson's approach lies – to connect the concrete expressions of the motifs step by step to more and more abstract formulations, and finally to tie together the whole with a quite general definition which sums up their function (in Propp's sense) in the flow of events narrated.

Two examples: 'The rendering of services' and 'Deception'

In spite of the theoretical poverty which stunts the realization of the *Motif-Index*, it is inconceivable that a researcher of the competence of Stith Thompson, heir to the experience and wisdom of a pleiad of forerunners, could go wrong at every point of this gigantic enterprise. More plausibly, his intuitions have in practice provided a corrective for his faulty conception, at least enough to persuade him that he was on the right track and to give him the courage to continue. Detailed examination would make it possible to determine, among the competing classificatory procedures observable at different points, those which are valid and those which are not, or those which, when better articulated into a coherent structure, would acquire a validity which they do not have as they stand. In lieu of such a detailed investigation, we will give two examples: the first to illustrate the drawbacks of the principle of selection in terms of the striking detail; the second to demonstrate the fruitfulness of a classification in terms of function, in a chapter of the *Motif-Index* where the functional point of view has almost prevailed.

As our first example, we will choose a category of events whose importance in the world of the folktale is indisputable: the rendering of a service, of assistance in all its forms. How is this treated in the *Motif-Index*? Reading through the table of contents we observe first, at the end of chapter N: 'Chance and fate', a sort of appendix, N 800 to N 899, entitled 'Helpers'. No doubt many readers have wondered what these helpers are doing in this chapter. We might explain this in the following way: among the happy chances of existence should be included the interventions of a providential saviour; in a wider sense, any case in which assistance is received can be assimilated to this kind of fortune. Suppose now that the accent of the motif seems to be not on the patient who benefits from the help – the receiver of the assistance – but on the agent who provides the assistance – the helper; it will then seem appropriate to have a separate listing for this category of characters. No doubt they would more appropriately be placed in a chapter called 'Services', but the very generality of this action, occurring in a very large number of situations of all varieties, makes it harder to perceive: of itself it is too banal to be judged to be characteristic of the motifs which it underlies, and it has thus been forgotten in the list of chapters. A few pale reflections of this missing chapter have been grouped together in the section 'Helpers' and this not very cumbersome section finds an inconspicuous sanctuary nearby, at the sign of 'Chance and fate'.

Our helpers are lodged in two sub-sections: N 810: 'Supernatural helpers', and N 820: 'Human helpers'. Before we ask about the appropriateness of this distinction, it is worth noting that the opposition between the supernatural and the human does not exhaust all conceivable kinds of helpers: the section 'Helpers', as given in chapter N, has been deprived of its most extensive category, shifted to chapter B: 'Animals', with the heading 'Friendly animals' (B 300 to B 599). Why this special treatment? A remark in the Introduction: 'Just as the motifs in Chapter B suggest some possible relation to the institution of totemism . . .' (p. 20), suggests that Thompson thought it useful to group all animal motifs together in chapter B because this would make investigations on the institution of totemism easier. In any case, we deduce that the relevant distinction, in the system of thought of the *Motif-Index*, is the opposition between 'Animal helpers' and 'Non-animal helpers', which would coincide with an opposition of value between 'More interesting helpers' and 'Less interesting helpers'. Among these less interesting helpers, the same criterion can be used again to distinguish 'Supernatural helpers', the more interesting ones, from 'Human helpers', the more banal ones.

As poor relations of the section 'Animal helpers', the sub-sections 'Supernatural helpers' and 'Human helpers', furthermore, only collect otherwise unclassifiable scraps of each category: the cases which have been put here are just those examples of non-animal helpers for which there is no really striking detail that would have allowed them to be placed elsewhere. Let us suppose that the helper provides his protégé with a magical device: since this detail allows the motif to escape from banality, it can be entered in chapter D: 'Magic', under the heading D 810: 'Magic object a gift'. Or suppose that the helper is a ghost come back from the grave to help someone dear to him: this detail, besides allowing the embarrassing problem of whether the helper is human or supernatural to be sidestepped, qualifies the motif for inclusion in chapter E: 'The dead', under the heading E 300: 'Friendly return from the dead'. Or suppose that the assistance provided, independently of the nature of its agent or instrument, has as its goal helping the hero to succeed in his quest, or in the trials preliminary to his quest. This circumstance is elevated to the rank of a detail which has enough independent interest to be a motif: chapter H: 'Tests', offers the following headings: H 970: 'Help in performing tasks', H 1233: 'Helpers on quest'; H 1235: 'Succession of helpers on quest'. As a special case, if the helper is *gifted* – an ally possessing superhuman powers – and puts his talents at the disposal of the hero for the winning of a princess' hand, this bundle of circumstances disqualifies the motif for chapter H, where we might have looked for it, and instead earns it a place in chapter F: 'Marvels', under the heading F 601.2: 'Extraordinary companions help hero in suitor tests'.

Each additional detail, each new characterization bearing on an actor, the means of action, its ends, or on other circumstances, gives further impetus to the centrifugal force which disperses motifs to the farthest recesses of the index, further and further from the central idea of 'Service'. We must sift through chapter R: 'Captives and fugitives', to find section R 150: 'Rescuers'; through chapter Q: 'Rewards and punishments', to find section Q 150: 'Immunity from disaster as reward'; through chapter V: 'Religion', to find the helping activities of the guardian angel (V 232) or the Virgin Mary (V 250), etc.

We can mention as a final example the case of the wife who gives her own milk to her husband who has been condemned to death by starvation, suckling him through the bars of his cell or a crack in the wall. This act of assistance has twice caught the attention of the authors of the *Motif-Index*. We find it first under number R 81 in the chapter 'Captives and fugitives', not, in fact, in the section R 100 to R 199: 'Rescuers', where we might well expect it to be, but in section R 70: 'Behavior of captives': are we to conclude that this motif, by Thompson's criteria, is more interesting for classification because of the prisoner who sucks than because of the wife who gives suck? Be that as it may, the motif reappears under another number, this time as evidence of conjugal devotion. Given that a wife who is devoted enough to save her husband's life is *a fortiori* a faithful wife, the motif is listed under the heading 'Faithfulness in marriage' (T 210). The scrupulous reader may be wondering what should be done with variants of the same motif where the husband of the heroine is replaced by her father. There is no reason to worry, the authors have solved this problem: the daughter who suckles her father through the bars of his prison cell is accommodated under T 215.2, in chapter T: 'Sex'!

Let us now consider one of the chapters of the *Motif-Index* which, because of its theme, comes closest to one of the major categories of actions which might be envisaged for a *New Index*. It will be seen this time that the outlines of a coherent and homogeneous classification have begun to take shape, although still blurred by all sorts of irrelevant intrusions.

Chapter K: 'Deceptions', occupies half of volume iv, that is, about a twelfth of the whole work. It is divided into two parts: the first, untitled, sketches in a categorization of deceptions according to the context which triggers them: 'Contests won by deception', 'Deceptive bargains', 'Thefts and cheats', 'Escape by deception', 'Capture by deception', 'Fatal deception', 'Deception into self-injury', 'Deception into humiliating position', 'Seduction or deceptive marriage', 'Dupe's property destroyed', 'Deceptions connected with adultery', 'Deceiver falls into own trap'; the second part, entitled 'Deception through shams', lists: 'Deception through bluffing', 'Deception by disguise or illusion', 'Impostures', 'Hypocrites', 'False accusations', 'Villains and traitors', 'Other deceptions'.

This bifurcation is of itself rather remarkable. Thompson has perceived that a deception can be characterized from two points of view: that of its end or that of its means. We glimpse the beginnings of a system of hierarchical classification in which a general end will be specified by the means used to realize it, and this means itself by a further specification of its nature. To carry this out, the *New Index* we are imagining should place the chapter 'Deceptions' at a level in the hierarchy intermediate between chapters devoted to very general types of action (call them A, B, C) which define the goals of the deception, and chapters devoted to more particular types of action (call them x, y, z) which serve as means for the deception. These relations can be represented as follows:

Goals of the deception:

$$A \qquad\qquad B \qquad\qquad C$$

$$\cdots \quad \cdots\text{ by} \qquad \cdots\text{ by} \qquad \cdots\text{ by}$$

$$\text{deception} \qquad \text{deception} \qquad \text{deception}$$

DECEPTION

Means of the deception:

$$\text{by } x \qquad\qquad \text{by } y \qquad\qquad \text{by } z$$

How are these categories of actions – A, B, C for the ends, x, y, z, for the means – given in the classification of the *Motif-Index*?

The second part, 'Deception through shams', appears to be difficult to salvage, the terminology used is so fuzzy. No doubt 'Deception through bluffing' is very likely to correspond to a category of enticements: the deceiver pretends to be stronger than he is, and so intimidates or seduces his partner; but from this we should conclude that 'Seduction' and 'Intimidation' are two categories of action intermediate between bluff and deception. There may be deception through 'seduction', and seduction through 'bluff', or deception through 'intimidation', and intimidation through 'bluff'. Simi-

144

larly, 'Calumny' is a form of deception well defined in terms of the means used: to achieve some end (escaping from suspicion, getting rid of a rival, sowing discord, etc.) the deceiver dupes a dispenser of justice by falsely accusing someone innocent. The other notions, however, are unusable, for we are never sure whether they are to be taken in a broad or narrow sense: does the category of 'Disguise' apply just to cases of material disguise, i.e. change of clothing, or can it be extended to any operation intended to have appearance taken as reality? Does the category of 'Imposture' reduce to cases where the deceiver manages to pass for someone else in order to obtain an advantage which he does not deserve? Just what is a 'Traitor', given that the entry in which this term occurs assimilates it to the case of a 'villain'? Does the role of the 'Hypocrite' belong alongside those of the impostor, the traitor, and the calumniator, who all have recourse to some form of hypocrisy? In reality, Thompson has glided from a categorization of deceptions, envisaged as *actions*, into a categorization of deceivers, envisaged as *characters*.

The *Motif-Index* is more successful in its elaboration of the goals of deception. Two major classes of situations are seen to emerge here. The first corresponds to interpersonal relations which are in appearance peaceful, contractual, cooperative: competition, the commercial transaction, that other variety of 'commerce' which is constituted by the *liaison amoureuse*, or marriage. At the basis of these relations there is the *rendering of services*, and the effort of the deceiver is aimed at misrepresenting the apparent equality of the services exchanged to his own advantage: sometimes a pseudo-creditor schemes to obtain unjustified payment for merchandise that is worthless ('Sale of worthless articles', treated as a sub-category of 'Deceptive bargains'), sometimes a debtor tries to elude a creditor ('Deception in payment of a debt'). The category of 'Contests won by deception' is reducible to the first case: by sleight of hand the cheat pretends to have won, and thus to have earned a reward which he does not deserve. Similarly, the heading 'Seduction or deceptive marriage', when once freed of its reference to the sexual theme, is reducible to the category of 'Deceptive bargains': the deceiver obtains the consent of his victim (and the services that come with it) by deceiving her about the quality of the merchandise he offers in exchange.

The other major class of situation corresponds to overtly hostile interpersonal relations. In one case, the deceiver is involved in protecting himself against an aggressor ('Escape by deception'); the rest of the time, the deceiver is the aggressor whose trickery is used against a victim: his scheming is then directed either against the possessions or the person of the victim. Against the possessions, by 'Theft', or by 'Dupe's property destroyed'; against the person physically, by murder ('Fatal deception'), by injury ('Deception into self-injury'); against the person morally, by 'Deception into humiliating position'.

Receiving a service (deserved or not); avoiding the obligation (legitimate or not) to furnish a service; performing an aggressive act (deserved or not); avoiding an aggressive act (deserved or not): these seem to us to be the four (or eight) major categories of *ends* for which deception serves as *means*, and which it may also serve to specify, while being itself specified by other actions such as intimidation, seduction, etc. which serve as its means.

Thus there can be observed the outline of a categorization of events, actions, passions, which, if systematized more rigorously, could furnish chapter-headings for an index of homogeneous categories. The *Motif-Index* has the appearance of a mass of dough worked on by different sorts of yeast, which have caused blisters, disproportioned swellings, confused amalgamations, but behind which we can still make out guidelines which could provide a coherent ordering if they were followed out to their furthest consequences. Might we do better? It can be hoped that we would, but it must first be understood that it is not sufficient to accumulate an enormous mass of documents, and then to knead this material in every possible way in the hope of bringing out its inherent organization. A better approach would be to begin by thinking clearly about the notions of narrative and plot, establishing an anthropologically valid system of the major categories of events, actions, and roles. This universal framework might then be applied in the analysis and classification of corpora defined with reference to specific cultures. Thus, on the same model, a series of partial indexes would be constructed, which would then be coordinated in an *Index of indexes*. Would these new compilations have the kind of utility which Thompson claims for the *Motif-Index?* No doubt they would not, but perhaps the question is premature: what is important is that our classification of motifs would truly be a classification, and no longer merely the unconscious projection of our prejudices. An organization of the traditional narrative material which respected its internal logic would raise new problems as much as it would solve old ones. The only thing we can be sure of about future research is that it will cease to be interested in the things by which we are obsessed, and will attend to details which we consider to be insignificant, or which we do not even perceive.

Notes

1. *Cahiers de littérature orale* 2 (Publications Orientalistes de France, Paris, 1977), pp. 15–24.
2. Antti Aarne and Stith Thompson, *The Types of the Folktale – A Classification and Bibliography* (Academia Scientarum Fennica, Helsinki, 1964).
3. Stith Thompson, *Motif-Index of Folk Literature*, new enlarged and revised edition (Indiana University Press, Bloomington, 1956), 6 volumes.
4. Zeitschrift 'Folk' (G. Hirzel Verlag, Leipzig, 9-11-1937).
5. FFC, vol. LXIV, 1955, p. 161.

8. What is a description?*

PHILIPPE HAMON

A reader recognizes and identifies a description without hesitation: it stands out against the narrative background, the story 'comes to a standstill', the scenery 'is foregrounded', etc. Nevertheless the reader is not able to define it as a specific unit, using precise formal and/or functional criteria, the only criterion appealed to being in general vaguely referential (a description describes *things*, a narrative describes *acts*) or morphological (the description is alleged to use adjectives, the narration, verbs: on this view Rimbaud's *Départ*,[1] a text which has hardly any verbs, would not be a narrative, and a sentence like 'a tree stood there' would be). This is not very satisfactory. We will begin with these various intuitions of our average reader, and attempt to sharpen or refine them. According to them, the description: (a) forms an autonomous whole, a sort of 'semantic unit'; (b) is more or less an appetizer, supplementary to the narrative; (c) can be freely inserted into a narration; (d) lacks any specific signs or marks; (e) is subject to no *a priori* constraints.

Our analysis will touch on a certain number of important problems: the position of realistic discourse within a typology of discourses, the notion of a genre and of constraints, the opposition between narrative and non-narrative, the relations between realism and description, etc. It is quite clear that the problem of description is not specific to realism. Utopian literature, for instance, like science fiction and fantasy, uses description extensively. Nor is it a specifically 'literary' problem. It is clear also that problems of the literalness (*littéralité*) of a description must be distinguished from those posed by its literarity (*littérarité*). (The former is, perhaps, .a problem of text grammar: under what conditions is an utterance to be considered as a description?) Similarly, we will not take up here the difficult problems connected with the distinction between a *linguistic description* and a descriptive *metalanguage*, nor problems which are *intersemiological* (for instance, in a paraphrase of a painting, the description 'There is a yellow table beneath the green fruit bowl' is 'possible', although in normal direct description it is next to 'impossible'; or consider the relation of text to picture in a fashion magazine or encyclopedia article, etc.). Finally, we will leave aside *diachronic*

* This is a revised version of the article published in *Poétique*.

problems related to the study of description: where, when, how, does a given type of description appear, why does a given period choose a given descriptive theme, such as, for example, the 'portrait' or 'character' in the seventeenth century (Lanson, in his *Art de la prose*, treated these as 'fixed forms' of classical prose), or the 'garden' at the end of the eighteenth century, or the romantic landscape with ruins, the machine, or the street in the nineteenth century, etc.

Classical rhetoric offers us little help in defining description, preoccupied as it was above all (especially in classical and French neoclassical authors) with the problem of establishing a classification of figures or tropes on the microscopic level (metaphor, metonymy, synecdoche, zeugma, oxymoron, etc.). Dumarsais does not mention it by name; as for Fontanier, he defines description (in *Figures du discours*, Paris, Flammarion, 1968) as follows: 'it consists in making an object visible and in making it known through the details of all the most interesting circumstances . . . it gives rise to *hypotyposis* when the object is presented so vividly, so energetically, that there results the stylistic effect of an image, a painting'. This is hardly precise: in jumping from description to hypotyposis, and from hypotyposis to painting, rhetoric, like all cataloguing, involves us in an endless loop of definitions.[2]

We can tentatively define a description as a textual unit having the following properties: it is continuous or discontinuous, a relatively autonomous expansion, characteristically referential; it is interchangeable with, and in certain conditions equivalent to, a *word* (a common or proper noun, a name) or a *deictic pronoun* (him, this, that . . .):

$$\text{deictic} \leftarrow \quad \begin{array}{c} \text{common noun} \\ \\ \text{proper noun} \end{array} \quad \rightarrow \text{description}$$

This unit has overall semantic autonomy, independent of its stylistic setting and of the meaning of its constituent elements (a description is thus a *hierarchy*); and it can, on the level of the utterance, have a single, collective, function (*actant collectif*). This immediately poses a number of problems, of which we will consider only a few in this article: (a) how is a description incorporated in a larger textual ensemble (a narrative or macro-description)? Does it possess a *demarcative–configurative apparatus*, signs or signals which demarcate, introduce, conclude? (b) how does a description function internally? Can a typology be developed, and, if so, on the basis of what criteria? (c) what is the role of a description in the overall functioning of the text which contains it (a narration, for example)? (d) does a description tend to occupy particular *strategic positions* in the text (this is the problem of its distribution)?

I

Let us begin with the first point. We will take most of our examples from Zola,[3] for several reasons: traditional criticism (the average reader) considers him to be the archetypical example of the realistic–descriptive author; his own critical writings on description and realism are numerous; his theoretical assumptions are clear, and directly accessible, as are his rough drafts and the preparatory materials for each novel.[4]

Consider, for example, a description of a locomotive that is to be inserted at a certain point in the story.[5] This description will have the form of a textual fragment composed of a certain number of sub-themes (the wheels, the rods, the levers, etc.), of qualifying predicates (big, gleaming, iron, steaming, copper-coloured, etc.), of verbs (roars, whistles, shudders, turns, lunges, etc.), whose internal arrangement we will observe in detail below. Since the author, according to the principle of 'objectivity' or 'impersonality', is supposed to be invisible behind his utterance, and not to look as if he is guiding it for his own ends, the characters of his story will be assigned the task of seeing and will have to assume responsibility for doing so.[6] For this purpose the characters will have to do one or more of the following:

A. look at the locomotive: this requires, for example, for plausibility, if the locomotive is in a shed, that there be enough light, whether sunlight, moonlight, or artificial, that there be an open door or window, that the character be neither near-sighted nor blind, that there be, for example, a view from above through a skylight in the shed roof, etc. The description has to be felt by the reader to depend on the *vision* of the character who is responsible for it, on his *ability to see*, and not on the *knowledge* of the novelist, on the contents of his files.

This explains the frequent occurrence in Zola's books of open doors and windows (in *Pot-Bouille* they are always open), of covered but open markets, of greenhouses, shop windows, glass-walled offices, etc. The unhampered freedom of view that is indicated in the text authorizes the author's unhampered description. Indeed, we often find, instead of the character who views a scene, an impersonal observer: 'one could see, through the glass panes . . . far off the sun could be seen . . . X and Y were visible through the half-open door', etc.[7] It also explains why there are so many indoor scenes that take place in a 'harsh light', so many 'precise' landscapes and panoramas, so many characters with 'piercing' looks. Here, for instance, is the countryside of Plassans: 'a crystal light, as limpid and icy as spring water, flowed from the pale horizon. In the distance was the Viorne . . . it was a whole region magnified by the clearness of the air and the peace of cold' (I, 209). A suburban landscape is described as follows in the *Confession de Claude*: 'what surrounded me, the streets, houses, trees, the sky, seemed to have been carefully scrubbed. The landscape was clean, brand new, gleaming white and clear' (C.L.P. I, 64). In *Lourdes*, we are given numerous descriptions of the city through the eyes of Pierre, who contemplates panoramas washed 'in the crystal air' (C.L.P. VII, 120). Witness also the views of Paris, in *Une Page d'amour*, as seen from the heights of Chaillot[8] (the author's preparatory file contains many photographs): 'so pure was the light that one could make out the finest details; Paris . . . gleamed like a crystal' (II, 850); further on, Paris is 'a city as white and clear as if it were embedded in crystal' (II, 907), in a light 'as limpid and cold as water from a spring, as if Paris were placed under glass' (II, 1088); or the landscape of *Germinal*: 'in the distance, in the bright sun, he could see the gantries over some pits . . . in the transparent morning air . . .'.

The author, feeling the need to justify his character's prolonged gazing at his surroundings, has to appeal to a desire to see, and a capacity to see, and makes the character a 'spy', or 'curious', an 'amateur' engineer, or a painter who 'is interested' in modern subjects, etc., and these psychological characterizations are present only to provide an *a posteriori* justification for the description which is their cause, not their consequence. By definition a description is an interruption in the syntagmatics of the narration due to a paradigm (a catalogue, an enumeration, a lexicon), and thus a prolongation of the act of looking of the character who is assigned the description. We are to suppose that the character is 'absorbed', 'fascinated', 'loses track of time',[9] because of what he is looking at, and that he has been able to abstract himself for a while from the plot; the 'delay' in the text is justified by a 'delay' invoked by the text: an 'idle period' in an activity, a 'breather', a 'pause', etc. We thus find many scenes where someone is waiting to meet someone, where there is imposed inaction (an illness, a convalescence, temporary immobility), and characters who are onlookers, idlers, carefree strollers, loafers, etc. Two possibilities are especially common: (a) a stationary character (leaning on something, lying down, squatting, sitting, standing motionless) before a panorama or an object which is moving or changing; (b) a moving character (walking, visiting, a tourist, an explorer)[10] observing a fixed but complex scene (a street, a landscape, a monument, a flat).

The sentences which introduce descriptions will be, for example, of the form: 'X, having nothing to do, leaned on the windowsill; down below he saw the locomotive, which . . .', and the type of character which is the antithesis of this is the blind man. To summarize this system of justificatory themes which is so frequent in Zola, we have the schematic introduction to a description shown on p. 151.

B. speak of the locomotive: in this case, the character is not the writer's eye, but his spokesman. A character who knows the locomotive describes it, with technical terms if necessary, to someone who does not know it, or does

X {
with nothing to do
absent-mindedly
during a pause
having arrived early
by chance
automatically
taking a break
unable to move because of an accident
walking aimlessly
}

{
walked up to
let his gaze stray to
leaned on
glanced at
entered
had his eye caught by
noticed
let his eye run over
caught sight of
spied on
lost track of time
while gazing at
}

a locomotive

{
through a/the
window
opening
open door
glass door
shop window
limpid air
transparent atmosphere
}

{
by the light of
the moon
the gas jet
the sun
a lightning flash
a candle
}

Character + expression indicating a pause + verb of perception + the object being described + expression indicating a transparent medium not know it well; the description will resemble a detailed specification or parts list.[11] This leads to the use of types of characters like intruders, beginners, apprentices, untrained people, interacting with technicians, specialists, professionals, natives, characters who are glib, garrulous, didactic, pedantic, gossipy, etc. A typical introductory sentence for such a description is, for example: 'X, who knew what he was talking about, for he had been driving it for a long time, was explaining to young Y how the locomotive worked: those rods . . .'.[12] The antithetical, and complementary, character type is the one who does not speak at all (the mute).[13] This type of introduction can be represented schematically as shown on p. 153.

In this fictional universe of spoken description, the information which circulates and is originated or transmitted by a speaker generally in the form of a pseudo-soliloquy, confidences, gossip, or technical explanations to some uninformed third party, is thus most often in semi-direct discourse.[14] We note that one or another psychological characterization ('curiosity', 'the joy of learning something new', etc.) can also be appealed to here.

C. act themselves on the subject being described (with or without the presence of an interested onlooker). This explains the use of characters who are men at work, technicians, people in action, busy people, characters who are moving into or out of a dwelling, or remodelling one, people introduced in the setting of their activity. A typical introductory sentence for such a description is: 'X and his workmen were busy trying to get the locomotive started; its rods and wheels . . .'. Here the description will take the form of a series of actions exemplifying to some degree of explicitness the professional qualifications of the person performing them: the pork-butcher will be shown making blood sausage in his *charcuterie*, the priest saying mass and decorating his church,[15] the smith working metal in his forge, etc. Here, there is no use of semi-direct discourse, but rather a listing of technical acts where the text runs through the tools and the details of the setting to be described as the character works on or with them. Thus, in this case, the description is organized in advance, much as it would be in the corresponding set of technical specifications.

Classical rhetoricians, always quick to criticize description (according to Boileau, it should be brief; according to everyone, it should be strictly subordinate to the story), admit 'Homeric' description as the only valid kind. Lessing, in the *Laocoon* (Paris, Hermann, 1964, pp. 111ff.) had already made similar remarks about Homer and his way of 'dramatizing' descriptions. In general, in the *before* and *after* of such descriptions, there is an effort to respect the before and after of a genuine technological manual. Note, for example, the description of sacramental objects to be used in the mass, in *La Faute de l'Abbé Mouret*: 'La Teuse spread out above the chasuble the stole, the maniple, the girdle, the alb and the amice . . . Father Mouret . . . was

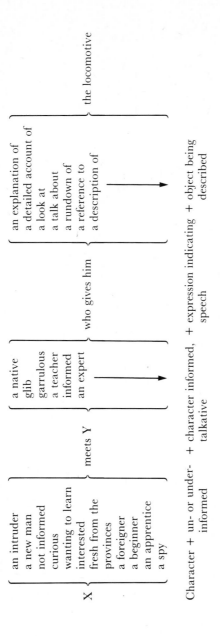

X
{ an intruder
a new man
not informed
curious
wanting to learn
interested
fresh from the provinces
a foreigner
a beginner
an apprentice
a spy }

meets Y

{ a native
glib
garrulous
a teacher
informed
an expert }

who gives him

{ an explanation of
a detailed account of
a look at
a talk about
a rundown of
a reference to
a description of }

the locomotive

Character + un- or under-informed + character informed, talkative + expression indicating speech + object being described preparing the chalice on a little table, a large old chalice of silver gilt, with a bronze foot, which he had just taken out from the back of a deal cupboard where the holy vessels and linen, the holy oil, missals, candlesticks, crosses, were kept . . .' (I, 1217). Here a simultaneity, a list, is replaced by a successivity.

Similarly, in a ploughing scene from *La Terre*, Zola furnishes, in the form of activity by his protagonist Jean, a list of the main parts of a plough: 'Digging in the share, with his hands on the plough handle, he called to his horse with the harsh croak he used to goad it . . . the ploughshare and coulter had a hard time parting the strip they were cutting in this full-blade ploughing. The thickly clodded earth could be heard grating against the mould board' (IV, 736). Here the character is essentially a tool-bearer.

The character type that would be the antithesis of this is the helpless or paralysed individual.[16] This suggests the paradigm shown below.

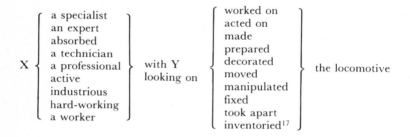

A typical introductory sentence would thus contain: an active character + a spectator + a verb of action + the object or scene being described. Recapitulating the three preceding examples, we obtain the formula for an introductory unit shown below.

Character A (or two characters A and B) conjoined with an object or scene C		(a) A works on C with B present (b) A talks to B about C (c) A looks at C		there is a transfer of information to A (or to B in case (b))

Note that the motifs of the three headings (a), (b) and (c) (working, talking and looking) can quite easily be permuted, omitted, or combined in various ways. For instance: 'X (a neophyte or apprentice) *watches* Y *taking apart* a locomotive and Y *explains* to him in detail how it works'. Differences in focus in the narrative (which may be centred on the actor, the watcher, or the speaker, etc.) provide a supplementary source of variation available to the author.

Furthermore, it will be noted that this thematics, which we can call the *pseudo-thematics* of description, may be subjected to a logic of its own.[18] For example, in the passage from *seeing* to *speaking* or *doing* the author may have to make a detour through a way station of the opposing thematics (not see; not speak; not do) (see diagram below).

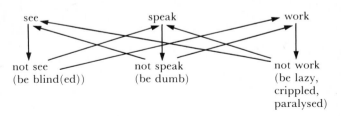

The opening pages of *Germinal* provide a good example: an ignorant stranger (Etienne) arrives in an unknown region; he assimilates it through the sense of *sight*; however, the darkness of night does not allow him to see everything; he approaches some workers whom he *watches* as they work, by firelight; an accident with a machine brings about a *pause* in the work, during which a worker who is a native and is well-informed (Bonnemort) *speaks*, describing the region to Etienne. Finally, instead of making use of contraries and contradictories as intermediate stages to diversify the pseudo-thematics, the text may involve the interplay of themes and their converses: seeing without being seen, being seen and speaking, working and being spoken of (quoted, referred to), being spoken of and seen without speaking (as is the historical figure, such as the character of Napoleon III, in Zola's work) etc.

While description requires from the author a true narrative stage-setting, a *savoir-faire*, and requires from the reader and the author considerable 'lexical competence' (description, which is the vehicle by which the lexicon of work is introduced, is also a reflection of work on the lexicon), it is, in addition, the point in the text at which, in the most 'natural' way possible, an ideological competence may be inserted: that is, the narrator's knowledge of the system of dominant values, rules, laws, etc., which governs his society. This will be evidenced by the incorporation in the text of evaluative comments, which will tend to accompany especially the triple thematics that serves as justification (seeing; speaking; working). Thus, for instance, the character's *seeing* may be the occasion for aesthetic evaluation of what he is looking at (the sight may be magnificent or sinister, beautiful or ugly, harmonious or chaotic, etc.), or comments about the effect of the sight on the looker (pleasure or displeasure, joy or distress, aesthetic enjoyment or boredom, etc.); similarly, the character's *words* may be accompanied by comments about grammatical or stylistic norms, rules or laws (his speech may be correct or incorrect, fluent or stumbling, simple or oratorical, pleasant or unpleasant, creative or stereotyped, suitable or unsuitable, etc.); and finally, the character's *work* may be accompanied by references to the rules and laws of technology (careful or shoddy work, in conformity with practice or not, successful or not, liberating or alienating, creative or mechanical, etc.). Almost always, the description also appears as a *normative space*, a domain of law, which reflects not only the narrator's lexical and linguistic knowledge, but also his knowledge of the laws, rules, rites, rituals, etiquettes which organize all aspects of social convention.

To sum up, all of these sequence-types (even the one involving *action* on the object or setting being described, which is simply the manifestation of a pseudo-power) represent a transmission (a making-known) of some kind of knowledge, which is of the general form shown below.

We see that even before it begins the description must be justified, and thus it comports various kinds of plausible *padding* serving as pretext, in which the author is led to introduce a whole series of themes, each one calling up a flood of others (to introduce description D he must introduce character X, who must observe setting S. Thus there must be a view from above, or a light. But it must also be mentioned that this character is interested in setting S, and that he has the time to inspect or scrutinize it. Thus there must be . . .). We will thus consider as themes which are *imposed* (required),[19] implicit, or *a posteriori*, in the realist discourse of Zola: (a) transparent media: windows, glass partitions, open doors, bright light, sunlight, clear air, wide vistas, etc.; (b) character types such as: the painter, the aesthete, the street idler, the stroller, the spy, the gossip, the neophyte, the intruder, the technician, the informer, the person exploring a place, etc. (We find in Jules Verne's *Twenty Thousand Leagues Under the Sea* a trio of characters who exemplify the principal functions of description (naming, classifying, enjoying) and the principal thematic roles (the sailor, a specialist in fishing, has excellent eyesight; the professor and his servant possess knowledge and speech): 'Our admiration stayed at a maximum. We were continually calling out. Ned Land would name the fish, Conseil would class them, and as for myself, I would fall into raptures over their lively movements and beautiful shapes' (chapter XIV).) (c) typical scenes such as: arriving ahead of time for a meeting, discovering a secret, visiting a flat, intruding upon an unknown place, taking a walk, pausing, resting, leaning out of a window, climbing up to a height, fitting up or modifying an interior or exterior, etc.;[20] (d) psychological motivations such as: absence of mind, pedantry, curiosity, interest, aesthetic pleasure, talkativeness, idleness, gazing vacantly, fascination, etc.

All of these themes, clearly, function purely as demarcations, as devices marking the introduction to a description, and they constitute an *empty* thematics, one entirely predetermined by the author's postulates (verisimilitude, etc.), whose function is above all that of avoiding gaps between description and narration, of filling in the chinks in the narrative by making the interruptions plausible.[21]

This *introductory* thematics of a description logically determines the set of themes that will *conclude* the description: if it begins by noting the existence of a light, it will close by noting the disappearance of the light. We will thus have the following set of possible conclusions: the disappearance of a light (artificial or natural); the closing of a door or window; the arrival of the person being waited for; coming down from the height, etc. These are merely the logical converses of the introductory themes.[22]

Let us consider two examples. The first comes from *La Faute de l'Abbé Mouret* by Zola:

But Father Mouret did not have the time to respond to this challenge from the Philosopher. A door suddenly opened at the far end of the vestibule; a dazzling opening was created in the blackness of the wall. It was like a vision of virgin forest, a break in a huge wood, bathed in sunlight. In that brightness the priest could see clearly, in the distance, a few precise details: a large yellow flower in the middle of a lawn, a sheet of water falling from a high rock, a gigantic tree full of flitting birds; the whole scene overwhelmed, lost, aflame, in such a flood of green, such a riot of vegetation, that the entire horizon was no more than a plant in bloom. The door slammed, everything disappeared.

The second is from Maupassant's story *La Petite Roque*:

The mayor came out also, took his hat, a large soft hat of grey felt, with a very wide brim, and stood for a few seconds at the threshold of his house. Before him lay a vast lawn with three large bursts of colour, red, blue and white, three wide beds of flowers in bloom, one in front of the house, and one on each side. Further off, the first trees of the wood stretched up to the sky, while on the left, beyond the Brindille, broadened here into a pond, could be seen long meadows, green, flat country, crossed with ditches and with rows of willows like monstrous squat dwarfs, always pruned close, bearing on their enormous short trunks a quivering bouquet of thin branches.

On the right, beyond the stables, the sheds, all the outbuildings belonging to the estate, began the village, a rich one, inhabited by cattle breeders.

Renardet went slowly down the steps of his house, and, turning to the left, walked up to the water's edge, then paced along it, slowly, his hands behind his back . . .

Note, in the second example, the theme of the *threshold*, the raised *steps*, the *pause* ('stood for a few seconds'), the *descent* from the vantage point. Also to be emphasized is the tendency for description to be a quantified ('a few seconds') 'halt' in the narration. This measurement is as much metalinguistic as referential; it is more a programming of the time it takes the reader to read the description than of the time of the incident: time is here deprived of all functionality.

It is not the complexity of reality which induces the prolongation (and hence the closing) of the description, but the limits of the lexicon available to the author, the exhaustion of what is in his working files, or the intrusion of the story (the full thematics). It is noteworthy that an author has at his disposal many devices for demarcating his descriptions, which may operate singly or in combination: a blank space, a new paragraph, an editorial intrusion of the type 'we will now describe the landscape which . . .', various kinds of preterition ('an indescribable scene was taking place . . .').[23] The delimitation of a description can also be aided by a break in the distribution of certain markers (changes of pronoun or tense), by the use of a specialized vocabulary ('in the distance', 'on the left', 'to the right', 'higher up', etc.). With Zola, a description often ends with a term in the singular (a 'precise' detail), after a context full of plurals (some . . . some . . . some . . .), or the opposite; rhythmically, there may be a long sentence after a series of short ones, or the opposite. An exhaustive study of description would require a detailed examination of all of these stylistic devices for opening or closing.

II

It is clear that description does not call for the same kind of 'linguistic consciousness' (or 'competence') on the part of the author or reader as does narration. A narrative structure, being a dialectics of correlated classes (inversions and transformations of elements of content), being an oriented vector, calls for predictions from the reader of a *logical* type: the opening of a door implies its closing, a lack implies the removal of the lack, a departure calls for a return, an order calls for compliance or refusal, a disjunction of entities implies a conjunction of entities, etc. A descriptive system, on the other hand, sets up *lexical* and *stylistic* expectations, where what are expected are semiotic sequences, where the notions of inclusion, resemblance or contiguity seem more important than the notions of transformation or inversion. (The term 'rose' will invoke, by referential contiguity, 'bouquet', 'petal', 'stem', 'thorn', 'flower', 'flower bed', 'garden', etc.; or, by lexical derivation, 'rosier' (rose bush), 'roseraie' (rose garden), 'rosière' (Rose Maiden), etc.; or, by institutionalized analogies, virginity, candour, purity, etc.; or, by phonetic resemblance, 'arrose' (sprinkle), 'ose' (dare), 'pose' (place, put), 'chose' (thing), etc.) Thus, a story is to be *understood*, primarily, while a description is to be *recognized*, although it must not be forgotten that there are procedures of *recognition* for narrative, involving the genres with their stereotyped frameworks. Narrative involves the level and domain of *semantics*, while description involves the linguistic–semiotic domain, to adopt Benveniste's fruitful distinction. Description, one might say, is the lexicographical consciousness of fiction. To describe is almost always to actualize a latent lexical paradigm based on an underlying system of referential knowledge about the world (for example, the reader's knowledge of terms applying to gardens, or to flowers). The elements of a descriptive system are organized globally as a *permanent equivalence* between a lexical *expansion* and a lexical *condensation* into a term. Thus, as we read a succession of botanical terms, of flower names, this sequence should be perceived as equivalent, for the duration of the reading, to the word 'garden'. A description organizes the persistence in memory of a single sign by means of a plurality of different signs.

No doubt the most 'expected' linguistic grouping in a description is the combination adjective + noun (e.g. the white flower, the flower is white). This group contains many potential variations, and it may be interesting to see which is the preferred actualization in a given text: a flower whitens, the whiteness of a flower; the white flower; the flower, white; the flower which is white; a white of flower; a whiteness flowers; the flower in its whiteness; a floral whiteness; the flower is whiter, less white, as white as . . ., etc. Often, a description is just the intrasemiotic exploration (itself accompanied by an intersemiotic exploration: the copying or paraphrasing of a picture, the intertextual 'rewriting' of a learned text, etc.) of a transformational field. For Bachelard, the realist mentality is primarily characterized by 'the piling up of adjectives on a single noun' (*Formation de l'esprit scientifique* (Paris, Vrin, 1970), p. 111). Finally, there is an important factor of internal cohesion in descriptions which should not be overlooked: the introductory theme (IT) can, by its phonemic constitution, function to 'seed' the description it introduces, can give rise to a succession of anagrams. The thematic word will then operate as the phonetic *maquette* (model – the term is Saussure's) of the description.

As we have seen, a description is often the result of the combining of one (or more) characters (C) with a setting, a milieu, a landscape, a collection of objects. This setting, the global introductory theme of the description (IT), triggers a series of sub-themes, a vocabulary (V) whose constituents bear the relation of metonymic inclusion with the IT, in a sort of 'branching metonymy'. A description of a garden (principal IT) all but entails the enumeration, the 'declension', of the various flowers, paths, beds, trees, tools, etc. which constitute this garden. Each sub-theme can in turn give rise to a predicative expansion, whether qualificative or functional[24] (PE), which serves as a gloss on this sub-theme. The formula for a description is accordingly:

$$C + F + IT (V + PEq/PEf)$$

where F, as we have seen, is most frequently of the form: 'look'/'speak'/'act', and where each of the units may be more or less disjoint with the others, may be absent, or may permute.

The sequence $IT \rightarrow V \rightarrow PE$ can be viewed as parallel, all in all, to the sequence *entry → definition → examples and cross-references* in the organization of a dictionary article. This accounts for the fascination felt by all descriptive writers for the dictionary (Zola for the nineteenth-century Larousse, Ponge for the Littré, etc.), a text which is not *read*, but *consulted*; and it leads to the danger that the descriptive text will also turn into a text 'to be consulted', hence one where the reader can skip over the descriptions. In general the object to be described (the introductory theme term, the pivot word or 'pantonym' which triggers the description, the lexeme which generates the vocabulary) is announced at the *beginning* of the description. It remains memorized, as it were, the common denominator for the whole description. Often, the role assigned to the title (cf. 'The Soap', 'The Meadow', 'The Carnation', titles of poems by François Ponge) is that of setting up a system of expectations designed to facilitate (or frustrate) the readability of the following description. However, the term can be delayed to the end of the description, or even omitted (with the description then approaching the riddle: the question taking the form of a definition-description, the answer that of a name), so that the description ramifies luxuriantly without the reader knowing what is being spoken of.[25]

Consider, for example, the following, from Paul Verlaine's 'La Bonne Chanson', where the introductory theme *cela* is placed at the end of the text with the main verb *poursuit*, and retrospectively assigns to the descriptive enumeration the semantic status of *object of the narrator's quest:*

> Le foyer, la lueur étroite de la lampe;
> La rêverie avec le doigt contre la tempe
> Et les yeux se perdant parmi les yeux aimés;
> L'heure du thé fumant et des livres fermés;
> La douceur de sentir la fin de la soirée;
>
> La fatigue charmante et l'attente adorée
> De l'ombre nuptiale et de la douce nuit,
> Oh! tout cela, mon rêve attendri le poursuit
> Sans relâche, à travers toutes remises vaines,
> Impatient des mois, furieux des semaines!

(The hearth, the narrow beam of the lamp; the reverie with finger on temple and eyes lost in the beloved's eyes; the hour of steaming tea and closed books; the sweet feeling of evening's end; the charming fatigue and the adored waiting for the nuptial dark and the sweet night, Oh! all that, my tender dreaming pursues it untiringly, through all vain delays, impatient with the months, furious with the weeks!)

The same type of riddle-construction is to be found in the presentation of the octopus in the *Travailleurs de la mer* of Hugo.

The following celebrated fragment by Paul Eluard in *Poésie Ininterrompue* is an example of a description reduced to a PE:

Nue effacée ensommeillée/Choisie sublime solitaire/Profonde oblique matinale/... Pavée construite vitrifiée/Globale haute populaire/Barrée gardée contradictoire ... (Cloud effaced drowsy/Chosen sublime solitary/Deep oblique matinal/... Paved built vitrified/Global high popular/obstructed guarded contradictory ...).

Let us take as an example the description of a bed of roses in *La Faute de l'Abbé Mouret*.[26]

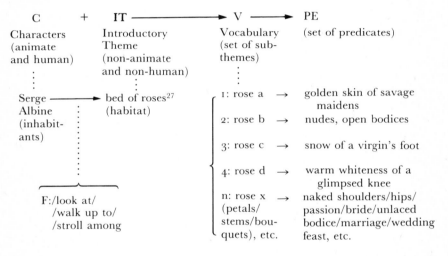

Another example would be the description of the locomotive *Lison* (IV, 1127ff.).

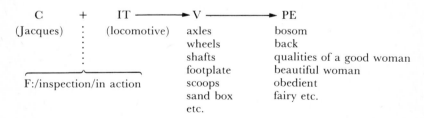

Or the description of the greenhouse in *La Curée* (I, 486ff.) which is the scene of the incestuous relations of Renée and Maxime.

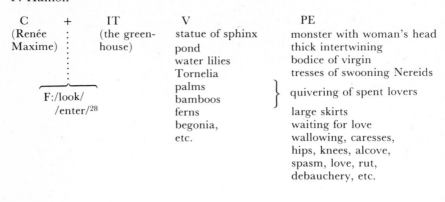

To be precise, every description has the form of a metonymically homogeneous lexical block whose extension is related to the *available* vocabulary of the author, not to the degree of complexity of the reality itself; it is above all an extendable lexicon whose limits are more or less artificial, and constituted by items whose appearance is more or less predictable. The author has at his disposal a certain number of possibilities for regulating the amount of predictability and adjusting the semantic homogeneity of the description.

Type I

The more technical the description becomes, using monosemic terms (scoop, rod, throttle, axle, etc.) or proper nouns (Nymphea, Tornelia, Begonia, etc.), i.e. the more it becomes a professional idiolect, the acuter the problem of its *readability* becomes. For example, if I want to describe a boat (IT), the paradigm (V) of technical words corresponding to the theme *boat* (boom, jib, rudder blade, joiner, staysail, etc.) may be somewhat incomprehensible to the reader, may not be part of his available vocabulary, and so may exclude him from the communicative process by transforming the description into a futile cryptogram (there will be a meaning only for the specialist, who does not really need it), into a series of desemanticized terms.[29] Consequently, the author will in general adjoin systematically, term by term, to this paradigm of technical words a succession of qualifying predicates (PE) which explain, paraphrase, or illustrate metaphorically, and which will clarify and counterbalance the obscurity of the elements of the paradigm through references to a certain number of clichés, common terms, codes (cultural, sensory, literary, etc.) or stereotyped associations. The description will thus be an authoritative matching of two lexical paradigms or sets, one desemanticized and of low predictability, the other semanticized and of high predictability.

162

Paradigm V	Paradigm PE
Specialized lexicon: set of themes, more or less desemanticized technical terms	Set of semanticized explanatory predicates
Unreadability	Readability
poor communication	good communication
low predictability	high predictability
specialized technical idiolect	clichés, comparisons, or institutionalized metaphors; vocabulary of high frequency, or accessibility – the basic available lexicon[30]

The types of predicates most often used to semanticize the technical lexicon of description will involve comparison, paraphrase, explanatory apposition and the anthropomorphic metaphor. For example, to take the case of the boat again:

> a stay will be: a long sinew of steel stretched to the breaking point
>
> a boom will be: the long piece of polished wood supporting the main sail
>
> the rudder blade will be: the submerged part of the rudder, as sharp as a razor blade
>
> the fore-topmast staysail will be: the small triangular sail stretched between the mast and the front of the boat, as full as the wing of a sea bird, as white as snow, etc.

Here we are very close to the dictionary article, the setting up of an equivalence between a name and its expansion; the description turns pedagogical, explaining the less known by the better known, and a metaphor plays a role somewhat like that of the cross-reference in a dictionary article.

Type II

Conversely, the introductory theme and the paradigm of the specialized lexicon which is to develop it may be easily identifiable (the lexicon may be immediately available: for example, for the IT *garden* the set V: bed, tree, thicket, flower, petal, compost, etc., or for a *portrait* the set: hair, eyes, nose, profile, clothing, etc.).[31]

The semantic field and the stereotyped vocabulary function here as a norm, or a genre, which restricts the reader's range of expectations and predetermines lines of least resistance for his reading (the appearance of the IT *garden*, in narration of the non-deceptive variety, makes it very probable

163

that words (V) will appear like: bed, tree, thicket . . .). The metaphorical predicates (PE) will then be selected so as to counteract this banality and strong predictability, and will systematically be kept at as great a distance as possible from the corresponding themes and sub-themes of V which are their point of departure. Thus the details of the Paris Halles are described by Zola as elements in a 'gigantic working drawing', which stand out against the 'phosphorescent vellum' of the sky, etc., with references to lexical fields from the plastic arts; similarly, the animate will be described with reference to the inanimate, the concrete with the abstract, the natural with the cultural, etc. In contrast to type I, the set PE will be intentionally 'poetic' here, with low predictability, and selected from technically specialized vocabularies. Thus

> the flower bed : unrolls its thick-pile carpet as precise as a blueprint
> the flower is : an opal stalagmite
> the soil is : a mixture of sienna and yellow ochre, etc.

Here description approaches the fantastic – the unknown is used to obscure the known.[32]

Type III

Here the author accepts a certain amount of unreadableness in his description, combining a specialized lexicon of technical terms and a series of predicates also taken from a specialized technical lexicon. Instead of introducing redundancy of content in the narrative, instead of neutralizing the unreadableness of one series of terms by the readableness of another, the description introduces a sort of semantic blank space into the text, which may be interpreted differently by different readers ('unreadable', 'obscure', 'poetic', 'hermetic', etc.). Thus, in the description of a garden, a *syringa* (a term from the vocabulary of gardening) will be described as having the colour of *ceruse* (white-lead, a term from the vocabulary of painting), etc. The description develops in this case through the confrontation of two kinds of specialized technical discourse in V and PE.

Type IV

Here the author accepts maximal readability. An IT triggers the appearance of a stereotyped lexicon which is predicated with a series of equally stereotyped terms or clichés. For example, for the IT *portrait*, the description will mention a *forehead* which is 'white as snow'. In such a case the description is quite close to tautology (with reduced information, redundancy of content, maximum predictability), pleonasm, or cliché (phatic communication).

Type V

The description is content with being purely a list of technical terms (hence unreadable) without any explanatory predicates intended to shed light on it. To continue with the same examples, the IT *boat* will be described only with the help of its specialized vocabulary: jib, boom, stay, etc. Here the description is close to the sales brochure, the classified advertisement, or the parts catalogue. Conversely, the description may consist exclusively of a series of more or less unreadable predicates or metaphorical paraphrases, taken from other specialized technical lexicons, or from quite distant semantic domains. Thus, the IT *garden* would trigger the appearance of predicates like: 'constellation of ochre', 'patches of ceruse', etc., without any appearance of the basic theme of V, whether known (roses) or unknown (syringas), which could serve as intermediary between IT and PE. Consider, for example, this description of a brook by Saint-Pol-Roux:

> On a Rivulet Flowing into the Lucerne
> . . . True water,
> First water,
> Candid water,
> Lily and swan water,
> Sweat of the shadow water,
> Baldric of the meadow water,
> Innocence passing water,
> Ingot of the firmament water,
> Litanies of the morning water,
> Coddled by the basins water,
> Cherished by the ewer water,
> Lover of the jars water,
> With an eye to christening water,
> For the pedestalled statues water . . .

In either case, the risk is that communication will be poor, but the first case (with a purely technical vocabulary) generally has unfavourable connotations for the reader (the description is 'dry', 'technical', 'bookish', etc.), while the second case (a pure series of metaphors) generally has favourable connotations (the description is 'poetic').

The description may present itself as an unadulterated sequence of predicates (PE) that are highly readable (institutionalized comparisons or metaphors, clichés, various kinds of stereotypes . . .) and avoid technical vocabulary, denomination, the 'right' name, the monosemic introductory themes of V, either intentionally, or else because this vocabulary has not been established by usage. Certain sensory objects (a perfume, a wine) or aesthetic objects (an abstract painting, a symphony) sometimes do not provide the author with a reality already cut up in terms of a vocabulary or

165

technical lexicon. In the absence of V, usage and culture will furnish a set of stereotyped predicates which take the place of obligatory descriptive signs for the object in question. Thus feminine *beauty* will be described with reference to an institutionalized predicative paradigm, for example a pictorial one (Albani's brush, the art of Raphael, Ingres' line . . .) or a sensory one (satin, jet, alabaster, lilies, roses, grain . . .). Beaujolais (a desemanticized proper name) will be 'full-bodied', 'fruity', 'subtle', 'light', etc. In the absence of a fixed vocabulary V felt by the reader as connected to IT by the metonymic relation of inclusion (as parts of the same whole), the description may be based on the stable and closed vocabulary associated with the five senses of smell, sight, hearing, touch and taste, which will preorganize it and serve as its specific and 'imposed' mark.[33] Thus the IT 'Chevret', the name of a type of cheese (the word being a proper noun that is partially semanticized, cf. 'chèvre': goat), will be described thus:

sight : thin, bluish rind; pink spots
touch: smooth regular consistency
smell : slight goat odour
taste : nutty flavour[34]

(Note here the description partly combined with a metonymic lexicon predictable from IT: inside/outside:consistency/rind.) The description terminates when the list of the senses has been exhausted. A series of pivots may be used to introduce these predicative expansions, of the type:

it was like (the whiteness of snow/the rumbling of thunder/the cutting edge of a razor, etc.); it looked like; it was reminiscent of; it resembled; it was a kind of; one might have thought one was seeing, etc.

The description then takes on a highly personalized appearance; this is the technique of impressionism, and also that which is often used in fantasy, adventure, science fiction, or in the riddle: it avoids specialized terminology in favour of a gloss using 'ordinary' words.

It is quite clear that the typology we have presented is abstract, and that it is necessary to allow for sub-types; only rarely does a description have a homogeneous appearance, and in general the author combines several procedures within a single description.

To summarize, he essentially works with:

condensation (single term)	⟷	expansion (sentential paraphrase)
readability (clichés, words of high frequency)	⟷	unreadability (available specialized vocabulary[35])

presence of an introductory lexicon (V)	⟷	absence of V
presence of explanatory predicates (PE)	⟷	absence of PE
predictable appearance of lexical occurrences of V after IT	⟷	unpredictability
reinforcement of effects (readability or unreadability of V is reinforced by that of PE)	⟷	neutralization (the readability or unreadability of V is destroyed or corrected by its converse in PE)
metonymically coherent lexicons (flower/petal/stem/bouquet . . .)	⟷	metaphorically coherent lexicons (flower/woman)

III

We will treat the third point only briefly: what is a description for, what role does it play in the overall economy of the context (often a narrative one) in which it is embedded?[36]

Being the crucial point at which the readability of a narrative is organized (or destroyed), a description thus has the appearance of a kind of highly organized semantic network. To consider again the three examples from Zola used earlier, we have, in the description taken from *La Faute de l'Abbé Mouret*, reading vertically, a series of metonymic relations: foot – knee – hip – bodice etc., for PE; and rose a, rose b, rose c, bouquet, petal, etc., for V. Horizontally, we have a series of metaphorical relations between V and PE (the roses are assimilated to parts of the female body), at a higher level between C and V,[37] and a semantic redundancy between C (human) and PE (human). The description is thus the point at which a metaphorical assimilation of human/non-human, and redundancies involving human/human and non-human/non-human intersect. It is the author's job to vary and differentiate these relations.[38]

In the example from *La Curée* also we find these metonymic and metaphorical relations within V, within PE, between V and PE, between C and PE.[39]

In the example from *La Bête humaine* there is a quasi-amorous relation between C and IT (human/human),[40] for the locomotive is assimilated, through a whole set of metaphorical predicates, to a woman, since women are one of the obscure obsessions of Jacques (one of the first titles conceived for the novel was *L'Inconscient*).

In the example from *La Petite Roque* we observe an echoing of the predicates describing the character ('*large* hat', 'with a very *wide* brim') in the predicates describing the landscape seen by the character ('*large* bursts', '*wide* beds', 'widened into a pond'). In addition, the colour of the flowers (blue–red–white) is an ironic allusion to the mayor's function in the republic, just as the elevation of his residence alludes to his high social status, while his name, Renardet, serves as a clue whose meaning will only be clear retrospectively: the mayor is the author of the 'bestial' crime who is sought during the story.

If narration can be defined as: (a) meaning which is stored (which accounts for its high redundancy and its easy memorizability); (b) meaning which is transformed (which accounts for its discursive organization into complementary logical classes), then the description is the point where the narrative stops, is suspended, but also the indispensable point where it is 'preserved', where its information is pulled together, where it 'sets' and is reduplicated, where the characters and the setting, in a kind of semantic 'gymnastics', to use Valéry's term, participate in a redundancy. The setting confirms, sharpens, or reveals the character as a bundle of simultaneous significant features, or else it introduces an indication (or a red herring) concerning what is to happen: Albine is *like* a rose, the roses are *like* women, the roses are *like* brides, Albine will *be* a bride, Albine will *die* amidst the roses, etc.; Renée and Maxime, the incestuous lovers, are *like* intertwined plants, the plants of the greenhouse are (artificially) intertwined[41] *like* lovers; *Lison* is, for Jacques, what he unconsciously denies (transference) that a woman should be. The existence of Renée is as *artificial* as the setting before her eyes, etc. The description orients our reading of the story by indirectly communicating information about the future of the characters. We can, then, say that the role of description is, on the one hand, to organize narrative,[42] and on the other hand, through the redundancy which it introduces into the narrative, to act as its memory.[43]

A certain number of marks, of stylistic processes, can become the rhetorical leitmotivs, the 'imposed' signs of these descriptions, and promote semantic circulation (and cohesion) between the environment and its inhabitants, between the human and the non-human.[44] Among these can be mentioned:

(a) metaphors which are alternatively anthropomorphic, zoomorphic, or reifying, according to the type of use the author wishes to make of this relation of environment and inhabitant (the themes of the 'bête humaine', the man-plant, the man-machine). (Note that, in the example from *La Petite Roque* cited above, the protagonist Renardet has the name of an animal, and the trees he is looking at are compared to monsters, to dwarfs.) The systematic use of *anaphors* (textual units referring to other, discontinuous units already introduced or to be introduced), or of 'connectors' ('like', 'similar to', 'resembled, 'seemed', 'a sort of') reinforces both the internal cohesion of the description and its ties with the narrative as a whole.

(b) a dynamicizing and anthropomorphizing of the lexicons, lists, and vocabularies, through the use of durative forms (imperfects, gerundives, present participles, various locutions) and of pronominal forms of the type 'un arbre se dressait' (a tree was standing) 'une plante se tordait' (a plant was writhing), 'un fossé se creuse' (a ditch lies deep (literally: digs, scoops itself)), 'un mur se hausse' (a wall rises, raises itself).[45]

(c) contamination in the use of certain marks, those of narration ('then', 'before', 'after', 'soon', 'meanwhile', 'while', etc., whose function is to mimic the flow of time) which have a tendency to replace the expressions which are more appropriate for indicating location ('in front of', 'behind', 'above', 'below', 'to the left', 'on the right', 'nearer', 'further', etc.). In this way, the reading process itself is signposted.

Thus, for example, the following two celebrated descriptions from Flaubert's *Madame Bovary* are supported by the scaffolding of a pseudo-narrative movement (of technological nature, perhaps corresponding approximately to the manufacturing process for the objects in question):

The newcomer still had his hat in his lap. It was one of those composite examples of headgear, where traces can be seen of the bearskin, the lancer's chapska, the bowler, the beaver and the cotton nightcap, one of those specimens, in short, whose mute ugliness has the expressive depths of an idiot's face. It was egg-shaped and stiffened with bulging ribs, it began with three circles of sausages; then there were alternating diamonds of velveteen and rabbit fur, separated by a red strip; after that came a sort of sack which terminated in a polygon stiffened with cardboard, covered by some complicated braidwork, from which there hung, at the end of a long, too-thin cord, a small knot of gold threads by way of a tassel. It was new; the peak was gleaming . . .

They had gone to Yvetot to find a pastrycook for the tarts and sweetmeats. Since he was new in the region, he had been especially careful in his work, and for the dessert he himself carried in an elaborate creation which elicited oohs and ahs. The base, to begin with, was a square of blue pasteboard representing a temple and with porticoes, and rows of columns, and stucco statues all around it in niches spangled with stars of gold paper; then as the second storey stood the *donjon*, a massive tower of sponge cake, surrounded by minor fortifications of angelica, almonds, raisins, and orange segments; and finally, on the top layer, which was a green meadow where there were rocks and lakes of jam and nutshell boats, there could be seen a small cupid, perched on a swing of chocolate, supported by two posts with two real rosebuds on top serving as the knobs.

Note, in the initial demarcative position in these two descriptions, the stereotyped justificatory thematics of the *new* (a new pupil; a new pastry-cook). The appeal to novelty is quite often justification both for having the newcomer look at, speak of, etc., the world (thematics of the intruder, the Huron, the *ingénu*, the provincial, etc.), and for having the natives look at, speak of, act on, etc., the intruder.

The realist attitude is based on a linguistic illusion, the belief in the possibility of a language which is monopolized exclusively by its referential

function, a language in which signs would be the adequate analogues of
things, a kind of codebook reproducing faithfully the discontinuity of reality.
But of course this project of realistic description – to reproduce with signs a
non-semiological reality – is only justifiable in a few quite marginal areas;
language, actualized as a succession of written, or spoken, signs, can 'imitate'
nothing but language, sounds, or those aspects of reality which are reducible
to a symbol. At best, a realist text would be composed of (a) speech that is
tape-recorded and transcribed (but such transcription already brings in
supplementary information: it is different because it is deferred, hermetic and
distorted); (b) effects due to various kinds of *motivating* factors (articulatory,[46]
auditory (onomatopoeia), visual (calligrams or diagrams)). It is easy to show
the marginal and precarious nature of such procedures, to show that
language is not monopolized by a single function but is a *hierarchy* of
functions, that it is not merely vocabulary, but also syntax, that it is not just
denotation, but also rhetoric. Zola does not, and most 'realist' writers do not,
explore these possibilities systematically (not until Ponge do we get this);
instead they develop a language which is metaphorical rather than 'motivated' in the above sense, a language which parades as a stylistic achieve-
ment, as artistic, rather than disappearing behind the information it is
conveying.[47]

Let us conclude: we defined a description above as a unit which triggered a
proliferation of themes introduced to enhance plausibility (the look, the
transparent air, the spoken explanation, the open window, etc.), which
constitute what we called an *empty* or *pseudo-* thematics. We then saw that the
description is the point where the narrative comes to a temporary halt, while
continuing to organize itself (with foretokens of what will happen, redundancy of content, metonymic duplication of the psychology or fate of the
characters): it can thus be seen that the fundamental characteristic of realist
discourse is to deny, to make impossible, the narrative, any narrative. This is
because the more it becomes saturated with descriptions, the more it is
concomitantly forced to multiply its empty thematics and its redundancies,
and the more it becomes organized and repetitious, thus becoming increasingly a closed system: instead of being referential, it becomes purely
anaphoric; instead of evoking the real ('things' and 'events') it constantly
evokes itself. The major problem of the realist author is thus to turn this *empty*
thematics into a *full* one, to bring it about that this tangential proliferation of
looks, of transparent media, etc., actually has a *role* to play in the story, does
not remain simple filler material, and to bring it about that the anaphoric
redundancy of content becomes a dialectic of content. This is not always
easy.

Notes

1. Cf. the analysis of this text given by J. C. Coquet in *L'Homme* 9(1) (1969).
2. For the rhetoricians, description was, with *étymologie*, a fundamental process of *amplification* (see E. Faral, *Les Arts Poétiques du XIIème siècle et du XIIIème siècle* (Paris, Champion, 1972), pp. 75ff.). Its principal object was either praise or blame. The first principles of a reflection on description can be found in Ricardou, *Problèmes du nouveau roman* (Paris, Seuil, 1967), pp. 91ff.; G. Genette, 'Frontières du récit', *Communications* 11 (1968); R. Barthes, '*L'effet de réel*', *Communications* 11 (1968) [translated in this volume]; and M. Riffaterre, 'Le poème comme représentation', *Poétique* 4 (1970). See also F. Rastier, 'Situation du récit dans une typologie des discours', *L'Homme* (Jan.–March 1971). See also Ph. Hamon, *Introduction à l'analyse du descriptif* (Paris, Hachette, 1980).
3. The references in roman numerals refer to the five-volume edition in *Bibliothèque de la Pléiade* (Paris, Gallimard). Those with C.L.P. followed by a roman numeral refer to the edition in fifteen volumes of the complete works of Zola, published by the Cercle du Livre Précieux.
4. Zola wants above all to *describe*, i.e. to transmit information about a society – its décors, places, landscapes, objects. 'Ah! To see and paint everything' is the cry of the painter Claude in *L'Oeuvre* (IV, 46). 'With me the drama is quite secondary', Zola writes in his preparatory dossier for *Nana* (II, 1666, cited by H. Mitterand). Other statements: 'The goal to be attained is no longer to tell a story, to string ideas or deeds one after another, but rather to render each object which is presented to the reader in its line, its colour, its odour, the integrated totality of its existence' (*Romanciers Naturalistes*, C.L.P. XI, 160); 'naturalist novelists . . . want to get away from the story . . . refuse this banality of narrative for narrative's sake' (C.L.P. XI, 170). These comments can be placed alongside Flaubert's remark: 'The narrative is a thing which I find quite tiresome' (in a letter dated 2 May 1872). For the 'scientific' value which Zola accorded to description (and which we will not study here) see for example his article 'On description' reprinted in *Le Roman expérimental* (C.L.P. X, 1299ff.). Zola's initial postulate was, therefore, *exhaustivity*: to depict the parts of the theatre hidden from sight after painting the stage and the front (*Nana*), to depict Paris after Plassans, the slums of *L'Assommoir* after the fine quarters of *Pot-Bouille*, and the dream of depicting the 'vast ark' haunts many of Zola's characters (Lazare, Sandoz, etc.).
5. With Zola (and quite a few novelists) the description often exists before the narrative. The text recycles and incorporates a preceding text, that of the novelist's *file*, where he has already assembled the materials of his novel. The problem of the insertion of a description is thus often connected with this writing and composing habit, a problem analogous to that of the insertion of a *quotation*, or an *anterior discourse*, already organized – a problem of joinery, how to erase or remove as much as possible the traces of the joints. The description is thus the most favourable location for (a) an instance of intertextuality; (b) the introduction of *knowledge*, and of the texts of the period documenting the received, official knowledge.
6. Zola says this quite straightforwardly in the notes and first drafts for his novels: certain characters serve only to 'give' the description of some object, landscape or setting. Certain scenes serve only to 'place' the description of some milieu. Certain décors will be provided 'with the help' of some character or other.
7. On this theme of transparency, cf. our 'Zola romancier de la transparence' in

Europe (May 1968). Some examples: ' A suddenly opened door gave him a glimpse of the generator furnaces in bright light . . .' (*Germinal*, III, 1136); 'The door, wide open, revealed seven furnaces with double hearths. Amidst the white vapour . . .' (*Germinal*, III, 1154); '[she] lit the candle . . . now the candle lighted the room, which was square, with two windows, and filled by three beds. There were a cupboard, a table . . .' (*Germinal*, III, 1143). We might note in passing that a favoured mark of the description is the use of numerals – that is, of a quite special semiotic system.

8. The elevation thus has, with Zola (cf. the mine tip in *Germinal*, Helen's window in *Une Page d'amour*, Montmartre in *Paris*, etc.), a function which is the opposite of that which it has with Stendhal, for example, where it is a (euphoric) theme rather than a (technical) alibi introduced to justify *a posteriori* a ramifying description. An interesting problem arises here. Rousset for Flaubert, and Ricardou for Ollier, have noted the importance of *windows, elevated viewpoints*, etc. It seems necessary to go through *all* the 'realist' writers to see if they all use this 'empty' thematics. If this were the case, we could speak of *constraints* on realist discourse, and of the specific marks of this type of discourse (windows, transparent things, looking, the raised place, etc.). Cf. certain titles of works belonging to the 'Nouveau Roman': *La Jalousie* (the lattice/blind), *L'Observatoire de Cannes*, *Le Voyeur*, etc., and the obsessive reference to windows in the metalanguage of western 'realistic' discourse in general, from the 'window' of Alberti to Zola's theory of the novel as screen and the novel as window. See A. Robbe-Grillet, 'Temps et description', in *Pour un nouveau roman* (Paris, Gallimard), in the collection 'Idées' (1964). Concerning the setting-up of a characteristic topos for the naturalist text, constituted so as best to repartition the information needed to make the text readable (the topos consists of (a) a private closed place containing a mirror; (b) an intermediate place consisting of a window; (c) an open public place, containing other windows), see our 'Note sur un dispositif naturaliste', in *Actes du Colloque sur le naturalisme, Cerisy, juillet 1976* (Paris, UGE, Collection '10–18', 1978).

9. The expression 'X s'oublia à regarder . . .' occurs constantly in Zola's works: 'There he forgot himself for an instant . . . a need to see came over him' (III, 808–9). Claude Lantier 'forgot himself before an effect of the light' (I, 618). See, for example, II, 1479; III, 717; II, 176; II, 1264; IV, 367, etc. It indicates the *oubli* by the author at these moments of the dynamic capacities of his characters (as supports of the narrative, as participants in a dialectic of actors) which he is using here merely as convenient introductory signs for descriptions.

10. Compare the numerous scenes in Zola where a character or couple methodically 'explore' an environment or décor which is new to them (Serge and Albine in the Paradou, Pascal and Clotilde in the environs of la Souleïade, Florent in les Halles, etc.). We might call this the 'Robinson Crusoe ploy' of the realist novelist, with the proliferation of the description being justified by the curiosity of a character introduced into an environment which he does not know. This kind of 'ambulatory description' – the term is used by R. Ricatte à propos of the Goncourts – this know-how in the pedagogue's art of getting the reader to know, should no doubt be viewed in the broader context of a certain kind of pedagogical discourse which uses a character who moves through various environments and acts as the support for a series of descriptions. Recall that the motto of Verne's Nautilus was 'Mobilis in Mobile', and indeed this teaching device has a long history, extending from the *Voyage du jeune Anacharsis* of Barthélémy, at the end of the eighteenth century, to the *Tour de France par Camille et Paul* (1977), and including the *Tour du monde en*

quatrevingt jours by Verne, and the *Tour de la France par deux enfants* by G. Bruno (1877).

11. The verisimilitude of 'spoken' descriptions can, of course, vary from one literary genre to another. Cf. Valéry (*Tel Quel*, p. 565 in the Pléiade edition): 'Description is lacking in the classical drama – is it *natural* for a character to mouth the picturesque?'

12. The frequency of the verb 'explain' and its synonyms is extraordinarily high in Zola. Here are a few examples: 'He raised his voice to give some explanations; he turned to the machines . . .' (*Assommoir*, II, 536); 'Pierre now forgot himself as he painted a charming portrait of bygone Lourdes' (C.L.P. VII, 91); 'He was explaining Plassans to Father Faujas' (*Conquête de Plassans*, I, 953); 'he explained to him . . . he was not short on details' (*Ventre de Paris* I, 794); 'Albine amused herself at naming the objects that he touched', for Serge wanted 'to see everything, to have everything explained' (*La Faute de l'Abbé Mouret* I, 1331, 1334); in the presence of Pauline, Lazare 'named the species with a joyous pedantry' (*Joie de Vivre*, III, 863); 'Gilquin was explaining to him . . . explained' (*Son Excellence Eugène Rougon*, II, 90, 96); 'The zinc worker explained to him . . . pointing to the different pieces' (*Assommoir*, II, 411); 'Speaking rapidly, he explained to him about the slaughtering, the five enormous stone slabs . . .' (*Ventre de Paris*, I, 794).

13. 'Miette, silent, looked and listened' (I, 29); 'Serge, voiceless, looked on' (I, 1327). Any indication of the momentary muteness of a character can often be also the herald of a visual description, speech deferring to sight. But a motif belonging to this demarcative thematics may be polyfunctional: the mention of muteness can serve either as an *introductory* or as a *concluding* sign for a description (a silence after a loquacious 'explanation' of the object of description).

14. Semi-direct style is a well-known stylistic procedure which allows the author to *divert* to his own ends the thoughts and words of his characters, to replace direct discourse (dialogue) by the characters with his own proliferating monologue (with generalization of the imperfect tense, elimination of the introductory typographic signs, etc.). It would be interesting to explain why Zola's characters speak directly so little, even though this would seem to be an essential requirement of 'realism'. When they speak, it is always in monosyllables, in exclamations, in clichés, in stereotypes (the priest's Latin, the bourgeois' clichés, technical jargon, ready-made formulas, etc.). Semi-direct style is thus essentially a *demarcative* sign which quite often reinforces a boundary (between the story and the discourse, between the utterance and the act of utterance) and introduces a description.

15. Concerning the character-type, quite frequent in Zola's universe, of the priest–decorator, see our article in *Cahiers Naturalistes* 42.

16. The disabled, the mute, the blind, define a *hierarchy* in Zola's work: there are no blind people, few mutes, but many invalids. Simply numbering these types of characters will thus place the theme of *looking* at the top of the hierarchy. The disabled and the mute can *look* (and thus more easily be the support of descriptions), but not the blind man: furthermore, all the introductory construction types use at some point the reference to a look.

17. How is a department store to be described, with all its employees and the objects it contains? Nothing could be easier: all that is needed is to imagine a scene where inventory is being taken (*Au Bonheur des dames*). Curiously, French civil and commercial law, with respect to industrial counterfeiting, prescribes a 'seizure-description': a consulting engineer, a bailiff, and a police official conduct a search on the premises of the alleged infringer and establish a description of the object or

machine in dispute. The subdivisions of the description are introduced by the typical formulas: 'I see that . . .', or 'The consulting engineer X informs me that . . .', where we encounter the same demarcative thematics (looking, the character as warrant, speech) as earlier. In the case both of verisimilitude and of civil law what is involved is the need to *authenticate*.

18. This logic can function within a single thematics: thus the character who serves as the looker can see and be seen, see without being seen, be blind and be seen, look and 'be blind' (in the figurative sense), etc.

19. Here we meet again the notion of *constraints*, which is fundamental, although it would profit from redefinition, in stylistics and in any theory of literature. However, common sense tells us that there is nothing less bound, nothing that is *a priori* less constrained than realist discourse; that description seems incapable of being subjected to regulation. Like the referent which it has as theme, like the information which it is its goal to communicate, realist discourse appears at first glance to be amorphous, unbounded, unstructurable, unstructured; no theme or 'figure' would seem to be obligatorily present, no schema or mark would seem to be characteristic of it. This is the source of Valéry's critical remarks. Nevertheless, it would appear to be the case that it is not free of a certain number of *a priori* constraints (on the place, organization, thematic content, demarcative signs, etc., of descriptions), of what we might call, following certain linguists, 'grammatical servitudes', or 'selectional restrictions'. Cf., on the level of realist discourse in general, our article 'Un discours contraint' in *Poétique* 16 (1973).

20. Syntagmatically, such scenes will tend to be placed at the beginning of the novels (*Germinal, Conquête de Plassans* etc.) so as to furnish the reader right off with the necessary information concerning the settings and background against which the action takes place. Their *place* is thus also often predetermined.

21. This pseudo-thematics, due to the scruples of an author attached to the dogmas of objectivity and credibility, thus constitutes what we might call the class of 'shifters' of realist discourse; these are the signs, internal to the *utterance* ('énoncé') (to the message considered as a coherent autonomous entity), which point to an *act of utterance* ('énonciation'), to a knowledge (that in the files of the author).

22. Cf. for example the discontinuous description (every time there is a lightning flash) of the banks of the Seine in the early pages of *L'Oeuvre*: 'a bright flash illuminated . . . one could see the sad-looking time-worn façades, in very sharp detail, a stone balcony . . . a blinding flash . . . everything disappeared . . . another flash . . . the sky darkened' (IV, 11–13). The description ends when the storm is over; or rather the opposite: the storm (and the lightning flashes which allow the character to *see* the scene) is over when Zola has finished his description. With Jules Verne, in *Vingt Mille Lieues sous les mers*, we find in succession descriptions of the 'cultural' interior of the Nautilus (the luxurious quarters of Nemo, the glass cases where the different kinds of shells are arranged and labelled, the machines, the library, the museum), and of the 'natural' exterior (the fish, the plants, the undersea landscapes), with the crystal porthole, now open, now closed, and the light from the lamps inside, or from the spotlights outside, now on, now off, serving to justify the passage from one description to the other.

23. The preterition can be 'true' (in that it introduces no listing, no description), as in this declaration of Balzac's introducing a stagecoach in *Un Début dans la vie*: 'This coupé was enclosed in a system of glass windows that was unwieldy and bizarre, whose description would take up too much space for us to speak of it here'; or else it can serve to introduce a long descriptive passage: 'What a spectacle! What pen

could describe it'; 'What an indescribable spectacle'; 'I could observe neither miralets, triggerfish, nor tetrodons . . .' etc., in *Vingt Mille Lieues sous les mers*.

24. Encyclopedia writers, and the promoters and architects of modern design, are quite familiar with this factorization of objects – for instance of a fan – according to its specific requirements both *functional* (it circulates air, should be silent, etc.) and *qualificative* (it should be stable, attractive, compact, etc.). A cheese will be described in terms of its shape, size, weight, appearance, differences from related varieties, etc., and of its uses: when to eat it, with what wines, foods, etc.; see Androuet, *Guide du fromage* (Stock, 1971). Cf. also the article by P. Boudon, 'Sur un statut de l'objet', in *Communications* 13 (1969). In similar fashion, in 'literature', a rose will be large, light, damasked, etc., or it will fade, droop, wither, tremble, await the beloved's hand, etc.

25. This procedure can even generate a narrative, a quest for knowledge, a quest for the names of things. Cf. J. Perret's *Le Machin* in his collection of stories *Le Machin* (Paris, Gallimard, 1955).

26. I, 134off. Here is a fragment: 'Around them, the roses were in bloom. It was a wild profusion, amorous, full of red laughter, pink laughter, white laughter. The living flowers opened up like naked bodies, like bodices disclosing their treasures. There were yellow roses, their blooms recalling the golden skin of barbarous maidens, straw-coloured roses, lemon-coloured roses . . ., the white rose, barely dyed with a hint of lacquer, snow of a virgin's foot as she tests the water of a spring; the pale rose, more secret than the warm white of a half-glimpsed knee, than the reflection of a young arm lighting a wide sleeve; the pure rose, blood under satin, naked shoulders, naked hips; all the nakedness of woman caressed by light . . ., *lie-de-vin*, almost black roses pierced this bride's pureness with a wound of passion . . .'. It will be noted that the French here simultaneously treats roses as flowers and roses as tints of the colour rose. It is known that Zola, while preparing *La Faute de l'Abbé Mouret*, had various horticultural catalogues and manuals at his side.

27. For Propp (*Morphologie du Conte* (Paris, Seuil), p. 107) the study of the habitat of the characters in a story does not strictly speaking belong to morphology, because it concerns the study of the variables of narration, as do the 'attributes' of the characters.

28. 'They saw the strange world of plants which surrounded them' (I, 486).

29. The sole function of a series of incomprehensible technical words may be to signify technicalness, or exoticism, and the appropriateness or precision of each of the terms may matter little. This is particularly clear in the case of descriptions in exotic or science fiction novels. This will, nevertheless, have an important consequence, in that it will force the author to create, in order to justify such descriptions, characters who are scientists, pedants, experts, technicians, etc., in the speech, or looks, of whom this profusion of technical terms will appear authentic. Description is a competition between competences, the lexical competence of the narrator and the lexical competence of the reader.

30. Concerning the matter of availability and frequency, see for example Gougenheim, Rivenc, Michéa and Sauvageot, *L'Élaboration du français fondamental* (Paris, Didier, 1956), and P. Rivenc: 'Lexique et langue parlée', in *Le Français dans le monde* (June 1968).

31. The readability of a description is often enhanced in that V follows a stereotypical order: from top to bottom (coat of arms), from near to far (landscape), from the physical to the moral (portrait), etc., or in that the description forms a *topos* composed of fixed motifs; thus there is the topos of the *locus amoenus* (blue sky,

flowing water, birds, walled garden, flowers, a shaded cottage, etc.: cf. Curtius, *La Littérature européenne et le moyen-age latin* (Paris, P.U.F., 1956), pp. 240ff.) which so often appears as the first scene of films or comic strip narratives. Or consider the different *topoi* formed by certain culturally valued moments or dates (sunset, dawn, noon, midnight, Christmas, 14 July, etc.) which have engendered so many descriptions. All this explains why the reader generally skips descriptions.

32. A good example of this kind of description is provided by the well-known text of Breton, *L'Union libre*, which is wholly based on the recurrence of the schema IT + (highly predictable) V + (not very predictable) PE, for example: 'My woman with hair of wood-fire . . . with hourglass waist . . . with rosette mouth . . . my woman with champagne shoulders' etc. This text is comparable to a homologous one by Rabelais, the description of Quaresmeprenant (*Quart Livre*, xxx and xxxi): 'The toes were a sort of organized spinet, the nails a sort of gimlet, the feet a sort of cittern. The heels a sort of bludgeon . . . the buttocks a sort of harrow . . . the skull, a sort of gamebag . . .'. Note the 'parodic' order of V, going from bottom to top, and the homogeneity of PE (tools and artefacts) which contrasts with the heterogeneity of the PE in Breton's text.

33. On the use of this vocabulary circuit of the five senses, or the four elements, to structure a description, cf. Curtius, p. 242. Note above, in the excerpt from *La Petite Roque*, the use of a standard topological frame, a true *topos* in all the senses of the word, which spreads out and organizes the description of the landscape, and programmes its development: the reader knows that after 'before him', 'further off', 'on the left', he can expect to find 'on the right'.

34. See Androuet, *Guide du fromage*, p. 278. Zola composed a celebrated description of cheeses in *Le Ventre de Paris* (i, 833) where the different varieties are described in particular with the help of a series of 'musical' predicates (the muffled booming of cantal . . . like a broad bass voice . . .). The difference between Androuet and Zola is that the latter uses a jumbled sensory code (synesthesia), favours an unexpected sense – the sense of hearing, avoids numbers (Androuet, speaking of Chevret: '45 per cent fat . . . 9 cm square, 2 cm high; or 8 cm high, 3 cm high, on average. Average weight: 150 gm . . .'), and avoids 'functional' description (Androuet, for Chevret: 'end of meal, snack'). Scientists, and advertising writers, who are faced with the task of describing unknown objects, are directly concerned with the techniques of description and its three major problems: (a) that of creating and using a stable and fixed repertory (V) of terms felt to be in a metonymic relation with IT; (b) that of imposing the automatic appearance of this lexicon V after IT; (c) that of creating and using a fixed repertory of descriptive and metaphorical predicates, either comparative (partial inclusion) or differential (non-inclusion), which is entirely predictable after V. This is the price of readability (of communication).

35. The unreadability of a 'technical' lexicon may be partially compensated for by a morphological 'motivation', as in the series of French terms derived from 'goudron' (tar): 'goudronner', 'goudronneuse', 'goudronnage', etc. See J. Dubois, 'Les problèmes du vocabulaire technique', *Cahiers de Lexicologie* 9 (1966).

36. Let us not forget that description can exist by itself (as with the poems of Ponge, advertising, the encyclopedia article), although this was energetically condemned by most classical rhetoricians.

37. 'Albine was a great rose' (i, 1341). Metaphor, besides its role in increasing or diminishing the readability of a technical vocabulary, is the 'imposed' feature aesthetically connoting description. More than just a 'reality effect' ('effet de

réel'), description is the point of fixation of an 'effet de poésie', the reader recognizing the metaphor as such before he grasps its content.

38. A predicate of PE can be in a metonymic relation (the same area of reality: here, garden plants) with a sub-theme of IT, and thus reinforce the semantic cohesion of the description: like certain roses 'similar to cabbages' (1, 1341). For Jakobson (*Essais*, (Paris, Éditions de Minuit), p. 61), 'the development of a discourse can proceed along two different semantic lines: a theme (topic) leads to another whether by similarity or by contiguity. No doubt it is best to speak of a metaphoric process in the first case and of a metonymic process in the second.' The internal functioning of description would certainly profit from being compared to that of 'spun-out metaphor' (see on this point the article of M. Riffaterre, in *Langue française* 3 (Sept. 1969)). A description is never a realistic copy, some utopian reproduction of a reality, but rather an *a posteriori* rationalization which is always in search of a metaphoric vocabulary. Witness this passage, in which (in addition to the proliferation of the 'empty' thematics, the justificatory pretext: looking 'without seeing', 'crystal', 'clarity', etc.) the word 'corbeil' (flowerbed; dress-circle) has triggered a cascade of theatrical metaphors: 'Renée had rested her head . . . and was looking lazily . . . without seeing. On the right . . ., on the left, below the narrow lawn which sloped down, interrupted by flowerbeds and clumps of bushes, the lake slept, with the clarity of crystal, without a fleck of foam, as if it had been sliced cleanly around its edge by the gardeners' spades; and on the other side of this bright mirror the two islands . . . raised up against the pale sky the theatrical lines of their pines, of their trees with evergreen leaves whose dark verdure was reflected in the water, like the fringes of curtains that had been hung along the horizon . . . a décor which seemed to have just been painted . . .' (1, 322). Indirectly, it is the destiny of Renée which is indicated to be an artifice.

39. Renée is 'a burning daughter of the hothouse', 'she seemed the white sister of this dark god' (the sphinx).

40. 'He was in love, really in love, with his machine' (IV, 1128).

41. Corresponding to the artificial conjunction, *contra naturam* (the sign of a 'deranged' society) of the exotic plants in the hothouse, is the incestuous conjunction of the two lovers. Artifice and incest are thus two redundant modes, equally penalized and discredited, of the conjunction of objects. (It should not be forgotten that there is in the greenhouse a marble *sphinx*.) Description is certainly the location at which the narrative connotes itself euphorically or dysphorically; a correlation of narrative functions (of the type: departure/return) is in fact, of itself, neither euphoric nor dysphoric, for the reader. For these reasons, description is certainly the fundamental *tonality operator* in the narrative text.

42. We borrow this term from Barthes (from 'Le discours de l'histoire', *Information Sur les Sciences Sociales* VI (4 August, 1967, Mouton)). It organizes the utterance by referring anaphorically either to something which has already been said, or else to a later fragment of the text. A description is thus the equivalent of 'we have already seen that . . .' or 'we shall soon see that . . .'. Jakobson had already mentioned this role of semantic reduplication which is played by description: 'The realist writer carries out metonymic digressions from the plot to the atmosphere and from the characters to the spatio-temporal framework. He is fond of synecdochic details' (*Essais*, p. 63). Similarly we find in Wellek and Warren (*La Théorie littéraire* (Paris, Seuil, 1971)), p. 309; *Theory of Literature* (Harvard, Harcourt Brace Jovanovich, 1900): 'The décor is the setting; and any setting, especially a domestic interior, can be considered as a metonymic or metaphoric experience of

an individual.' In one type of realist–veridical narrative, the miser will be named Gobseck ('gober' = swallow, 'sec' = dry), will have dirty clothes, will live in modest circumstances, etc. In a narrative of the *deceptive* type, the description will introduce red herrings and will reject this anaphoric and redundant aspect of content (for example, a miser will be called M. Donnant (Mr Giver), will live in a sumptuous town house, wear fine clothes, be of agreeable appearance, etc., with cultural stereotypes playing an important role here).

43. We leave aside other functions: (a) the demarcative, emphasizing the divisions within the narrative; for example the descriptions of Paris in *Une Page d'amour*, or the description of the Bois de Boulogne at the beginning and the end of *La Curée*; (b) the dilatory, delaying what follows, putting off an expected dénouement; (c) the decorative, the 'effet de réel', the poetic effect, etc., which can be added by any description in any narrative.

44. Of course all of this should be viewed in the context of the 'philosophical and scientific' justifications which Zola puts forth (the influence of the environment on the individual, the contamination of man by his setting). The problem is to determine whether it is his writing technique (the author as artist) and his postulates (to describe) which have imposed this philosophy on the author, or vice versa.

45. These stylistic tics are a part of the style of the period ('artistic writing') but they are perhaps an inevitable accoutrement of description as such, and in general. They often help to turn a setting, a landscape, into a collective participant, strongly anthropomorphized (like the garden in *La Faute de l'Abbé Mouret*, les Halles in *Le Ventre de Paris*, etc.), whose semantic function as *actant* (positive Subject or negative Subject, Proponent or Opponent, positive Emitter or negative Receiver, etc.) will have to be defined by analysis.

46. These are brought out by, for example, P. Guiraud in his *Structures étymologiques du lexique français* (Paris, Larousse, 1967).

47. Valéry saw quite clearly that the realist attitude led to a certain 'gymnastics' which, as much as any other, vaunts itself as 'literature': 'the desire for "realism" leads one to seek ever more powerful means of *rendering*; rendering leads to technique. Technique leads to classification, to order. Order leads to the systematic . . . And thus, starting from the aim of exactly reproducing some fact, one arrives at a sort of gymnastics which incorporates the false and the true' (in *Tel Quel*, Pléiade edn, p. 584). Description is without a doubt one of the most characteristic and appropriate signs of literature. Cf. Ricardou, *Problèmes du Nouveau Roman*, p. 105: 'Description constructs a fictitious world.' See also R. Barthes, *S/Z* (Paris, Seuil, 1970), p. 61.

Part IV

9. On the circularity of song

(with reference to the twelfth- and thirteenth-century *trouvères*)

PAUL ZUMTHOR

We will leave aside problems relative to the origin, immediate or distant, of what Roger Dragonetti once called the 'grand chant courtois'. We will consider this form here, not in terms of its development, but rather from a synchronic and global point of view, taking the period of its early maturity, when it evidenced the greatest homogeneity: the last quarter of the twelfth and the first half of the thirteenth centuries.

The poets who were designated by the term 'finders' (in the nominative singular, *trouvère*) in the language of that period gave us the earliest poetry, in the strict sense of the word, which appears in the French language: I understand by this a mode of saying entirely and exclusively referred to an 'I' who, although his existence is often only grammatical, still establishes the framework and the conditions of the discourse independently of any narrative context.

This art reaches fruition in the *chanson*, a complex form which, essentially, defines it: the form obeys subtle rules, inherited from the troubadours of Aquitaine, but which seem purified by an imagination that is even more controlled or more abstract – a more ascetic expressive intention. Furthermore, the most typical *chanson* is that which might, at first glance, be called a *chanson d'amour*: that, let us say, which is marked by various formal constants, such as the use of the word 'amour' itself. I will not pursue this topic now; but the purpose of this article is to examine the matter more closely.

The *chansons d'amour* (which form by far the largest part of this poetic corpus) exhibit, from one example to the next, innumerable surface combinations, but these derive from a deep structure which is almost invariant. Various methods are available for use, and have been used, in an attempt to define this structure: by the very fact that it is a 'deep' structure, it is not available to direct observation, and can only be described inductively, and not without the risk of ambiguity.

The most important feature, but also the hardest to deal with, is the musical aspect of this 'song'. Words and melody are the product of a single impulse, they generate each other in a relationship which is so intimate that any analysis has to treat both simultaneously.[1] Unfortunately, no more than a tenth of the texts have come down to us along with their melodies, and the deciphering of the latter raises problems which are still more arduous than the establishing of the former. We thus have no choice, except in a few untypical cases, but to focus our observations – like an archaeologist studying potsherds – on the linguistic half of the *chanson*, in the hope of restoring the original harmonious design from the few surviving fragments.

It would be totally impossible to construct, in a few pages, a model,[2] properly so called, that could do rigorous justice to the reality of the semantic micro-universe manifested in the *chanson*. We can at best attempt to determine a perspective, a standpoint from which such a model might be constituted – bearing in mind that no model can provide an exhaustive interpretation of a poetic text, that the text always, in one way or another, goes beyond the methodological framework with which we apprehend it. The construction of a model is never more than an instant in a dialectic process.[3]

To help the exposition (even though this study is meant to remain theoretical, and not to be concerned with any particular text), I believe it will be useful to cite a few lines which can serve as a sort of emblem for what follows. They are taken from the excellent edition of the songs of the Châtelain de Couci (c. 1200) by Alain Lerond.[4]

Here is the beginning of the first stanza:

> Bele dame me prie de chanter,
> Si est bien droiz que je face chançon;
> Je ne m'en sai ne ne puis destourner,
> Car n'ai pouvoir de moi se par li non

(Literally: Belle Dame asks me to sing. It is thus right that I make (a) song: I have no way of escaping, for I have no power over myself except through her/it.)

The last line contains a noteworthy ambiguity, in that 'li' (her) can be anaphoric as well to 'dame' as to 'chançon'.

The beginning of the second stanza:

> Preuz et sage, je ne vous os conter
> La grant dolor que j'ai, s'en chantant non;
> Et sachiez bien ja n'en orrez parler.[5]

(Literally: discreet and prudent, I dare not tell you, except by singing, the great pain I have, and you can be certain that you will never hear me speak of it.)

'Parler' here is clearly opposed to 'chanter', which is the key term in these first two stanzas. That of the third stanza is 'fine amor' (perfect love); of the fourth, 'joie'; of the fifth, 'cuer' (heart). We thus observe, within a homogeneous semantic field, a kind of imperceptible shift along a curve that is almost closed: from the song to the heart.

This thematic structure is common. Another song of the same poet[6] is built on a series of leitmotivs (alternatively in nominal and verbal form, except for the conclusion, which is wholly nominal): stanza i: 'chant', 'chanter'; ii: 'coeur', 'aimer', 'voir' (heart, love, see); iii: 'coeur', 'aimer', 'désir'; iv: 'aimer', 'voir', 'coeur'; v: 'chanson', 'amour'. It would be as easy as it would be pointless to give many more examples. We find here a type of discourse which is polarized by the use that is made of the verb 'chanter' and the words which are formally or semantically related, to such an extent that the text in its entirety looks like an expansion, and a strictly limited one, of these words.

This impression has to be verified and refined. Some concrete examples are indispensable. For instance, 'chanter', at the first reading of the texts, appears as a dynamic term whose extremely dense semic nucleus is surrounded by a vast space of possibility in which shifting connotations are continually at work, some of them difficult for us to perceive. The contexts where, in a hundred or so of the songs, the relevant words occur, are grouped below, as briefly and schematically as possible.[7]

The distribution of the three formally related words 'chanter', 'chanson', and 'chant', from the beginning to the end of a poem, show a 'topographical' tendency that is rather clear: out of 87 occurrences of 'chanter', 40 are found in the first stanza; out of 15 of 'chant', 10 occur in the first stanza; out of 42 of 'chanson', 12 are found in the first stanza of a poem and 22 in the final *envoi*.

It is noteworthy (in conformity, it might appear, with the theory of the rhetoricians, who at that time particularly stressed the composition and the qualities of the *exordium*) that the initial stanza of the *chanson* is generally the most structured, with a pattern which allows a restricted number of variants. As for the *envoi*, in general it does nothing more than develop a clichéd formula. We can therefore presume that the locations of the words 'chant' (designating the action of singing) and 'chanson' (its result), and to a lesser extent the place of the verb 'chanter' itself, convey a particular meaning. An examination of the micro-contexts reinforces this assumption. In the first stanza, 'chanter' belongs either to narrative discourse or to allocutive discourse.[8]

In narrative discourse the verb is predicated of a subject mentioned by name and belonging (with a few exceptions) to the class of birds: 'le rossignol chante'[9] (the nightingale sings), 'j'entends les oiseaux chanter' (I hear the birds sing), are typical. Most often, 'chanter' reappears later in the stanza, but with the 'allocutive' function – that is, like a vocative or imperative, the verb opens the discourse to the expectation of a response (which will be the song itself); it creates the possibility of contact, between the singer and his audience, but also, at a deeper level, between the sound that is heard and the meaning that will gradually be discovered. This allocutive 'chanter' has the form of an announcement, with or without a causal explanation: either simply 'je chante' or 'je chanterai'; or 'ma dame (l'amour, etc.) me fait chanter' or 'le désir me prend de chanter', with an indication of the reason: 'je chante pour me consoler'. There are very few other combinations.

Similarly, 'chant', in first stanzas, is always either 'le chant des oiseaux', or 'je veux (re)commencer mon chant' (note that 'vouloir (to want), is, for the *trouvères*, one of the terms which, in other contexts, expresses erotic desire). 'Chanson' hardly appears in an initial stanza, except in the expression 'chanson faire', where the absence of determiner before the noun could be interpreted as a shift towards a verb ('faire chanson' = 'chanter'); in the *envoi*, on the other hand, there are two solutions: either 'chanson finir', symmetrical to 'chanson faire', or else, and more frequently, in allusive discourse, the *'chanson'* is apostrophized, with an imperative following that indicates speech or even movement ('Chanson, dis à, va auprès de . . .': Song, say to, go to).[10]

The range of possible choices thus seems extremely limited to the modern reader, in spite of the role of variations which allow different combinations of these predetermined elements. But the word 'choice' is inappropriate here: it implies the voluntary renunciation of something, of a freedom which would otherwise be total. What is involved here, however, is an act from which any negative aspect is absent, one that has become habitual through tradition, but still deliberate, an act of placement, and as it were of positive definition, of fixation of a certain kind of discourse: the quite explicit setting up of an *isotopie*.

The fact that the verbal elements of this lexical group ('chanter', 'chanson faire', 'mon chant commencer') occur most often in the infinitive heightens the effect: the 'theme' which is introduced in this way, and for which the poem will be, on various levels, the development, is treated almost as a substantive, as if it constituted the very 'substance' of the song. When the infinitive is lacking, we always find a present (the timeless present of a poem free of any narrative burden), or, more rarely, the future (covering the duration of the act of singing, and in a way anticipating it).

In initial stanzas, 'chanter' is most often associated with two other elements, one of them a cliché which, with some exceptions, does not reappear in the text of the chanson (birds and verdure: the 'springtime motif'); the other constituting the first evocation of any of the motifs which relate to the lover's complaint, a motif which will be repeated and developed in a succeeding stanza. 'Chanter' is thereby doubly marked in the *exordium*: it is the one element which is both predictable and recurrent.

The second and succeeding stanzas of the chanson do not provide so rigorous a frame for 'chanter', 'chant', and 'chanson'. Nevertheless, analysis of their contexts allows us to determine the semic structure of these words in their various occurrences. We obtain in this way a curious prismatic image, in which the denotations are diluted in a conflux of connotations that are at once sharp, stable, few in number, and mutually supporting.

In a short summary, we can characterize the spectrum of 'chanter' as follows: (1) 'produce a welcome harmony of sound (evoking joy and love)'; (2) 'perform the song'; (3) 'manifest an exalted emotion'; (4) 'tell one's love'; (5) 'love' (transitively or absolutely). We observe a continuous semic shift from (1) to (5): from the material to the ideal, from an action of the body to the passions of the heart. Furthermore, globally, the data reveal a very strong predominance of nuances (4) and (5) in poetic discourse: in all, there are 62 occurrences out of 87! Nuance (4) was identified 52 times. This high frequency is not at all surprising: the seme 'say' relates 'chanter' to that metalanguage integrated in the poem itself which is so characteristic of love songs, which have a strong tendency to refer to themselves in the course of their development.[11] Nuance (5) is found in contexts where permutation is possible between *chanter* and *aimer*: this may be explicit in the text (e.g. 'Or chant, or l'aim' (Now I sing, now I love her), from Gautier d'Epinal, chanson IV);[12] or it may be suggested implicitly by the use of antonymy, as 'chanter/pleurer' in the first stanza of chanson VII by the Châtelain de Couci.[13] Between (4) and (5) there is, in any case, no sharp break, no more than between (3) and (4), or (2) and (3). The semantic dynamism of *chanter* tends toward an identification of song with love as the goal of singing: the discourse is based on this identification, and defined by it, in virtue of this goal.

The situation is analogous with 'chant' and 'chanson'. For 'chant' we have: (1) 'harmony produced by birds'; (2) 'the act of performing the song'; (3) 'the act of telling one's love'; (4) 'what one says in the song, the message (erotic connotation)'.

This final nuance appears in certain limiting cases, where the 'chant' is presented as a property of the *chanson*, relative to the 'Dame'; thus, from Richard de Sémilli:

> chanson, par amors trouvée,
> salue moi la vaillant,
> et si ton chant ne li grée . . .[14]

(Song which is sung by (i.e. through the power of) Love, greet for me the virtuous one, and if what-you-say-to-her (your message) does not suit her . . .)

The range of 'chanson' is much tighter – as if, in the lexical group in question, the substantive had less freedom than the verbal terms ('chanter', and the deverbal 'chant'); as if the singer's flexibility were the consequence rather of the spontaneity of an action (the action of the voice) than of the permanence of an object. 'Chanson' appears in fact only in three kinds of contexts: (1) in the figure of apostrophe (the allocutive function): 20 occurrences out of 42; (2) in groups of the type 'faire ('finir' etc.) chanson':

17 occurrences; (3) with a possessive determiner referring to the nameless subject, 'ma chanson', grammatically related to a verb expressing the notion of conveying information, of manifesting ('apprendre ma chanson', 'ma chanson est ouïe', etc.: make known my song, my song is heard): 5 occurrences.

On a semic analysis, we can categorize these contexts as follows: (1) the poem, conceived of as the result of the act of singing ('faire chanson'); especially as a self-determined act, which elevates the subjectivity involved in and by that act to the status of a living thing (apostrophe); (2) the poem, conceived of as emanating from a subject ('ma chanson'). The word possesses considerable homogeneity of meaning, as well as a certain obscurity which is explained by the structure of its semic nucleus, which evokes the pair 'chanter'–'chant', which in turn evokes 'chanson'.

There is, then, absence of any external referent. Even when, in the course of the poem, 'chanter'–'chant'–'chanson' occur in apparently quite explicit sentences that are close to 'naive' communicative language, they remain semantically tinted by their typical uses, and cannot be stripped of the ambiguous values which (as the poem unfolds in time) they have acquired or will acquire at their favoured, predictable locations: the *exordium* and the conclusion. This lexical trinity thus constitutes an absolute, which is 'self-diffusive' (in the sense of the Scholastic expression referring to the Good), that is, it creates its own meaning, which it radiates throughout the poem to the point where the poem, far from illuminating it (indicating its referent), is illuminated by it (refers to it, in some mysterious fashion).

The usual interpretations of this poetry have a different starting-point: the thematic group whose basic element, on the level of expression, is the lexical pair 'amour'–'aimer'.[15] Semic analysis of these terms (without going into much detail) gives the following overall result.

The content of *aimer* (total occurrences: 220) is essentially bisemic, for this verb designates either an action of the grammatical subject of the song (153 times) or of another subject (67 times). In the second case, the connotations can be varied; the emotional denotation is always obvious and is close to or identical with the 'naive' meanings (those occurring outside of the semantic universe of the *chanson*). The first case is different: we find rather a semantic spectrum analogous to that of 'chanter'.

We can distinguish: (1) contexts where an expression of the type 'aimer (la dame)' interacts, in textual proximity, with 'chanter' (used neutrally or transitively): 90 occurrences; (2) topic sentences where 'aimer' and 'chanter' seem interchangeable from one *chanson* to the next (predominant type: something commands me to love, I must love): 8 occurrences; (3) sentences where there is an explicit or implicit relation established between 'aimer' and 'chanter' (on the pattern: 'j'aime, je chante', or 'aimer ma chanson'): 10 occurrences; (4) absolute use of 'aimer', with no formal or semantic specification (45 occurrences), so that an action is designated independently of any particular circumstance, without an object.

From whatever angle this distribution is viewed, it seems obvious to me that the connotative (if not denotative) sets represented by 'chanter', on the one hand, and 'aimer', on the other, have a large area of overlap. One might well carry the metaphor further and state flatly that 'aimer' (1) (involving the grammatical subject of the song) is included in 'chanter'.

The analysis of 'amour' raises more delicate formal problems, because of the large number of its occurrences (340), and because the majority of these involve a rhetorical ambiguity, with the word (which normally lacked an article in Old French) being interpretable as a personification. Consequently 'amour' almost always fluctuates in context, in a sort of shadow-play, occurring, for the duration of a syntagm, now with one, now with the other of the two nouns which are most regularly personalized in the apostrophe, 'dame' and 'chanson'. The absence, in 235 occurrences, of any determiner, reinforces this ambiguity to the point of making 'amour' a nuclear term, concentrating an undifferentiated semantic energy which arises from the very sources of the 'chant'. A limited number of examples (about 15) are as clear in this respect as anyone could wish: they involve more or less clichéd formulas, such as 'bonne chanson' in alternation with 'bonne amour', and above all introductory or concluding formulas of the type 'commencer (or 'finir') amour'. I believe that this provides a key.

While 'aimer' (admitting this hypothesis) is included in 'chanter', the latter set of meanings, more extensive than the former, intersects with another one, that of 'trouver' (75 occurrences), in other contexts. I will not develop this point, but it is worth mentioning, if only because it justifies the name *trouvère*. Here again we can speak of a (continuous) semantic spectrum: (1) 'discover, ascertain (in the situation created by the 'chant')' (18 occurrences); (2) 'obtain through the act of singing' in such formulas as 'trouver merci' (23 occurrences); (3) 'exercise a transitive action whose object is the *dame*', in very ambiguous sentences where the semes 'say', 'obtain', or even 'see', overlap inextricably (e.g. the type: 'je ne trouve au monde plus belle') (22 occurrences).

These three semic constellations are distributed in strikingly equal fashion.[16] The result is that a line like 'chanson par amors trovee', cited above, is to be considered as (magnificently) tautological, with each of the terms implying the other two in a closed chain for which 'chanson' constitutes the lock. 'Chanson', a substantival form of 'chant', designates the area of unequivocal meaning where all the semantic fields set up in the course of the poem intersect; it indicates the heart of the poem, hidden under the powerful rhetorical musculature and the sleek melodic surface; the nucleus of energy responsible for the force of the voice and the efficacity of the message, that is, its organization and intentional ambiguity.[17]

These equivalences mark the entire discourse. They rule out any genuine transitivity. There are flashes of apparent transitivity, in series of sentences (where it is generally explicit and as it were camouflaged as informative communication), which constitute the stanza and, beyond, the poem itself. But these occurrences are finally captured, woven into the texture from which they had appeared to be escaping; they have no existence outside of the text itself. There is no prolongation, no 'beyond' for the song. The gates of paradise close, a paradise echoing with birds, brightened with verdure, but without water, without those shimmering, infinitely reflected aquatic images introduced by later tradition into the universe of poetry.[18] The world of the *chanson* is an austere one, where the voice is the servant of thought ('pensée' is another key term) which reflects itself. This *pensée* does indeed aspire towards a culmination, a completion, a kind of final rest after the extreme tension of the poet's song. This completion is named endlessly, almost always in negative, conditional, or optative sentences, or else in sentences projected by the verb into the future, rarely into the past. It is 'joie', a term whose indefinability is sufficiently demonstrated by the wealth of contradictory commentaries it has provoked – unless it is identified with a kind of vital exaltation, arising from the sources of being; but this does not help very much. The first *trouvères* took the form of the word from everyday speech, but they gave it the content (inherent in the system of the *chanson*) of the 'joi' of the troubadours, a word which has been thought to derive from Latin *jocus*, meaning 'play'. But that is of little importance. 'Chanter', which is 'aimer' (and vice versa), an action without an object, as it is carried out (that is, as it perpetuates its process for the length of a certain number of stanzas), creates its own substantification, the *chanson*, which is 'amour' (and vice versa). 'Joie' refers both to this action and to these substances: it is the action, the substance, as felt and reflected on by the subject, and consciously and dangerously experienced by him.

Whatever meaning is assumed, in the concrete textual occurrences, by 'chanter', one cannot neglect the seme 'say, utter' which it carries, and which it is doubtful that poetic usage completely eradicates – the same applies to the seme 'emotion' in 'aimer', etc.: these permanent values themselves participate in the poem and, by their interference, produce the equivocal delight of this 'joie'. From this point of view 'chanter' belongs to the category of presentational terms, so abundant with the *trouvères*, who use them for all kinds of distancing effects: 'voir', 'ouïr', 'dire', (see, hear, say) introducing, in the first person, a descriptive or gnomic sequence. 'Dire' is an approximate and very weak substitute for 'chanter';[19] 'ouïr' is its converse; 'voir' is used for sham descriptions of various circumstances. 'Chanter' dominates and polarizes this group, includes it in its sphere of influence. In so doing, it functions as a verbalizing clause, giving the whole discourse the aspect of an allocution, like an interpersonal process, anterior or posterior to any communication in the strict sense, an expanded version of a pure vocative. To be sure, this discourse is prolonged, is counted out over three, five, six stanzas. It unwinds in a series of spirals which are more than mere repetitions: the voice expands, creates its own space, which must be filled. But what fills it, and finds its dimensions there, is not an object, a 'complement', through which the song would be 'dispatched', as 'I say' or 'I know' are 'dispatched' through 'that time is passing'. The space is occupied by the circumstances attached to the song by the anecdotic link of an apparent causality, of a fictive accompaniment, of an anteriority or posteriority which are interchangeable (to the extent that, from one manuscript to another, we find differences in the number and order of the stanzas): relations which are all grammatical rather than real, and are further blurred (intentionally, I think) by the extreme poverty of the connective devices which implement them. Moreover, the means–end relation is almost totally absent, and this can be considered as a positive mark of this style. The circumstance is degraded to the role of insignificant pretext, indifferent in principle (although tradition determines the range of choices rather narrowly), a support for the reality of the voice, and a justification on the formal level for the spinning out of a design. The design is perpetuated until the return and the closure of the last line of the *envoi*: the return is provisional, a furtive turning by the *pensée* back on itself; the closure is merely formal, while the intentional content persists. The song ceases; but it has no 'end', in any of the senses of this word. That is why there are always other songs (which today seem to us, superficially and mistakenly, so similar to one another!) and a discourse among the poets on their own singing.

If one wanted to define reductively the use of 'chanter'–'chant'–'chanson' by our *trouvères* in rhetorical terms, it would be more appropriate to speak of catachresis than of metaphor. It is less appropriate to say that 'chanter' and 'aimer' are in the relation of what is compared and what it is compared to, than to say that 'chanter' has two signifieds which are indistinguishably blended, and unnameable in any other way. Moreover, the same thing is true of most of the alleged metaphors of this poetry: this could be the subject of another essay. But these speculations (which are to an extent justified by the apparent primacy of rhetoric in mediaeval writing) may be taking us away from what is essential. Poetic practice of the twelfth and thirteenth centuries,

187

in spite of what certain critics have said, hardly utilizes iconic motivation, which tends to make of the sign a symbol by manifesting or suggesting a resemblance between the signifier and the signified. The motivation of signs (which, of itself, is inseparable from poetry) is achieved with the help of an expressive register existing prior to the poem: a network of formal or semantic relations seen as beyond question, and providing a basis for the participation of the singer and his audience in a common meaning, as well as for the resulting pleasure.

This was, no doubt, the conception of Dante when, in about 1300, looking back on an art whose classical period was coming to a close, he attempted, in *De Vulgari Eloquentia*, to define the song (*cantio*):[20] 'Fictio rhetorica musicaque poita': this *poita*, from Middle Latin *poire*, awkwardly fashioned from Greek *poiein*, proclaims the logical priority of the 'chant' over the fiction which it actualizes. The specific quality of the poem is a *convenientia*, a collaboration, a coming together, whose effect is to bind everything, thanks to the melodiousness of the voice, into the unity of the 'same': aspiring to flower from analogy into identity.

Harald Weinrich has recently proposed a reversal of customary perspectives for the study of literary phenomena.[21] Instead of starting from the author (the producer of the artistic communication) or the text (the communication itself), he suggests that from the beginning there should be an analysis of the reader (the receiver). This novel viewpoint sheds light on the origins of the genre of the *roman*, towards the end of the twelfth century: the *roman* is defined by the fact that it is addressed to a female readership, which is the source of the coherence of this genre, in that it is *intended* for women readers. It might be tempting to extrapolate his conclusion and apply it to the *trouvère*'s *chanson*: is not the coherence of the melodic discourse established by the 'dame' who is referred to in the *chanson* (in the second, but also often in the third person)? I do not think that this is possible. The uttering voice is a pure succession of harmonious sounds: it is essentially *in time*. The song elevates a fragment of duration into an absolute value. But time can only flow within a space, and that is why the world, i.e. this poetry, exists. The space in question is a meaning space – and the words I am using here do not come from merely abstract reflection. The space I am speaking of is marked in the text: the ultimate circumstance, the limit toward which the objectless actions, grammatically introduced as the sentences of the poem succeed each other, tend, is a *place*: 'aimer en haut lieu', many of these poets sing. The adverbs of place 'ici', 'là', 'où', dot the poem's landscape and are often interpreted as rhetorical substitutes for the *dame*. But the relation is really the opposite; the *lady* is a substitute for the places:

de haut lieu muet la cançons que je cant

(The song I sing comes from a lofty place.)[22]

188

The *dame* is no more the object of the discourse than the *je* is its subject: no more nor less than on the syntactic level. The song integrates the *dame*, she is a formal and semantic component of it on an elementary level (the level on which one might, eccentrically, take the *chanson* as an object lesson), but not really a thematic component. It may happen, to be sure, that some descriptive detail present in a stanza, a proper noun, an allusion in the *envoi*, seems to refer to a specific individual. The case is rather rare, but it cannot be denied that it occurs. It amounts to some kind of social use of the system, for particular ends, that are foreign to poetry: the *chanson* then partakes of the *roman*, the narrational. The system of the chanson is not affected.

The *chanson* is thus its own subject: a subject without a predicate. This difference might be discussed in logical terms. Although a concept can be the totality of the signified of a subject, it never forms the whole signifier of a predicate.[23] Song, which ends only by coming to its own beginning, is its own totality, that is, in this context, its own meaning.

There is no doubt that this is the way in which the audience of the *trouvères*, at the time when this poetry was most alive, carried out the decoding of the sung message. The only testimony to this which we have, admittedly indirect, is the didactic or polemical passages in certain *chansons*, where song judges itself: but this testimony is quite clear.

The poem is a mirror of itself. The poem flows to its end, and, if it loses itself at some end-point, that terminus is itself.

> Aisi-m perdei com perdet se
> Lo bel Narcissus en la fon.

(. . . and I lost myself as beautiful Narcissus lost himself in the pool.)

Thus sang in Provençal Bernard de Ventadour, whose songs, more than others, provided the *trouvères* with the rules of their art. But what the singer loses himself in is not water that flows: it is a 'miralh', a mirror, which is his eyes, which are 'Amour', which is the 'Chant'. What you see in Love, in Song, is not you, it is Love itself, it is Song itself, it is you turned into song, universalized like the voice which sings you.

That is why, to cite again the same poet (who represents a model which is often more explicit or more primitive, easier to see the workings of, than the *chanson* of the *trouvères*):

> Lo vers, aisi com om plus l'au,
> vai melhuran toda via

(This song, the more one hears it the richer it becomes en route.)[24]

As it proceeds to unfold its length, song tends toward its own perfection.

If, after the examination of key terms, we went on to study thematic motifs, it would be easy to isolate one of the most frequent ones, which, I believe, is clearly the most central: it is an insistent affirmation, integrated into the fabric of the discourse, and expressed in formulas such as the typical 'the song comes from the heart', or inscribed in the textual syntax of the poem, as we observed above for a chanson of the Châtelain de Couci (which exhibits as it were the rhetorical inversion of this, the *ordo artificialis*: the song is reabsorbed in the heart, in its return movement).

Is the heart to be seen here as the seat and source of the emotions? No doubt it is, in a certain sense. But it is rather to be seen (as the syntax indeed suggests, for the word generally occurs without determiners or modifiers) as the archetypal heart, the place of the first light and of the processions of life, the receptacle of energies of which feeling and action are no more than superficial, accessory, and contingent consequences. Likewise, in another figure of the same kind, *the eyes* (and only these) are associated with the *heart*: like the heart, they have as their function and their only power that of receiving and manifesting brightness. Antithetically, in opposition to the heart there is the body: opacity and inertia are opposed to the outpouring of radiance, to solar limpidity; in opposition to the occasional, to the moment of action, is its immanent cause. Song rises to us from the heart, loaded with a meaning which is the song itself, and includes us in the circularity of this unutterable exchange: a little like the way in which the figures in a painting by Memling look at the scene represented, with a gaze that always reaches beyond things, that incorporates them in its lucidity.

Notes

1. R. Dragonetti, *La Technique poétique des trouvères* (Bruges, 1960), pp. 381–537.
2. In the sense of A. Greimas, *Sémantique Structurale* (Paris, Larousse, 1966), p. 163.
3. Cf. the remarks of R. Barthes and N. Ruwet in *Langages* 12 (1968), pp. 6–7 and 60–1.
4. Paris, P.U.F., 1953, p. 95.
5. This is the reading of four manuscripts out of five; the fifth gives the variant 'deporter', which modifies the sense of the line – 'I cannot be happy about it' – but hardly that of the whole passage.
6. Lerond edn, pp. 68–70.
7. I give here only the results of this comparative study, not the successive phases it went through. To give a few figures, the corpus had 100 songs, about 4,000 lines, half octosyllabic, half decasyllabic; there were in all 87 occurrences of 'chanter', 42 of 'chanson', 15 of 'chant', 75 of 'trouver', 220 of 'aimer', 340 of 'amour'.
8. I adapt freely for the purposes of my analysis the 'Categories of the theory of grammar' of M. A. K. Halliday, in *Word* 17 (1961).
9. In this and succeeding cases I give theoretical formulas, a sort of architopic, which one might well introduce by an asterisk, as is done with reconstructed historical forms.
10. 'Chanson' has the function which, in other poems, at the same point, is performed by the word 'messager', or a name.

11. Most of the time, the self-references are of the categorial or taxonomic type (sometimes one could as well speak of them as advertisements), either positive (the song defines itself as a 'chanson', 'descort', etc.; it makes a qualitative judgement about itself: new, beautiful, truthful, appropriate, etc.) or negative (not like some other, not in a certain style, not in the Picard dialect, etc.). It is clear that 'chanter' occupies a central position in this terminology.

12. The edition of U. Lindelöf and A. Wallensköld (Helsinki, 1901), p. 68.

13. Lerond edn, p. 89.

14. The edition of G. Steffens (Halle, 1902), p. 335.

15. This type of interpretation is very old: it was introduced by the authors of *razos* who, at the end of the thirteenth and during the fourteenth century, attempted to give biographical explanations of the songs of the troubadours.

16. I exclude 'se trouver', used simply to introduce a modifier.

17. The desire for ambiguity (a surface ambiguity) is one of the undeniable characteristics of this poetry. This is particularly clear in the *trobar clus* of the troubadours, and this, rather than the *trobar leu* was the inspiration of the French *trouvères*. I find sufficient proof of this in the fact that the French *chansons* are so surprisingly poor in descriptions and comparisons.

18. There are rare exceptions, with the troubadours rather than the *trouvères*: the motif of the *fontaine*, in the twelfth and thirteenth centuries, belongs to other genres of poetry rather than the *chanson* proper.

19. It is, in fact, much rarer in the *chanson* than in lyrical–narrative genres like the *pastourelle*, where it is the normal term. The introducer, on the other hand, in the *chansons de geste*, is of the type 'voulez-vous ouïr chanson?' But this expression is something quite different, a topos similar to *arma virumque cano*.

20. See the relevant commentary of H. Dragonetti, *Aux Frontières du langage poétique*.

21. 'Für eine Literaturgeschichte des Lesers', in *Merkur* 21 (1967), 236, pp. 1026–38.

22. Moniet d'Arras, edited by H. Petersen Dyggve (Helsinki, 1938), p. 66. The example is complex (it is the first line of a Marian song adapting the tone of the amorous complaint). This makes it even more representative, bearing witness to the value attached to the mention of the place.

23. Cf. G. Frege, *Aritmetica e logica* (Milan, 1948), pp. 191–209.

24. The edition of M. Lazar (Paris, 1966), p. 102.

10. The autobiographical contract

PHILIPPE LEJEUNE

Is it possible to define autobiography? I had attempted to do so, in *L'Autobiographie en France*,[1] in order to be able to establish a coherent corpus, but my definition left a certain number of theoretical problems unresolved. I felt the need to refine and sharpen it, by trying to find stricter criteria. In doing this, I inevitably encountered the classical issues which the genre of autobiography always raises: the relation of biography and autobiography, the relation of the novel and the autobiography. These problems are irritating because of the repetitious nature of the arguments one encounters, the vagueness of the vocabulary used, and the confusion among problems belonging to independent domains. As a result of my new attempt at definition, I wound up trying to clarify the terms in which the problems of the genre are stated. When one wants to get things clear, one runs two risks: the first is that of seeming to repeat the obvious (since there is no alternative to going back to basics), the other is the opposite – the risk of seeming to want to complicate things with excessively subtle distinctions. I will not escape the first charge; for the second, I will try to provide a rational basis for my distinctions.

I had conceived my definition not *sub specie aeternitatis*, not by examining each text as a thing-in-itself, but from the point of view of a contemporary reader who is trying to see order in a mass of *published* texts, which have in common the fact that they tell the story of someone's life. The situation of the 'definer' is thus doubly relativized and limited: as regards *history*, the definition does not claim to cover more than the two centuries since 1770, and is concerned only with European literature; this does not mean that we should deny the existence of personal writing before 1770 or outside Europe, but simply that our present-day way of thinking about autobiography becomes anachronistic or irrelevant outside this area. With regard to the *text*, I am adopting the reader's point of view: my starting point is neither the problematic internal state of the author, nor an attempt to establish the canons of a literary genre. By choosing to start from the situation of the reader (which is my own, the only one I know well), I may be able to grasp the functioning of the texts more clearly (and the differences in how they function), since they were written for us, their readers, and since, as we read

192

them, it is we who cause them to function. I have therefore tried to define autobiography through a series of oppositions between the various texts which are available for reading.

Slightly modified, the definition of autobiography might be: 'a retrospective prose narrative produced by a real person concerning his own existence, focusing on his individual life, in particular on the development of his personality'.

This definition involves elements from four different categories:

1. Linguistic form: (a) narrative; (b) prose.
2. Subject treated: individual life, personal history.
3. Situation of the author: author (whose name designates a real person) and narrator are identical.
4. Position of the narrator: (a) narrator and protagonist are identical; (b) narration is retrospectively oriented.

Any work is an autobiography if it fulfils all of the conditions indicated in each of these categories. Genres close to autobiography do not satisfy all of these conditions. Here is the list of the conditions not fulfilled by other genres: memoirs: (2); biography: (4a); first person novel: (3); autobiographical poem: (1b); diary: (4b); self-portrait or essay: (1a and 4b).

It is evident that the different categories are not all equally restrictive: some of the conditions can be largely, though not totally, satisfied. The text should be *mainly* narrative, but we know the importance of speech in autobiographical narration; the orientation should be *mainly* retrospective, but this does not exclude passages of self-description, of diary, of reference to the time of writing, and quite complex temporal constructions; the subject should be *mainly* the writer's individual life and the growth of his personality, but the description of events, of social or political history, can also be included. This is a matter of proportion, or rather of hierarchy: there are natural transitions to the other genres of *littérature intime* (memoirs, diary, essay), and a certain latitude is left to the classifier in the examination of particular cases.

On the other hand, two of the conditions are a matter of all or nothing, and these are, of course, the conditions which oppose autobiography (but also the other forms of *littérature intime*) to biography and to the personal novel: these are conditions (3) and (4a). Here there is no transition or latitude. Either there is identity or there is not. There is no possibility of degrees, and any doubt imposes a negative conclusion.

For there to be autobiography (and more generally *littérature intime*), there must be identity between the *author*, the *narrator*, and the *protagonist*. But this 'identity' raises numerous problems, which I will attempt, if not to solve, at least to formulate clearly, in the following sections:

How can 'identity' between the narrator and the protagonist be expressed in the text? ('I, you, he')?

In the case of a narrative 'in the first person', how is the identity of the author and the narrator–protagonist manifested? ('I, the undersigned'). This will be the context in which to contrast autobiography and the novel.

Is there not a confusion, in most reflection about autobiography, between the notion of *identity* and that of *resemblance*? ('Certified true copy'). This will be the context in which to contrast autobiography and biography.

The difficulties encountered in these analyses will lead me, in the last two sections ('Autobiographical space', and 'The reading contract') to try to formulate the problem in different terms.

I, you, he

The 'identity' of the narrator and the protagonist which autobiography implies is most often marked by the use of the first person. This is what Gérard Genette calls 'autodiégétique' narration in his classification of the 'voices' of the narrative, based on works of fiction.[2] But he also clearly distinguishes a narration 'in the first person' without the narrator being the same individual as the protagonist. This is what he calls more broadly 'homodiégétique' narration. Continuing along these lines we see that conversely there can perfectly well be 'identity' of the narrator and the protagonist without use of the first person.

Two different criteria must thus be distinguished: one involving the grammatical person, and one involving the 'identity' of the individuals to whom the uses of the grammatical person refer. This elementary distinction is forgotten because of the polysemy of the word 'person', and it is camouflaged in practice by the connections which are *almost always* established between a given grammatical person and a given type of identity relation or of narration. However, this is only 'almost always' the case; the undeniable exceptions require us to rethink the definitions.

Because it raises the problem of the *author*, autobiography spotlights phenomena which fiction leaves in a state of uncertainty: in particular the fact that there can quite well be 'identity' between the narrator and the protagonist in the case of a third-person narrative. Since this 'identity' is not established within the text by the use of 'I', it is determined indirectly, but unambiguously, by the two equivalences: author = narrator, and author = protagonist, from which we deduce that narrator = protagonist, even if the narrator remains implicit. Such a procedure conforms literally to the original meaning of the word 'autobiography': it is a biography, written by its subject, but written like a simple biography.

This technique may be adopted for a variety of reasons, and has produced different kinds of effect. Speaking of oneself in the third person can imply either an enormous self-esteem (as is the case with the Commentaries of Caesar, or some works by de Gaulle), or else a form of humility (as with certain antique religious autobiographies, where the writer called himself 'the servant of God'). In either case the narrator adopts, with respect to the individual he once was, either the distance of historical perspective, or that of divine perspective, that is, of eternity, and introduces into his narrative a transcendence with which, in the last analysis, he identifies himself. Totally different effects of the same procedure can be imagined, of contingency, of dissociation, or of ironic distance. This is the case with *The Education of Henry Adams*, by Henry Adams, where the author describes in the third person the almost Socratic quest of a young American (himself) looking for an education. In all the examples given so far, the third person is used throughout the work. There exist autobiographies in which part of the text designates the protagonist by the third person, while in the rest of the text the narrator and the protagonist are merged in the first person: this is the case for *Le Traître* in which André Gorz uses these changes of 'voice' to express his uncertainty about his identity. Claude Roy, in *Nous*, uses this device in a more banal way to confer a chaste distance on an amorous episode of his life.[3] The existence of these bilingual texts, genuine Rosetta stones for identity, is valuable: it confirms the possibility of an autobiography in the third person.

Even within the personal register (first and second persons) it is clear that it is quite possible to write other than in the first person. What would prevent me from writing my life referring to myself as 'you'? In fiction, this has been done by Michel Butor, in *La Modification*, and by Georges Perec in *Un Homme qui dort*. There seem to be no autobiographies which have been entirely written in that way, but the device sometimes appears briefly in addresses by the narrator to the person he once was, to comfort him in a difficult situation, or lecture or disown him.[4] From such use to a whole narrative there is, to be sure, quite a distance, but the thing is possible. This kind of narration would clearly point up, on the level of discourse, the difference between the subject of discourse, i.e. the speaker, and the subject of the utterance treated as the addressee of the narrative.

These uses of the third and second persons are rare in autobiography, but they make it impossible to confuse problems of grammatical person with problems of 'identity'. One can therefore imagine a matrix conceived like that on p. 196.

It has been necessary, on the basis of exceptional cases, to dissociate the problem of person from that of 'identity'. This allows us to account for the complexity of existing or possible forms of autobiography. It can also induce uncertainty about the possibility of giving a 'textual' definition of autobiography. For the present, after this look at the exceptions, let us return to the

grammatical person / identity	I	YOU	HE
narrator = protagonist	classical autobiography (autodiégétique)	second-person autobiography	third-person autobiography
narrator ≠ protagonist	first-person biography (eye-witness account) (homodiégétique)	biography addressed to the subject	classical biography (hétérodiégétique)

REMARKS

(a) By 'grammatical person' should be understood the person which is given primary importance throughout the narrative. Obviously, an 'I' is not conceivable without a 'you' (the reader), but the latter is generally left implicit; conversely, a 'you' implies a (usually implicit) 'I'; and narration in the third person may contain intrusions by a first-person narrator.

(b) The examples given here are all taken from the gamut of referential narrative offered by biography and autobiography; we could have as easily used examples from fiction. I give Genette's categories at the appropriate points; it will be seen that they do not cover all possible cases.

(c) The case of a biography addressed to its subject is illustrated by certain academic speeches, where the speaker talks directly to the person whose life story he is telling, before an audience which is the true recipient, just as, in an autobiography in the second person, if such a work existed, the addressee (oneself at an earlier age) would be invoked to receive a discourse, with the reader as onlooker.

most frequent case, that of the classical autobiography in the first person ('autodiégétique' narration): we will encounter new reasons for uncertainty, this time concerning the way in which 'identity' is established between the *author* and the *narrator–protagonist*.

I, the undersigned

Let us assume, then, that all autobiographies are written in the first person, as one might infer from the constant refrain of the autobiographers: *I*. We find, for example, from Rousseau: 'I, I alone'; Stendhal: 'Once again you are backsliding into *I* and *me*'; Thyde Monnier: *Moi* (a four-volume autobiography); Claude Roy: *Moi, je* (as for me, I); etc. Even in this case we are faced with the following question: how is the 'identity' between the author and the narrator manifested? For the autobiographer, it would be natural to pose this question simply by saying 'Who am I?' But since I am a reader, it is no less natural for me to ask the question in another way: who is 'I'? That is: who is the one who is *saying* 'Who am I?'?

I hope I will be excused for recalling, before continuing the analysis, a few elementary linguistic notions. Unfortunately, in this domain, the simplest things are the ones which are most easily forgotten: they are taken as natural and they disappear in the illusion that they create. I will begin with the analyses of Benveniste, but will arrive at conclusions which are slightly different from his.[5]

The 'first person' is defined by a junction between two domains:

1. Reference: the personal pronouns (I/you) have reference only within a discourse, in the very act of utterance. Benveniste points out that there is no concept 'I'. 'I' refers, each time it is used, to the individual who is speaking and who is identified *by the very fact* of his speaking.

2. Utterance: the personal pronouns of the first person express *identity* of the subject of the speech act ('énonciation') and the subject of the utterance ('énoncé').

Thus, if someone says: 'I was born on . . .', the use of the pronoun 'I' because of the junction between these two domains, leads to an identification of the person who is speaking with the person who was born. At least, that is the global effect. This should not be taken to mean that the kinds of 'equivalences' established within these two domains are similar: on the level of reference (discourse as referring to its own production), the identity is immediate: it is instantaneously perceived and accepted by the hearer or reader as a *fact*; on the level of utterance ('énoncé'), what is involved is a simple relation that is expressed, i.e. uttered – that is, an assertion like any other, which one can believe or doubt, etc. The example chosen gives an idea of the problems that may arise: is the baby who was born in some hospital, at a period of which I have not the slightest memory, really the same person as *me*? It is important to distinguish these two relations, fused in the use of the pronoun 'I': as we will see below, failure to distinguish them has introduced a great deal of confusion into thinking about the problems of autobiography (see 'Certified true copy' below). Leaving aside for the moment the problems relevant to utterance, I will restrict my examination to those involving production ('énonciation').

The analyses of Benveniste are based on the situation of *spoken* discourse. In that situation, it might be thought that the reference of 'I' poses no problems: 'I' is the one who is speaking, and I, in my role as interlocutor or hearer, should have no trouble identifying that person. However, there exist two kinds of oral situations in which identification can be a problem:

(a) *Quotation*: this is discourse within discourse: the first person of the second discourse (the quoted one) refers to a context of utterance which is itself stated in the first discourse. In various languages, different signs –

quotation marks, dashes, etc. – identify embedded (i.e. quoted) discourse when writing is involved. Intonation has a similar function in spoken discourse. But if these indications are unclear, or lacking, there will be uncertainty: this is the case with re-quoting, and, in general, in the theatre. When la Berma acts in *Phèdre*, who is the one saying 'je'? The theatrical context can, to be sure, have the function of quotation marks, signalling the fictive nature of the person saying 'I'. But this is where we begin to feel dizzy, for even the most naive among us is tempted to ask whether it is not the person who defines the 'I', but rather perhaps the 'I' which defines the person – that is, whether there is no person except within the discourse. Let us fight off this dizziness for a moment. What we are touching upon here is the problem of the difference between the autobiographical novel and the autobiography, but also, within autobiography, the self-evident truth that the first person is a role.

(b) *Speaking at a distance*: this is, in this context, the conversation on the telephone, or through a closed door, or in the dark: there is no other way to identify the speaker than by his voice: 'Who is it?' 'Me.' ('Me who?' – in such a case dialogue is still possible, and can lead to identification. If the voice is delayed in time, as in a recording, or if the conversation, even when instantaneous, is one-way, as on the radio, then that possibility is lacking. Such a situation is equivalent to that of writing.

So far I have pretended to be following Benveniste, by straightforwardly imagining everything that might happen, in a situation of speaking, to keep the identity of the speaker unclear. No one would want to deny that 'I' refers to the act of speaking: but the speech act is not the final stage of reference – it raises in turn an identity problem, which, in the case of direct oral communication, we solve instinctively on the basis of extra-linguistic data. When oral communication is disturbed, identity can become problematic. However, in the case of written communication, unless it is intended to remain anonymous (as sometimes happens), the person who produces the discourse is supposed to allow himself to be identified on the basis of the discourse content itself, not merely on the basis of material clues, like the postmark, his handwriting, or his spelling idiosyncrasies.

Benveniste remarks (p. 261) that there is no concept of 'I': an accurate observation, if one adds that there is no concept of 'he', etc., either, and that, in general, no personal, possessive, demonstrative, etc., pronoun has ever *referred* to a concept, but that these rather merely perform a function, which is to point to a noun, or an entity capable of being designated by a noun. We therefore propose to refine his analysis by adding the following two propositions:

(a) The personal pronoun 'I' designates the utterer of the discourse token where the 'I' occurs; but this utterer is himself capable of being designated by a nominal (whether this is a common noun, determined in one way or another, or a proper noun).

(b) The opposition between having and not having an associated concept acquires its meaning from the opposition of the common noun and the proper noun (not of the common noun and the personal pronoun).

In another passage (p. 254) Benveniste justifies as follows, in terms of economy, the use of this first person which has no reference except in its use in a speech act: 'If each speaker, to express his feeling of irreducible personal identity, had his own personal call signal, as each radio station has its own call sign, there would be about as many languages as there are individuals, and communication would be impossible.' This is a strange 'if', for Benveniste seems to be forgetting that these personalized call signals actually exist, in the lexical category of proper nouns designating people: there are almost as many names as there are individuals. Naturally, the different names do not require different forms of the verb conjugation, and Benveniste is right to stress the economical function of 'I'; however, by forgetting to relate it to the lexical category of personal names, he makes it incomprehensible why each speaker, using 'I', is not as a consequence lost in the anonymous mass, and is still able to declare what he irreducibly is by naming himself.

The individual person and his discourse are connected to each other through the personal name, even before they are connected by the first person, as is shown by the facts of language acquisition by children. The infant speaks of himself in the third person, using his own name, long before he comes to understand that he too can use the first person. Later, each of us will call himself 'I' in speaking; but for everyone this 'I' will designate a particular name, which he will always be able to utter. All of the situations of identification, whether easy, difficult, or indeterminate, indicated above for spoken language, inevitably end up by cashing in the first person for a proper noun.[6]

In oral discourse, whenever it is necessary, there is a return to the proper noun: this is the introduction, performed by the person himself, or some third party (the French word for introduction, *présentation*, is itself suggestive, because of its inexactitude: physical *presence* does not suffice to characterize the utterer; there is not full presence without naming). In written discourse, likewise, the *signature* designates the utterer, as the address does the intended recipient.[7]

The problems of autobiography must thus be considered in relation to the *proper noun*. In printed texts, the whole utterance is assumed by a person whose *name* is customarily placed on the cover of the book, and on the flyleaf, above or below the title. In this name is summed up the whole existence of what is called the *author*: it is the only mark in the text of an indubitable 'outside-of-the-text', designating a real person, who thus asks that we attribute to him, definitively, the responsibility for producing the whole text. In many cases, the author's presence in the text is reduced to just this name. But the place assigned to the name is highly significant: by social convention, it is connected with the accepting of responsibility by a *real person*. By these words, which occur above in my definition of autobiography, I mean a person whose existence is legally verifiable, a matter of record. Of course, the reader is not going to go out and verify it, and he may very well not know who this person is, but his existence is beyond question; exceptions and fraud only serve to emphasize the general credence given to this variety of social contract.[8]

An author is not just a person, he is a person who writes and publishes. With one foot in the text, and one outside, he is the point of contact between the two. The author is defined as being simultaneously a socially responsible real person, and the producer of a discourse. For the reader, who does not know the real person, although believing in his existence, the author is defined as the person who is capable of producing this discourse, and he thus imagines him on the basis of what he has produced. Perhaps one really becomes an author only with one's second book, when the name written on the cover is the common denominator for at least two different texts, and thus gives the idea of a person who is not reducible to any particular one of his texts, and who, being capable of producing others, goes beyond all of them. As will be seen, this is very important for the reading of autobiographies: if the autobiography is the author's first book, he is an unknown – even if he is telling his own story in the book, he lacks, in the eyes of the reader, that sign of reality constituted by the prior production of *other texts* (non-autobiographical ones), which is indispensable to what we will call 'the autobiographical space'.

The author is thus a personal name, the identical name accepting responsibility for a sequence of different published texts. He derives his reality from the list of his other works which is often to be found at the beginning of the book under the heading 'by the same author'. The autobiography, a narration of the life of the author, presupposes *identity in name* between the author, as represented by his name on the cover, the narrator, and the one being spoken of. This is a very simple criterion, which defines, simultaneously, autobiography and all the other genres of *littérature intime* (diary, self-portrait, personal essay).

One objection comes to mind immediately: what about pseudonyms? The objection is easy to answer, once the pseudonym has been defined and distinguished from the name of a fictitious person.

A pseudonym is a name, which differs from that recognized by the law, which a real person uses to *publish* some or all of his writings. The pseudonym is an *author's* name. It is not exactly a false name, but rather a *nom de plume*, a second name, exactly like that which a nun adopts when she takes the veil. Admittedly, the use of a pseudonym can sometimes involve deceit, or be the result of a desire for discretion: but in such cases most often just one work is involved, and almost never is that work presented as the autobiography of an *author*. In general, literary pseudonyms are neither secrets nor hoaxes; the second name is as authentic as the first, it just signals that second birth known as published writing. When he writes his autobiography, the pseudonymous author will himself give the origin of his assumed name: thus Raymond Abellio explains that his name is Georges Soulès, and says why he chose his pseudonym.[9] The pseudonym is simply a differentiation, a splitting, of the name, which does not change the identity of the person at all.

The *pseudonym*, defined in this way as the name of an *author* (written *on* the cover of the book), must not be confused with the *name* attributed to a fictitious individual *within* the book (even if this individual is the narrator and figures as the utterer of the text in its entirety): for this individual is identified as fictive simply because he is incapable of being the *author* of the *book*. Let us take a very simple example: 'Colette' is the pseudonym of a real person (Gabrielle-Sidonie Colette), who is the *author* of a series of stories: 'Claudine' is the name of a fictitious heroine, who is the narrator of the stories which have her name in the title. If we cannot accept these narratives as autobiographies, this is obviously because of the second fact, not because of the first.

In the case of a fictitious name (that is, one different from the author's) given to a character who tells the story of his life, it can happen that the reader has reason to believe that the story of what happened to the character is exactly that of the author's life, because of parallels in other texts, or because of other information already in the reader's possession, or even because there are things in the text itself which make it ring false as fiction (as when someone says: 'Something happened to a close friend of mine . . .', and then tells the story of this 'friend' in a very involved, personal way). Even if there were all the reasons in the world for believing that the story was exactly the same, it would still be the case that the text in question was not an autobiography: autobiography supposes first of all that *identity* is assumed by the author on the level of the speech act ('énonciation') and, quite secondarily, that there is a *resemblance* on the level of the utterance ('énoncé').

Such texts as these would thus belong to the category of the 'autobiographical novel': I will use this term for any piece of fiction for which the reader may have reason to suspect, on the basis of what he guesses or thinks to be resemblances, that there is identity between the author and the *protagonist*, even though the author has chosen to deny, or at least not to affirm, that identity. So defined, the autobiographical novel includes both personal narratives (where there is 'identity' between the narrator and the

protagonist) and 'impersonal' narratives (where the protagonist is designated in the third person): it is defined in terms of its content. Unlike the
autobiography, an autobiographical novel can be so to various degrees. The
'resemblance' supposed by the reader can range from a vague 'family
resemblance' between the protagonist and the author to a quasi-
transparency which leads us to say that the protagonist is an exact likeness.
Thus, concerning *L'Année du crabe* (1972) by Olivier Todd, a critic has written
that 'the whole book is obsessively autobiographical beneath transparent
pseudonyms'.[10] Autobiography, on the other hand, does not admit of
degrees: it is a matter of all or nothing.

It can be seen how important it is to use a clearly defined vocabulary in
making these distinctions. The critic speaks here of a 'pseudonym' for the
name of the hero; for me, the term can only stand for the name of an author.
The hero can resemble the author as much as he wants to; so long as he does
not have his name, it makes no difference. From this point of view, the case of
L'Année du crabe is typical. The subtitle of the book is 'roman': novel; Todd's
hero is called Ross. On the jacket, the publisher informs the reader that Ross
is really Todd. This is a clever advertising gambit, but it does not change
anything. If Ross is really Todd, why does he have a different name? If it
really was him, why did he not simply *say* it was? Whether he coquettishly
helps the reader to guess that it is him, or the reader figures it out in spite of
the author, does not matter much. Autobiography is not a guessing game: in
fact, it is exactly the opposite. What is missing here is something essential, it
is what I have proposed calling the *autobiographical contract*.

Ascending from the first person to the proper name, I am now forced to
correct what I wrote in *L'Autobiographie en France*: 'How are we to distinguish
the autobiography from the autobiographical novel? It must be admitted, if
we restrict ourselves to an internal analysis of the text, that there is no
difference at all. All the devices that are used in autobiography to convince us
of the authenticity of the story can be imitated by the novel, and that has
often been done.' This is true as long as the text is considered without the
title page; when that is taken as part of the text, with the name of the author,
then a general textual criterion is available: 'identity' between the names of
the author, narrator, and protagonist. The autobiographical contract is the
affirmation in the text of this identity, referring in the last resort to the *name* of
the author on the cover.

The forms of the autobiographical contract are quite varied, but they all
manifest an intention to 'honour the signature'. The reader can quibble
about how much resemblance there is between the protagonist and the
author, but not about whether there is 'identity'. Everyone knows only too
well how much each of us values his own name.

A piece of autobiographical fiction can turn out to be 'exact', with the protagonist resembling the author; an autobiography can be 'inexact', with the individual described being different from the author. These are *de facto* matters (though we are still leaving aside the question of *who* is to judge whether there is resemblance, and how), which do not affect the *de jure* matter of the type of contract existing between the author and the reader. It can be seen that the contract is important from the observation that it in fact determines the attitude of the reader: if there is not an affirmation of identity, as is the case with fiction, then the reader will try to find resemblances, in spite of the author; if there is, as in the case of autobiography, he will tend to look for differences (errors, distortions, etc.). When confronted with a narrative that has the appearance of an autobiography, there is often a tendency for the reader to act like a detective; that is, to look for breaches of the contract, whatever kind of contract it may be. This is what is responsible for the myth of the novel that is 'truer' than autobiography: we always believe what we think we have discovered from the text in spite of the author to be truer and deeper. If Olivier Todd had presented *L'Année du crabe* as his autobiography, perhaps our critic would have been sensitive to the flaws, gaps, and rearrangements of the narrative. This indicates that all questions of *faithfulness* (this is the problem of 'resemblance') depend in the last analysis on the question of *authenticity* (this is the problem of identity), which itself is formulated in terms of the name of the author.

Identity in name between the author, the narrator, and the protagonist can be established in two ways:

1. *Implicitly*, with the connection between the author and the narrator, suggested by the *autobiographical contract*, which can take two forms: (a) *titles* can be used which can remove all doubt that the first person refers to the named author (*The Story of My Life, Autobiography*, etc.); (b) there can be an *initial section* of the text where the narrator makes commitments to the reader by behaving as if he was the author, in such a way that the reader has not the slightest doubt that the 'I' designates the name on the cover, even if the name is not repeated in the text.

2. *Overtly*, with the name that the narrator–protagonist gives to himself in the course of the narrative, and which is the same as that of the author on the cover.

It is necessary for identity to be established in at least one of these two ways; it often happens that both are used.

In symmetry with the autobiographical contract, we could posit the *fictional contract*, which would itself have two aspects: *overt practice of non-identity* (the author and the protagonist do not have the same name), and *attestation of fictivity* (the subtitle 'roman' (novel) generally has this function nowadays; note that 'roman', in present-day terminology, implies the fictional contract, while the word 'récit' (narrative) is indeterminate, and compatible with the

P. Lejeune

autobiographical contract). It will perhaps be objected that the novel has the potential to *imitate* the autobiographical contract: was not the eighteenth-century novel developed in fact by imitating the different forms of *littérature intime* (memoirs, letters, and, in the nineteenth century, the diary)? But this objection does not hold, if one remembers that such imitation cannot be sustained through its final term, that is, the *name* of the author. One can always pretend to be reporting, to be publishing the autobiography of someone whom one wishes to be taken as a real person; as long as that someone is not the *author*, the only one responsible for the book, this changes nothing. The only cases which will not be covered by this criterion are cases of literary hoaxes: these are exceedingly rare, and their rarity is not due to respect for other people's names or the fear of punishment. Who is there to prevent me from writing the autobiography of an imaginary person and publishing it under his name, also imaginary? That is in fact what, in a slightly different area, MacPherson did for Ossian! The case is rare because there are very few authors who are capable of giving up *their own name*. The proof is that even the Ossian hoax was short-lived, since we know who was the real author, for MacPherson could not resist putting his name on the title page as the adapter.

Assuming these definitions, we can classify all possible cases with the use of two criteria: the relation between the name of the protagonist and the name of the author, and the nature of the contract entered into by the author. For each of these criteria, three situations are conceivable. The protagonist (1) has a name different from the author's; (2) does not have a name; (3) has the same name as the author; the contract is (1) fictional; (2) absent; (3) autobiographical. By combining these two criteria, we theoretically get nine cases; in fact, only seven are possible, since two are excluded by definition: identity of the names cannot coexist with the fictional contract, nor a difference of name with the autobiographical contract.

The table on p. 205 gives all the possible combinations; the numbers refer to the descriptions below; in each box is given the effect which each combination produces in the reader. This matrix, of course, applies only to 'autodiégétique' narration.

1. Name of protagonist ≠ name of author

This alone excludes the possibility of autobiography. It is thus of little importance whether there is also an attestation of fictivity (1a or 1b). Whether the story is presented as true (as, e.g., an autobiographical manuscript found by the author–editor in an attic, etc.), or as fictitious (and believed to be true, connected with the author by the reader), in any case there is not identity between the author, the narrator, and the hero.

Name of protagonist / Contract	≠ name of author	= o	= name of author
fictional	1(a) NOVEL	2(a) NOVEL	////////
= o	1(b) NOVEL	2(b) indeter-minate	3(a) AUTOBIO-GRAPHY
autobiographical	////////	2(c) AUTOBIO-GRAPHY	3(b) AUTOBIO-GRAPHY

2. Name of protagonist = o

This is the most complex case, because of its indeterminacy. Everything depends on what contract the author chooses. Three cases are possible:

(a) Fictional contract (the book is identified as 'fiction' on the cover or title page): the 'autodiégétique' narrative is attributed to a fictitious narrator. The case cannot be frequent – no example comes to mind immediately. One might be tempted to cite *A la recherche du temps perdu*, but this fiction does not exactly correspond to the case in question, for two reasons: on the one hand, there is no clear indication of the fictional contract at the beginning of the book, and in fact numerous readers have mistakenly identified the author Proust with the narrator; furthermore, it is true that the narrator–protagonist has no name – except on just one occasion, where, in a single utterance, the possibility is offered of giving the narrator the same first name as the author (we can attribute this utterance only to the author, for how can a fictitious narrator know the name of his author?), and in this manner we are informed that the author is not the narrator. This strange intrusion of the author functions simultaneously as a fictional contract and as an autobiographical clue, and situates the text in some ambiguous intermediate region.[11]

(b) Contract = o: not only does the protagonist not have a name, but the author does not subscribe to any contract, autobiographical or fictional. There is total indeterminacy. An example is *La Mère et l'enfant*, by Charles-Louis Philippe. While the secondary characters in this narrative have names, the mother and the child have no family name, and the child does not have a first name. It is easy to imagine that they are Madame Philippe and her son, but this is not stated anywhere. In addition the narration is ambiguous (is the work a paean to childhood in general or the story of a particular child?), the time and place are quite vague, and we do not know who the adult is who is speaking of this childhood. The reader can read the book in whatever way he pleases.

(c) Autobiographical contract: the protagonist has no name in the narrative, but the author states explicitly his identity with the narrator (and hence with the protagonist, since the narrative is 'autodiégétique'), in an initial contract. An example is *Histoire de mes idées* by Edgar Quinet; the contract, incorporated in the title, is made explicit in a long preface, signed by Edgar Quinet. The name does not appear once in the entire narrative, but, because of the contract, 'je' always refers to Quinet.

3. Name of protagonist = name of author

This of itself excludes the possibility of fiction. Even if the narrative is, in historical terms, completely false, it will be a *lie* (which is an autobiographical category) and not fiction. Two cases can be distinguished:

(a) Contract = 0 (this is meant to include the contract indicated by the title and other peripheral material): the reader realizes the identity of author, narrator, and protagonist, although this is not stated explicitly. Example: *Les Mots*, by Jean-Paul Sartre. Neither the title nor the beginning indicate that the work is an autobiography. Someone is telling the story of a family. On page 14 of the *Folio* edition the narrator appears explicitly for the first time ('*Il m'intrigue: je sais* qu'il est resté célibataire . . .' (He fascinates me: I know he remained a bachelor); or 'Elle l'aimait, *je crois* . . .' (She loved him, I think)); on page 15, doctor *Sartre* appears in the story, who, on page 16, has a grandson: 'moi'. Because of the name, we grasp the identity between the protagonist, the narrator, and the author whose name is printed above the title: Jean-Paul Sartre. And the fact that this is the famous author, and not someone else with the same name, is established by the text itself, whose narrator claims the authorship on page 48 of *Les Mouches*, *Les Chemins de la liberté*, and *Les Séquestrés d'Altona*, and, on page 211, of *La Nausée*. The story itself will give us insights of the most varied kinds concerning this name, from daydreams of glory – 'This little Sartre knows his business; if he were to disappear, little does France know what she would be losing' (p. 80) – to familiar – and familial – distortions of his first name – 'André thinks that Poulou is showing off' (p. 188).

This criterion might be considered to be quite haphazard. Sometimes the first occurrence of the author's name in the narrative is far from the beginning, in a minor episode which, we feel, could be eliminated from the text with no change at all in its general aspect: thus, in the autobiography of Julien Green, *Partir avant le jour* (Grasset, 1963), only on page 107, in an anecdote about the awarding of prizes, does his name appear. It sometimes even happens that there is only a single and allusive occurrence of the name. This is the case in *L'Age d'homme*, where we understand 'Michel' for 'Micheline';[12] but still, almost always, the name appears. Naturally, in general, the autobiographical contract does not mention the name: one's own name is such an obvious thing, and it will be on the cover anyway. It is because of this inevitability of the name that it never receives a formal avowal on the part of the author (the *author*, just because he is an author, always assumes that the reader knows him to some extent), but still sooner or later shows up in the narrative. For all that, it may be explicitly given, or, since it is always the name of an author, it may be only implicit, when the narrator acknowledges having written the other works of the author of the book (thus, while Quinet does not name himself, he names his books, which amounts to the same thing).

(b) Autobiographical contract: this is the most frequent case, for, very often, even if the contract is not formally avowed at the beginning of the book, it is present in scattered form throughout the text.

An example is the *Confessions* of Jean-Jacques Rousseau; the contract, expressed in the title, is developed in the preamble, and confirmed all through the text by the use of 'Rousseau' and 'Jean-Jacques'.

I will here use the term 'autobiography' for texts which fall under cases 2(c), 3(a), and 3(b); as for the rest, we will read the texts which fall under cases 1(a), 1(b), 2(a), and, if we want, 2(b), as novels (but without forgetting that it is *we* who decide).

In this kind of classification, it is always instructive to think carefully about the limiting cases, which are more revealing than those whose description poses no real problems. Are the alternatives which I have rejected really impossible? Two problems are worth exploring here: that of the two blanks in the above matrix, and then that of the anonymous author.

The blanks

(a) Can the hero of a novel which is declared to be such have the same name as its author? There is nothing to prevent this situation from existing, and it is, perhaps, an internal contradiction which could serve as the basis for interesting effects. However, in practice, no example comes to mind of such an attempt. When the case does arise, the reader has the impression that there has been a mistake: thus, the autobiography of Maurice Sachs, *Le Sabbat*, was published by Corrêa in 1946 with the subtitle *Souvenirs d'une jeunesse orageuse* (Memories of a stormy youth); it was reissued in 1960 by Gallimard (and again in 1971 in the *Livre de Poche*), with the subtitle 'roman' (novel). Since the story is narrated by Sachs in his own name (he even gives himself as well as his pseudonym, his real name: Ettinghausen), and the

207

publisher is clearly responsible for the subtitle, the reader concludes that there has been a mistake; (b) In an autobiography which is declared to be such, can the protagonist have a different name from the author (apart from cases involving a pseudonym)? It is difficult to find an example;[13] and if, in his desire for an artistic effect, an autobiographer chose this device, the reader would always wonder whether he was not simply reading a novel. It is clear that in both these cases, if the internal contradiction was intentionally chosen by an author, it would never result in a text that would be read as an autobiography, or, really, as a novel either, but rather in a Pirandello-like game playing with the ambiguity. To my knowledge, this is a game which is practically never played in earnest.

In the above matrix, the diagonal going from lower left to upper right, comprising the two empty boxes and the central one, thus covers a zone of indeterminateness – extending from the 'neither one nor the other' of the middle box to the 'both at once' of the two blanks.

The anonymous author

This matrix supposes that the author has a name; a tenth case should therefore be envisaged, that of the anonymous author. But this case (along with the subdivisions generated according to whether the protagonist has a name or not, and whether a publisher establishes some contract with the reader in place of the missing author) is also excluded by definition, since the author of an autobiography cannot be anonymous. If the absence of the author's name is accidental (as with an unsigned unpublished manuscript found in an attic) there are two possibilities: either, at some point in the text, the narrator gives his name, and elementary historical research reveals whether a real person is involved, given that by definition an autobiography tells a story that is assigned to a particular time and place; or else the narrator–protagonist does not name himself, and then either the text belongs to category 2(b), or is just fiction. If the anonymity is intentional (as in a published text), then the reader has the right to be suspicious. The text may look true, may give all sorts of checkable or plausible details, may sound like the real thing, but all this can be counterfeited. At best, this would be a kind of limiting case, similar to category 2(b). Everything depends in such a case on the reader's decision. An idea of the complexity of the problem can be obtained by reading, for example, the *Memoires d'un vicaire de campagne, écrits par lui-même* (1841), attributed to l'abbé Epineau, who is supposed to have been forced by his ecclesiastical responsibilities to remain temporarily anonymous.[14]

Of course, in stating that it is impossible for an autobiography to be anonymous, I am only giving a corollary of my definition, not proving it to be correct. Anyone who wants to is free to claim that it *is* possible, but then he has to propose a different definition. Everything depends, clearly, on the connection that I have established, through the notion of the *author*, between the person and his name, as well as on the fact that I have chosen to define autobiography from the reader's point of view. For any reader, a text which looks autobiographical, but is not claimed by some individual, looks exactly like a work of fiction.

However, I believe that this definition, far from being arbitrary, brings out the essential point. What defines an autobiography, for the person who reads it, is above all a contract guaranteeing 'identity' sealed by the name of its signer. This is also true for the person who writes it. If I write the story of my life without giving my name, how is my reader to know that it was *me*? It is impossible for the autobiographical vocation and the passion for anonymity to coexist in the same being.

Thus the distinctions proposed here, and the focus on the name, have great importance on the practical level as classificatory criteria; on the level of theory, they necessitate a whole series of observations, which I will give only in outline.

(a) *The author and the person*: autobiography is the literary genre which, by its very content, most clearly exhibits the confusion between the author and the individual person, on which all of the theory and practice of Western literature since the end of the eighteenth century is based. This explains the passion for the name, which goes beyond simple author's vanity, for it expresses the cry for existence of personal identity itself. The deep subject of autobiography is the proper name. One recalls those drawings by Hugo, where his own name is spread in gigantic letters across a chiaroscuro landscape. The desire for glory, for eternity, so cruelly debunked by Sartre in *Les Mots*, depends entirely on the personal name which has become an author's name. Is it possible to imagine today an *anonymous* literature? Valéry was already dreaming of one fifty years ago, but he does not seem to have thought of turning that dream into a reality, since he ended up in the Académie Française. He offered himself the glory of dreaming of anonymity. The *Tel Quel* group, by calling into question the notion of the author (replacing it by the notion of the 'scripteur') makes a similar proposal, but has shown no greater interest in putting it into practice.

(b) *The person and language*: we saw above that it was legitimate to ask, with respect to the 'first person', whether it was the psychological person (conceived naively as being external to language) which expressed itself by using the grammatical person as instrument, or whether rather the psychological person was an *effect* of the act of utterance itself. The word 'person' contributes to this ambiguity. If there is no person outside of language, then, since language is other people, we would have to conclude that autobiographical discourse, far from referring, as everyone imagines, to an 'I' to be cashed as a series of personal names, is on the contrary an alienated discourse, a mythological voice by which each of us is possessed. Naturally, autobiographers are in general as far removed as possible from the problems of Beckett's hero in *L'Innommable* asking who it is inside him who says 'I', but such anxiety emerges in a few books, for example *Le Traître* by Gorz, or rather the sort of 'transcription' of it produced by Sartre (*Des rats et des hommes*). Sartre gives the name 'vampire' to these voices that possess us. No doubt the autobiographical voice is one example. We could then envisage – once the psychology and mystique of the individual are demythologized – developing an analysis of the discourse of subjectivity and individuality as a myth of our civilization. Everyone is, in fact, aware of the danger in this indeterminacy of the first person, and it is not an accident that we attempt to resolve the indeterminacy by anchoring it to the proper name.

(c) *The proper name and the 'proper body'*: in the development of the individual, acquiring his own name is doubtless as important a milestone as the 'mirror stage'. This acquisition occurs at a moment inaccessible to memory, or to autobiography, which can speak only of those second and inverted baptisms which consist, for a child, in the accusations which freeze him in a role by means of a label: 'thief', for Genet, 'Yid', for Albert Cohen (*O Vous, frères humains*, 1972). The name first received and carried, the father's, and above all the given name, which distinguishes you from your father, are without a doubt important facts for the history of the self. Proof of this is the fact that one's name is never neutral, whether one adores it or detests it, whether one is willing to have it from someone else or prefers to receive it only from oneself: this may go as far as a generalized system of games or evasions, as with Stendhal,[15] or a preference for the Christian name, as with Jean-Jacques (Rousseau); more banally, it may result in all those private or parlour or chance playings with this string of letters which each of us feels instinctively to contain the essence of his being. There is play with the spelling, or the meaning of a name: for example, with the bad luck of being called François Nourissier[16] [cf. 'nourricier' = nutritious, foster-father, 'nourisher']; or with its gender: is it Michel or Micheline Leiris (cf. note 12)? The name can be present in the voices of those who say it: 'Ah Rousseau, I thought you were good-natured', said Marion. There can be pondering by a child on the arbitrariness of his name, and an attempt to find another name which is essential rather than accidental, as with Jacques Madaule.[17] There can be a history of the name itself, often in what is for the reader tiresome detail, in those prefaces that read like family trees.

When, therefore, we look for something to distinguish fiction from autobiography, to serve as a basis for the referent of 'I' in first-person narratives, there is no need to appeal to an impossible region 'outside-the-text': the text itself provides, on its outer edge, this final term, the proper name of the author, which is at once textual and indubitably referential. This referentiality is indubitable because it is based on two social institutions: the legal identity of the individual (a convention which is internalized by each of us from early childhood) and the publisher's contract; there is hence no reason to doubt the author's identity.

Certified true copy

'Identity' is not resemblance. Identity is a *fact* that is immediately apprehended – accepted, or rejected – on the level of the speech act ('énonciation'); resemblance is a *relation*, and as such is subject to discussion and infinite qualification, and is established on the basis of the utterance ('énoncé').

The 'identity' in question involves three terms: the author, the narrator, and the protagonist. The narrator and the protagonist are the entities referred to, within the text, by the subject of the speech act, i.e. the utterer, and the subject of the utterance; the author, who is represented on the outer edge of the text by his name, is, then, the referent who is designated, through the autobiographical contract, by the utterer.

In dealing with *resemblance*, we are forced to introduce a fourth term into the equation to obtain symmetry with what we have on the utterance side, an extratextual referent who might be called the 'prototype', or, better yet, the *model*.

My thinking about identity has led me to draw a primary distinction between the autobiographical novel and the autobiography; for resemblance, it is the opposition with *biography* that will have to be sharpened. In both cases, in fact, our vocabulary is a source of error: 'autobiographical novel' is too close to the word 'autobiography', which is itself too close to 'biography' for confusion not to take place. Is not an autobiography, as its name indicates, just the biography of an individual written by himself? We tend consequently to perceive it as a particular case of biography, and to apply to it the historicizing approach of that genre. Many autobiographers, whether amateurs or established writers, fall naively into this trap, for this illusion is necessary for the functioning of the genre.

In opposition to all forms of fiction, biography and autobiography are *referential* texts: exactly like scientific or historical discourse, they claim to convey information about a 'reality' which is external to the text and hence to be subject to the test of *verification*. Their goal is not mere 'vraisemblance' but resemblance to the truth. Not the 'reality effect' ('l'effet de réel'), but the image of reality. All referential texts thus embody what I will call a *referential contract*, implicit or explicit, in which are included a specification of the area

211

P. Lejeune

of reality being treated and a statement of the manner and degree of resemblance the text is claimed to possess.

In the case of autobiography, the referential contract is in general coextensive with the autobiographical contract. Like the subject of the speech act and the subject of the utterance in the case of the first person, they are difficult to dissociate. Its formula is not 'I, the undersigned', but 'I swear by Almighty God that the evidence I shall give shall be the truth, the whole truth, and nothing but the truth.' The oath is rarely taken in such abrupt and total form: it is a supplementary proof of the author's honesty to restrict it to the *possible* (the truth as I see it, insofar as I am able to determine it, etc., given the inevitable memory lapses, errors, involuntary distortions, etc.), and to indicate explicitly the *domain* to which the oath applies (the truth about a given aspect of my life, without any commitments regarding other aspects).

It can be seen how this contract resembles that entered into by any historian, geographer, or journalist, with his readers; but one has to be naive not to see the differences as well. We need not speak of the practical difficulties involved in applying the test of *verification* in the case of auto-biography, due to the fact that the autobiographer is telling us precisely – and that is what makes his account interesting – what he alone is able to tell us. Biographical study can easily enable us to assemble other information and determine the degree of exactitude of the account. The difference does not lie here, but in the fact that, rather paradoxically, this exactitude is not of primary importance. In autobiography, it is indispensable that the referential contract be *made*, and *respected*, but it is not necessary that the result be an absolutely faithful resemblance. The referential contract can be, by the reader's criteria, imperfectly respected, without the referential value of the text disappearing – on the contrary – and this is not the case for historical or journalistic texts.

This apparent paradox is of course due to the confusion which I have maintained so far, following the example of most authors and critics, between biography and autobiography. To remove it, we must reconstitute our fourth term: the *model*.

By 'model', I mean the reality to which the utterance claims resemblance. How a text can 'resemble' a life is a question that biographers rarely ask themselves and that they always implicitly assume to have been answered. The 'resemblance' can hold on two levels: negatively – and on the level of the facts given in the narrative – there is the criterion of *exactitude*; positively – and on the level of the narrative as a whole – there is what we will call *fidelity*. Exactitude concerns *information*, fidelity *meaning*. The fact that meaning can be created only through the techniques of narrative and with the help of an explanatory system involving the ideology of the historian does not prevent the biographer from conceiving of it as the same sort of thing as exactitude,

212

bearing a relation of resemblance to the extratextual reality to which the entire text refers. Thus Sartre states shamelessly that his biography of Flaubert is a 'true story' ('un roman vrai').[18] The model, in the case of biography, is thus the life of a man 'just as it was'.

We can thus construct a diagram (see p. 214) to represent the biographical enterprise, in which the columns represent the text and the extratextual, and the rows the subject of the speech act and the subject of the utterance. Inclosed within the boundary lines separating the text from the extratextual is the author, who occupies the marginal position corresponding to that of his name on the cover of the book.

Comments on the diagram. In biography, the author and the narrator are sometimes related by the identity relation. This relation can remain implicit or indeterminate, or can be stated explicitly, for example in a preface (as in *L'Idiot de la famille*, where the biographer, Sartre, explains that he has a score to settle with his model Flaubert). It can also be the case that no relation of 'identity' is established between the author and the narrator. What is important is that, if the narrator uses the first person, he never does so to speak of the main character of his story, who must be someone else. When the protagonist is spoken of, the principal mode of narration is the third person, what Genette calls 'hétérodiégétique' narrative. The relation between the protagonist (in the text) and the model (the referent outside the text) is to be sure first of all a relation of 'identity', but it is above all a relation of *resemblance*. In fact, in the case of the subject of the utterance, the identity relation does not have the same *value* that it has for the subject of the speech act: it is simply a fact concerning the utterance, on a par with other facts. It does not prove anything, and it itself needs to be proved by resemblance.

We can already see here what will fundamentally oppose biography and autobiography: the relative importance of the relations of resemblance and 'identity'. In biography, resemblance is the basis for 'identity'; in autobiography, 'identity' is the basis for resemblance. 'Identity' is the actual starting point for autobiography; resemblance is the unattainable goal of biography. This explains the different functions of resemblance in the two systems.

This becomes obvious when we consider the diagram corresponding to autobiography (see p. 215).

The personal ('autodiégétique') narrative is seen here to be not at all reducible to the impersonal ('hétérodiégétique') narrative.

In the case of the personal narrative what does the equals sign connecting the subject of the speech act and the subject of the utterance (signal) stand for? It implies actual 'identity'; and this 'identity', in turn, entails a certain form of resemblance. Resemblance to whom? If the narrative is entirely in the past tense, the resemblance between the protagonist and the model can,

P. Lejeune

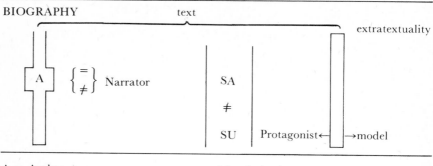

A = Author
SA = Subject of speech act
SU = Subject of utterance

= means 'identical to'
≠ means 'not identical to'
⟷ means 'resembles'

as with biography, be conceived exclusively as a verifiable relation between the protagonist and the model; but any narration in the first person implies that the protagonist, even if long-past experiences are being spoken of, is also the *present* individual who is producing the narrative: the subject of the utterance is a double subject, in that it is inseparable from the subject of the speech act; it only becomes simple, if at all, when the narrator is speaking of his current act of narrating, and never at the other extreme, to designate a protagonist independent of any present narrator.

It is thus clear that the relation expressed by the equals sign is not at all a simple relation, but rather a *relation between relations*; what is meant is that the narrator is to the protagonist (past or present) what the author is to the model; it can be seen that this implies that the ultimate standard of truth (if we are thinking in terms of resemblance) cannot be the past individual as thing-in-itself ('être-en-soi') (if in fact such a thing exists), but the *pour-soi*, the present consciousness of the individual, as manifested at the time of utterance. If the narrator errs, lies, forgets, or distorts, with respect to his relation to the history (whether remote or almost contemporaneous) of his protagonist, these errors, lies, omissions or distortions, if we perceive them, will simply be taken as further aspects of his nevertheless authentic speech act. Let us use the term 'authenticity' for this internal relation, which is characteristic of the use of the first person in a personal narrative; it is not to be confused either with 'identity', which concerns the proper name, or with resemblance, which involves a judgement of similarity between two different images that is made by a third party.

This detour was necessary to understand the inadequacy of our diagram for autobiography. The illusion involved is shared by all who think of autobiography in terms of biography. In constructing the diagram for

214

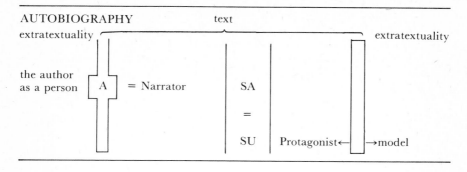

biography, I was led, because of the non-identity between the narrator and the protagonist, to distinguish two 'sides' for extratextual reference, putting the author on the left and the model on the right. The fact that the relations involved were *simple* – 'identity' on the author side and resemblance on the model side – allowed a linear representation. For autobiography, 'reference' exists on just one side (since there is fusing of the author and the model) and the relation which links identity and resemblance is in fact a relation between relations which cannot be represented linearly.

We thus have the following formulas:

Biography: A is or is not N; P resembles M.
Autobiography: N is to P what A is to M.
(A = author; N = narrator; P = protagonist; M = model)

Since autobiography is a referential genre, it is naturally also subject to the requirement that there be resemblance with the model, but this is only a secondary aspect. That *we* judge that there is no resemblance is not essential, as long as we are sure that resemblance was intended. What is important is not so much the resemblance between 'Rousseau at the age of sixteen' as represented in the text of the *Confessions*, and the Rousseau of 1728 as he 'really' was, but the attempt by Rousseau about 1764 to *depict*: (1) his relation to the past; (2) that past as it really was, with the intention of not changing anything.

With 'identity', the limiting and exceptional case, which proved the rule, was that of the *hoax*; with resemblance, it will be *mythomania*: that is, not just the mistakes, distortions, and interpretations that are an inevitable secretion of the personal myth in any autobiography, but the substitution of an account that is a barefaced *invention*, and lacking *in general* any exact

215

correspondence with the author's life. As with hoaxes, this is extremely rare, and the referentiality which is claimed for the narrative is easily undermined by research in literary history. But even if it is shown not to be autobiography, the narrative will retain its interest considered as fantasizing (on the level of the utterance), and the fraudulency of the autobiographical contract, considered as behaviour, will still be revelatory for us (on the level of the speech act), of a subject who still has autobiographical intentions, and whom we will continue to take as existing behind the phoney subject. This is equivalent to analysing, from a different point of view, not the relation of biography to autobiography, but that of the novel to autobiography, to defining what might be called *autobiographical space*, and the *three-dimensional* effect it produces.

Autobiographical space

It is now time to show the naivety of the illusion on which is based the widespread theory according to which the novel is truer (deeper, more authentic) than the autobiography. This commonplace, like all commonplaces, has no originator; each writer in turn has expressed it in his own way. According to Gide, for instance 'Memoirs are never more than half sincere, no matter how great the concern for truth: everything is always more complicated than people say it is. Perhaps we even come closer to truth with the novel.'[19] Or François Mauriac: 'But this is to seek in lofty regions for excuses for stopping my memoirs after only one chapter. Is the real reason for my laziness not rather that our novels express what is essential in ourselves? Only fiction does not lie; it opens slightly a secret door on a man's life and through it slips, beyond all control, his unknown soul.'[20] Albert Thibaudet has given to the commonplace the academic twist of 'parallelism', the ideal school essay subject, opposing the novel (deep and multifarious) to the autobiography (superficial and schematic).[21]

I will demonstrate the illusion on the basis of the formulation offered by Gide, if only because his work provides incomparable material for the demonstration. The reader need not worry: I have not the slightest intention of coming to the defence of the autobiographical genre, and proving the truth of the contrary proposition, namely that it is autobiography which is truer, deeper, etc. There would be no point at all in reversing Thibaudet's proposal, except perhaps to show that, in whatever direction it is read, it is still the same proposal.

The point is that when it *appears* that Gide and Mauriac are belittling the autobiography and glorifying the novel, in *reality* they are doing something quite different from setting up a more or less debatable schoolroom parallel: they are designating the autobiographical space within which they want us to read the body of their work. Far from being a condemnation of the autobiography, these remarks, so frequently quoted, are really an indirect form of the autobiographical contract: they give us the nature of the ultimate truth aimed at by these texts. The reader too often forgets that, in these judgements, autobiography presents itself on two levels: along with being one of the two *terms* of the comparison, it is the *criterion* used in the comparison. What is this 'truth' that the novel helps us to come closer to than the autobiography, if not the personal, individual, intimate truth of the author, that is, that very thing which is the object of any autobiographical project? So to speak, it is insofar as it is autobiography that the novel is declared to be closer to the truth.

The reader is thus invited to read novels not just as *fictions* which point to truths of 'human nature', but also as *fantasies* which reveal an individual. I will call this indirect form of the autobiographical contract the *fantasmatic contract*.

If hypocrisy is the homage which vice pays to virtue, these judgements are really the homage which the novel pays to autobiography. If the novel is truer than the autobiography, then why have Gide, Mauriac, and so many others not been content to write novels? When the question is formulated thus, things become clear: if they had not *also* written and published autobiographical texts, even 'insufficient' ones, we would never have seen what kind of truth it was that we were supposed to look for in their novels. These statements are therefore ruses, perhaps involuntary, but still quite efficacious: a writer sidesteps accusations of vanity and egocentrism when he shows how lucid he is about the limits and inadequacies of his autobiography; and nobody realizes that, in doing so, he has in fact extended the autobiographical contract, in an indirect form, to the totality of what he has written. Two birds have been killed with one stone.

A double blow, or rather, double *vision* – double writing, an effect, if I may be allowed a neologistic use of the word, of *stereography*.

Looked at in this fashion, the problem is completely different in nature. We are no longer asking which is closer to the truth – the autobiography or the novel. Neither is closer than the other: the autobiography is lacking in complexity, in ambiguity, etc.; the novel lacks exactitude. Is the answer then: one of them plus the other? A better answer is: each of them *in relation to* the other. What is truly revelatory is the space in which the two categories of texts are situated, and which is not reducible to either of them alone. This effect of three-dimensionality which is obtained by the procedure in question is the creation for the reader of an 'autobiographical space'. In this regard, the work of Gide and of Mauriac is typical: both have orchestrated, albeit, it is true, for different reasons, the spectacular failure of their autobiographies, so as to force their readers to read all the rest of their narrative production in the autobiographical mode. When I speak of failure, I intend no value judgement on texts which are admirable (Gide) or respectable (Mauriac), but simply echo their own statements, and observe that they have *chosen* to leave their autobiographies incomplete, fragmentary, full of gaps, and open.[22]

This form of indirect contract has become more and more widespread. Formerly it was the reader who, in spite of the denials of the author, took the initiative, and assumed responsibility for this type of reading; today authors and publishers orient the reader in this direction from the very start. It is revealing that Sartre himself, who briefly envisaged continuing *Les Mots* in fictional form, repeated Gide's words: 'It is about time I finally told the truth. But I can only do it in a work of fiction', and that he formulated the contract he would have proposed to his readers as follows:[23]

I then planned to write a story in which I wanted to present indirectly everything that I had previously thought I would say in a kind of political testament which would have been the continuation of my autobiography, which I had abandoned. The fictional element would have been quite minor; I would have created a character of which the reader would have been able to say: 'This man presented here is Sartre.'

This does not mean that, for the reader, there would have been exact identity between the protagonist and the author, but that the best way to understand the protagonist would have been to look in him for what came from me.

All these games, which clearly show the predominance of autobiographical intentions, can be found, to varying degrees, in many modern writers. It can also, naturally, be imitated within a novel. This is what Jacques Laurent does in *Les Bêtises* (Grasset, 1971), where he gives us both the piece of fiction that his protagonist is supposed to have written and various 'autobiographical' texts of the protagonist to read. If Laurent ever publishes his own auto-biography, the texts in *Les Bêtises* will create a dizzying number of 'dimensions'.

The reading contract

A stock-taking at the conclusion of our survey indicates that the nature of the problem we started with has changed:

Negative aspects: certain points remain vague or inadequate. For example, it can be asked how the fact that the author and the narrator are the same person can be established in the autobiographical contract when the name is not repeated (cf. above, p. 205); there may be scepticism about the distinctions I have proposed in 'Certified true copy'. Above all, the sections entitled 'I, the undersigned' and 'Certified true copy' consider only the case of autobiography using 'autodiégétique' narration, even though I noted that other kinds of narration are *possible*: would the distinctions established still hold in the case of third-person autobiography?

Positive aspects: on the other hand, my analyses seem to me to be productive whenever, going beyond the apparent structures of the text, they lead me to reexamine critically the positions of the *author* and the *reader*. The 'social contract' engaged in by the use of the author's name, and by the act of publication, the autobiographical contract, the fictional, referential, and fantasmatic contracts, all of the expressions used convey the idea that autobiography is a *contractual* genre. The difficulty I encountered in my earlier attempt was due to the fact that I was seeking in vain, on the level of the structures, modes, or voices of the narrative, some clear criteria to justify a difference which any reader in fact experiences. The notion of 'autobiographical contract' which I formulated at that time remained unanchored, because I failed to see that the proper name was an essential element of the contract. That something so obvious did not then occur to me shows that this kind of contract is implicit, and, because it seems to be part of the nature of things, hardly encourages reflection.

The approach to autobiography proposed here is, therefore, not based on an externally established relation between the text and what is outside it – for such a relation could be only a relation of resemblance, and would prove nothing. Nor is it based on an internal analysis of the functioning of the text, of the structure or of aspects of published texts; rather, it is based on an analysis, at the global level of *publication*, of the implicit or explicit contract proposed by the *author* to the *reader*, the contract which determines how the text is read, and produces the effects which, attributed to the text, seem to us to define it as an autobiography.

The level of analysis used is therefore that of the relation between *publication* and *published*, which is the parallel for the printed text to the relation between speech act and utterance on the level of oral communication. To be carried further, research on contracts between author and reader, on implicit or explicit publishing codes – on that borderline area of the printed text which in reality *governs* all of our reading (author's name, title, subtitle, title of the series, publisher's name, down to the ambiguous function of the preface) – such research should include a historical dimension which I have not given it here.[24] Chronological variations in these codes (which are due both to changes in the attitudes of authors and readers and to the technical or economic problems of publishers) would make it much easier to see that we are dealing with codes, and not with 'natural' or universal states of affairs. For instance, since the seventeenth century, behaviour with respect to anonymity and the use of pseudonyms has changed a great deal; writers who make claims that their fiction is really true do not play the game today according to the same rules that were used in the eighteenth century;[25] readers, on the other hand, have acquired a taste for trying to ferret out the presence of the author (or his unconscious) even beneath the surface of works which do not look autobiographical, so great is the extent to which fantasmatic contracts have created new reading habits.

This global level is the one on which autobiography is characterized: it is as much a way of reading as a kind of writing; it is an historically variable *contractual product*. The present study, in reality, is based totally on the types of contract in use at present: this explains its relativity, and the absurdity of trying to take it as universally valid. This explains also the difficulties we have encountered in this attempt to define our subject – I wanted to make explicit, in a system which was clear, coherent and exhaustive, and which accounted for all cases, the criteria determining a corpus (that of autobiography) which in reality is determined by multiple criteria which vary across time and from person to person, and are often mutually inconsistent. Anyone who managed to find a clear and total formulation for autobiography would in fact have failed. The reader, in the course of this essay which I have tried to make as rigorous as possible, will often have felt that this rigour was becoming arbitrary, and inadequate for an object which perhaps is more appropriately treated in terms of Chinese logic, as Borges describes it, than in terms of the logic of Descartes.

When all is said and done, this study seems to me more of a document to be itself studied – the attempt of a twentieth-century reader to make his reading criteria rational and explicit – than a 'scientific' text: a document belonging to an historical science of the modes of literary *communication*.

The history of autobiography would, on this view, be above all the history of how it is read; it would be comparative history, where the reading contracts proposed by various types of texts could be made explicit (for there is no point in studying autobiography in isolation, since contracts, like signs, have meaning only through their being in opposition), and confronted with the different kinds of reading actually applied to these texts. If, therefore, autobiography is to be defined in terms of something outside the text, this is not to be done by falling short of the text, by aiming at an unverifiable resemblance to a real individual, but by aiming beyond it, defining it in terms of the kind of reading it engenders, the inherent credibility it reveals, which can be elicited from the critical text.

Notes

1. Philippe Lejeune, *L'Autobiographie en France* (Paris, A. Colin, 1971).
2. Gérard Genette, *Figures III* (Paris, Seuil, 1972).
3. Claude Roy, *Nous, Essai d'Autobiographie* (Paris, Gallimard, 1972), pp. 33–9.
4. As, for example, Rousseau does in Book IV of the *Confessions*: 'Poor Jean-Jacques, in that cruel moment you hardly hoped that one day . . .'; cf. also Claude Roy, in *Moi, je* (Paris, Gallimard, 1970), p. 473, where he imagines himself speaking to the person he once was: 'Believe me, my child, you should not . . . You ought not to

have done it.' On this page, Roy, opposing the (present) narrator to the (past) protagonist, uses both the second and the third person to speak to the latter.

5. Emile Benveniste, *Problèmes de linguistique générale* (Paris, Gallimard, 1966) Section v: 'L'Homme dans la langue'.

6. Concerning the linguistic aspects of the problem of the proper name and the way it contributes, in the speech act, to reference, see Oswald Ducrot and Tzvetan Todorov, *Dictionnaire encyclopédique des sciences du langage* (Paris, Seuil, 1972), pp. 321–2.

7. The problem of reference in *written* speech acts, in which the utterer and the person to whom the discourse is directed do not share the same situation (and may not even know each other), is too seldom considered by linguists, or else is mentioned as something which should be studied – but which is not (cf. E. Benveniste, 'L'Appareil formel de l'énonciation', *Langages* 17 (March 1970), p. 18).

8. The case of hoaxes, or the problems of the author's identity (anonymity, the pseudonym), can be studied, to begin with, in the classic works of J.-M. Quérard, *Les Supercheries littéraires dévoilées* (1847), or A. Barbier, *Dictionnaire des ouvrages anonymes*, 3rd edn (1872). For an amusing inventory of recent hoaxes, see *Gulliver* 1 (November 1972).

9. Raymond Abellio, *Ma dernière mémoire, I, un faubourg de Toulouse, 1907–1927* (Paris, Gallimard, 1971), pp. 82–3.

10. Bertrand Poirot-Delpech, in *Le Monde* (13 October, 1972).

11. 'She would recover her voice, she would say: "My" or "My dear", followed in either case by my Christian name, which would have made, giving the narrator the same name as the author of this book: "My Marcel", "My dear Marcel".' Marcel Proust, *A la recherche du temps perdu* (Paris, Gallimard, Bibliothèque de la Pléiade, 1954) vol. 3, p. 75. The occurrence on page 157 is merely a repetition.

12. Michel Leiris, *L'Age d'homme* (Paris, Gallimard, collection 'Folio', 1973), p. 174.

13. In spite of appearances, this is not the case with Stendhal's *Vie de Henry Brulard*. This text poses very delicate problems because it is unfinished, and was not ready for immediate publication. Consequently it is difficult to decide whether Henry Brulard is a pseudonym or just the name of a character, since the text never reached the form of a manuscript conceived in terms of publication: the humorous titles were meant, not for the publisher, but for 'M. M. de la Police' in case of a surprise visit; the subtitle 'Novel imitated from *The Vicar of Wakefield*' had the same function of burlesque flimflam. The fact that this is a genuine autobiography, temporarily 'camouflaged', becomes obvious when we read the text itself. The name '*Brulard*' appears only three times in the text (Stendhal, *Oeuvres Intimes* (Paris, Gallimard, Bibliothèque de la Pléiade, 1955), pp. 6, 42, and 250). Two out of these three occasions reveal the camouflaging: on p. 6, 'Brulard' is written over Stendhal's true name 'Beyle'; on p. 250, the first version of the 'seven letters' of 'Brulard' was 'five letters'; and throughout this delightful passage 'Bernard' is to 'Brulard' as 'Brulard' is to 'Beyle'. The rest of the time, the family name is given as 'B.' (which can be applied to either 'Beyle' or 'Brulard') or else merely as Beyle, 'signing' the text as autobiography (pp. 60, 76, 376), or as 'S.' (Stendhal) (p. 247), which amounts to the same thing.

14. These anonymous *Mémoires*, in their second edition (1843) are prefaced by A. Aumétayer. The preface carries the ambiguity to the extreme.

15. Cf. Jean Starobinski, 'Stendhal pseudonyme', in *L'Oeil Vivant* (Paris, Gallimard, 1961).

16. François Nourissier, *Un Petit Bourgeois* (Paris, Livre de Poche, 1969), pp. 81–4.

P. Lejeune

17. Jacques Madaule, *L'Interlocuteur* (Paris, Gallimard, 1972), pp. 34–5.
18. Interview in *Le Monde* (14 May 1971).
19. André Gide, *Si le grain ne meurt* (Paris, Gallimard, collection 'Folio', 1972), p. 278.
20. François Mauriac, 'Commencements d'une vie', in *Ecrits Intimes*, (Geneva/Paris, La Palatine, 1953), p. 14.
21. Albert Thibaudet, *Gustave Flaubert* (Paris, Gallimard, 1935), pp. 87–8.
22. See my 'Gide et l'espace autobiographique', in *Le Pacte autobiographique* (Paris, Seuil, 1975), pp. 165–96.
23. Interview with Michel Contat, in *Le Nouvel Observateur* (23 June 1975).
24. Concerning this problem, see my 'Autobiographie et histoire littéraire', in *Le Pacte autobiographique*, pp. 311–41.
25. Cf. Jacques Rustin, 'Mensonge et vérité dans le roman français du XVIIIᵉ siècle', *Revue d'histoire littéraire de la France* (January–February 1969).

11. A complication of text: the *Illuminations*

TZVETAN TODOROV

Ma sagesse est aussi dédaignée que le chaos. Qu'est mon néant
auprès de la stupeur qui vous attend?

Rimbaud, Vies I

(My wisdom is as disdained as chaos. What is my nothingness next to
the stupor which awaits you?)

The real problem of the *Illuminations* is obviously not chronological but
semantic: what are these enigmatic texts about, and what do they mean? The
literature on Rimbaud is particularly copious, so one can hardly avoid
turning to it in search of an answer, and, although most writers have been
much more interested in Rimbaud's travels in England or the Harrar, in his
homosexual experiences or drug-taking, than in the meaning of his texts,
there do exist a number of studies devoted to the interpretation of the
Illuminations. Reading them, however, I have the impression that they fall
short of, or immediately overshoot, the real problem posed by this group of
'poems in prose'. Thus, to place in context my own reaction to this text, I
must summarize briefly the different attitudes it has inspired in the past, and
explain why they appear unsatisfactory to me.

I will use the term *Euhemerist criticism* for one form of reaction to Rimbaud's
text which, to my mind, cannot really be called an 'interpretation'.
Euhemerus was an ancient Greek writer who read Homer as a source of
information about the people and places described in the epics, as a factual
(and not imaginary) narrative; Euhemerist reading passes through the text
without the slightest pause, in a search for clues to some reality outside it.
Astonishing as it may seem, Rimbaud's work, though it seems so little
referential in its intention, has most often been read as a source of
information about the poet's life. This seems an especially precarious
undertaking in that his life is something we know little about, and the poetic
texts are often the only source we have: the biography is constructed from the
work, and yet some critics give the impression that they are explaining the
work from the life!

This can be seen from one of the texts from the *Illuminations* that are easiest
to understand: 'Ouvriers'. The expression 'cette chaude matinée de février'

223

(this warm February morning) and the indication that the scene of the action is not the south, prompt the following commentary from Antoine Adam: 'We are in a northern country, in February, and the temperature is mild. Now, in the period 1872–78, the temperature was especially mild in 1878 (the average in Oslo was 0 to 7 degrees). It has been said that Rimbaud travelled to Hamburg in the spring of 1878, and this vague indication, slightly modified, would fit the poem "Ouvriers".' To this Chadwick replies that the poem is to be dated to February 1873, because *The Times* mentions flooding in London in January, and the text also speaks of the water 'left by the flooding of the previous month'. Our critics have had to show ingenuity worthy of Sherlock Holmes, studying the weather reports over a ten-year period, and even so they are unable to prove their hypotheses, because of the poverty of the initial information (even when it has been 'slightly modified').

Clearly, the real problem lies elsewhere. Even if the textual indications matched the weather reports perfectly, going from one to the other would be extremely risky: it implies ignorance of the most elementary of distinctions, that between history and fiction, between documentary and poetry. Suppose that Rimbaud was not speaking of a real flood, or a warm winter that actually occurred? The very fact that we can ask these questions, and answer them in the affirmative, makes all the erudition of Adam or Chadwick beside the point. To learn this, it would have sufficed to read what Rimbaud himself has written: 'Ta mémoire et tes sens ne seront que la nourriture de ton impulsion créatice' (Your memory and your senses will be only the food of your creative impulse) ('Jeunesse IV').

Let us suppose, however, that the text does in fact describe Rimbaud's life. The reason I hesitate to call such a statement an interpretation is that it is, at best, a contribution to our knowledge of the poet's biography; it is not in the slightest an explication of his text. The 'satanic doctor' of 'Vagabonds' is, perhaps, Verlaine, as the commentators have all said, following Verlaine himself, and the water 'broad as an arm of the sea' in 'Les Ponts' is perhaps a description of the Thames, as is claimed, for example, by Suzanne Bernard; but the meaning of a text is not explained merely by giving the origin of its elements, even if the identifications are valid. The meaning of each word and each sentence is determined only in relation to the other words and sentences of the same text. It is embarrassing to have to state such a self-evident truth, but it seems not to be one for Rimbaud's commentators. Thus when Bernard says of 'Royauté', another especially clear text from the *Illuminations*: 'The text, in the present state of our knowledge, remains obscure', her comment seems to me totally beside the point: no unexpected discovery, no biographical key will make this work any clearer (nor does it need this), for the pretext which has nourished the 'memory' and the 'senses' does not contribute to the establishing of the sense.

A second attitude towards Rimbaud's text can be termed *aetiological criticism*. Here again, we cannot really speak of interpretation: rather than enquiring about the meaning of the text, the author asks what might have led Rimbaud to express himself as he did. Here instead of referential transparency we find a transparency oriented towards the poet, whose text is not really considered as an expression but as a kind of symptom. The most usual explanation of why Rimbaud wrote incoherently is his drug addiction. Rimbaud wrote under the influence of hashish. It is true that certain poems, for example 'Matinée d'ivresse', can give the impression of being the description of a drug experience. It is not obvious that this is so, but even if it were, it would add nothing to our understanding of the text. The statement that Rimbaud had taken hashish before writing some poem is as irrelevant to its interpretation as the information that he wrote it in the bathtub, or while wearing a red shirt, or with the window open. At best it is a contribution to the physiology of literary creation. The question that one should ask in reading 'Matinée d'ivresse' and comparable works is not: was the author drugged? but: how is this text to be read if one is not willing to abandon the search for its meaning? How is one to react to this incoherence, or this apparent incoherence?

Other specimens of aetiological criticism are those commentaries which say: if this text is strange, that is because it describes an operatic performance, or a painting, or an engraving; or (as Delahaye explains for 'Fleurs') because Rimbaud is lying in the grass on the edge of a pond, looking at the plants from close up. As for Thibaudet, he imagines in 'Mystique' an exhausted walker lying on his back on the ground, looking up at the sky. Here again the critic is content to identify (and such identifications are quite controversial) the experience which supposedly caused Rimbaud to write the poem, but he does not ask what the text means. Such statements, however, can be made in the framework of an interpretation, provided that we speak not of the picture which Rimbaud allegedly saw, but the one which his text creates – that we speak, that is, of the pictorial effect, not the pictorial pretext.

The other two critical attitudes which I wish to distinguish here do indeed involve interpretation: their object is to explain the meaning or the organization of the text. They do so, however, in a manner which seems to me to leave out what is most characteristic of the *Illuminations*, and thus to ignore the most important aspect of its message. This is fairly easy to see in the case of *esoteric criticism*. As with any obscure text, the *Illuminations* has received numerous esoteric interpretations that make everything clear: each element of the text – at least each problematic element – is replaced by another which is drawn from some variant of the universal symbolism, from psychoanalysis to alchemy. The strange 'son of the Sun' of 'Vagabonds' is really oneness, or love, or a pharaoh; the rainbow in 'Après le déluge' is the umbilical cord; the 'Fleurs' are the pure substance contained in metal. These interpretations are never confirmable, or refutable either, which gives them minimal interest; in addition, they translate the text bit by bit, with no attention to its articulation, and the final result, perfectly clear, provides no explanation for the initial obscurity: why would Rimbaud have found it amusing to encode these rather ordinary thoughts?

The fourth and last attitude towards Rimbaud's text deserves to be called *paradigmatic criticism*. Its starting point is the postulate, explicit or implicit, that continuity is without significance, that the task of the critic consists in gathering together elements which are more or less distant in the text, to show their similarity, or opposition, or relatedness; in short, that the paradigm is relevant, but not the syntagm. The text of Rimbaud, like any other text, is amenable to such operations, whether they are carried out on the thematic, structural–semantic, or grammatical and formal level. The only problem is that now there is no difference between the *Illuminations* and any other text. This is because the paradigmatic critic treats all texts as if they were *Illuminations*, lacking order, coherence, and continuity, since, even if he found these, he would not take them into account, and would set up in their place the paradigmatic order he himself has discovered. But what might already have seemed disputable in the analysis of other texts (the postulate of the irrelevance of the syntagmatic dimension, of discursive and narrative continuity) leads to an inadmissible result in the case of the *Illuminations*, since this approach provides no way to state the striking feature of this text, namely its surface incoherence. Because he treats all texts as if they were *Illuminations*, the paradigmatic critic can no longer say how the *Illuminations* itself differs from other texts.

I would like to formulate, in opposition to these various critical strategies, another position, which the text of the *Illuminations* seems to me to demand compellingly. It consists in taking seriously the difficulty we experience in reading the work; not considering it as some regrettable accident, a chance breakdown of the mechanisms that should have taken us to our goal – the meaning – but rather making it the very object of our enquiry; asking whether the principal message of the *Illuminations*, rather than lying in some content established by thematic or semic decomposition, does not lie in the *way* that the sense appears, or, perhaps, disappears. Whether, to view it on another level, an 'explication de texte' should not give way, in the case of the *Illuminations*, to a 'complication de texte', which would bring out clearly the impossibility in principle of any *explication*.

Whenever Rimbaud's text evokes a world, the author simultaneously does everything necessary to make us understand this world is not *real*. There may be supernatural and mythological beings or events, such as the triple metamorphosis in 'Bottom', the goddess in 'Aube', the angels in 'Mystique', or the hermaphrodite in 'Antique'; or objects and places whose size surpasses anything ever seen: 'This dome is an artistic steel structure about fifteen thousand feet in diameter' ('Villes ii'), 'the hundred thousand altars of the cathedral' ('Après le déluge'), the villa and its outbuildings which form a promontory as vast as Arabia ('Promontoire'), or the numberless bridges of various shapes ('Les Ponts'). Or there are simply objects which are physically possible but so improbable that we refuse to believe they exist: the boulevards of crystal in 'Métropolitain', the boulevards of theatrical stage boards in 'Scènes', the cathedral in the middle of the woods ('Enfance iii') and the 'castles of crystal and of wood which move on invisible rails and pulleys' ('Villes i'), the piano in the Alps and the Splendide-Hôtel at the pole ('Après le déluge').

When geographical indications occur, in order, it might seem, to slake the passions of an Euhemerus and allow identification of the places being spoken of, Rimbaud, as if in mockery, likes to blend regions and continents. The fabled promontory recalls Epirus and the Peloponnese, Japan and Arabia, Carthage and Venice, Etna and Germany, Scarbro' and Brooklyn, and, as if that were not enough, 'Italy, America and Asia' ('Promontoire'). The idol is at once 'Mexican and Flemish', the boats have 'Greek, Slavic, and Celtic' names ('Enfance i'); the aristocracies are German, Japanese, and Guarani ('Métropolitain'); Germany, the Tartar deserts, the Celestial Empire, Africa, and even the 'Occidents' come together in 'Soir historique'. Where is the country described in these texts? That is a problem never to be solved by learned dispute between the partisans of Java and the experts who favour England.

Often a phrase or word says openly that what is being described is only an image, an illusion, a dream. Improbable bridges disappear in the light of the sun: 'A ray of white, from out of the sky, annihilates this comedy' ('Les Ponts'); and the geographical locations of these fabulous cities are clearly given: 'What kind arms, what lovely hour will give back to me that region from which come my sleeps and my slightest movements?' ('Villes i'). The beings evoked in 'Métropolitain' are 'fantasmagories'. The dream is no longer for Rimbaud, as it was for Baudelaire, for example, a thematic element, but rather a reading device, an indication as to how one is to interpret the text one has before one's eyes. The characters in 'Parade' are dressed 'with the taste of a bad dream', and the mountains of 'Villes' are also 'of a dream'; 'postillion and dream animals' pass through 'Nocturne vulgaire' and 'Veillées' speaks of dreams. Furthermore, the theatrical and 'opéradique' vocabulary of the *Illuminations* has long been recognized; rather than taking this as proof that Rimbaud often went to the theatre during his stay in London, should we not regard this as a clue to the fictive, illusory

227

nature of what is being spoken of? Is it not non-existence, after all, which characterizes so many other things the poet mentions, from the 'impossible melodies' of *Soir historique* to 'inns which forever have already shut their doors' ('Métropolitain') and the invisible castle parks, where 'in any case, there is nothing to see' ('Enfance II')? All the regions of the *Illuminations*, and not just the arctic flowers in 'Barbare', deserve this incisive, definitive comment: 'Elles n'existent pas.'

But asserting the fictitious character of the referent is simply the most conventional way of raising doubts about the ability of a piece of writing to summon a world into existence. Besides this discrediting of the referent we observe a much more insidious tampering with the referential capacity of the discourse itself. The entities designated by the text of the *Illuminations* are essentially indeterminate: we do not know where they have come from or where they are going, and the shock effect is still more striking because Rimbaud does not even seem to be aware of this indeterminateness, and continues to use the definite article in introducing them as if there were nothing odd in this. *The* precious stones, *the* flowers, *the* main street, *the* stalls, *the* blood, *the* circuses, *the* milk, *the* beavers, *the* tumblers, *the* big house, *the* children in mourning, *the* marvellous images, *the* caravans: these objects and beings appear (in 'Après le déluge'), one after the other, without our knowing anything about them, and without the poet noticing our ignorance – since he speaks as if we were informed. How is a reader to know, with no help, what an 'operadic breach' is, what 'whistling for the storm' is, what these 'suffocating groves' are, and what 'rolling on the bark of mastiffs' ('Nocturne vulgaire') involves? Expressions like 'the girl with lip of orange' (*'Enfance* IV'), 'the peaceful animals' ('Enfance IV'), 'the old man alone, calm and handsome' ('Phrases'), 'the music of the ancients' ('Métropolitain'), 'the ornamental saps' ('Fairy') and so many others do seem to evoke a specific entity, but one which, for lack of further information, we know nothing about, and which we have a great deal of difficulty imagining. These things are perceived for the infinitesimal instant of an illumination.

Taken in isolation, each of the objects mentioned is undetermined, for the mention is too brief, a lightning flash. We thus begin to look for some relational determination, of one of the objects to others, or (what amounts to the same thing) of one part of the text to another. And it is here that the shock is most violent: in the *Illuminations* discontinuity has become a fundamental rule. Rimbaud has made absence of organization the organizing principle of these texts, and this principle functions on all levels, from the poem as a whole down to the two-word group. This is evident, for example, in the relations between paragraphs: there are none. If we suppose that each paragraph of 'Métropolitain', for example, is summed up by the noun which ends it – and this is a continual source of problems – what is the connecting relationship that unites into a single text 'the city', 'the battle', 'the country', 'the sky', 'your strength'? Or, in 'Enfance I', what justifies the transition from the idol to the girl, the dances, and the princesses? All of the poems, not just one, could have been given the significant title 'Phrases' ('Sentences').

It might be thought that at least a new paragraph signalled a change of theme and so justified the lack of continuity. But the propositions within the paragraph, or even within the sentence, are piled up in the same disorganized fashion. Let us read, for example, the third paragraph of 'Métropolitain', already quite isolated from its neighbours:

Lift your head: this wooden bridge, arched; the last kitchen gardens of Samaria; these illuminated masks under the lantern whipped by the cold night; the foolish nymph with the noisy dress, at the bottom of the rivers; these luminous notches in the sheets of peas – and the other phantasmagorias – the country.

What unites all these 'phantasmagorias' into a single sentence? What allows the linking up, within a single paragraph, of 'The beavers built. The "mazagrans" smoked in the small bars' ('Après le déluge')? It is hard to tell whether one should be more surprised at the incoherence of the city described in 'Villes I' or at that of the text which describes it, which juxtaposes, in a single paragraph, chalets, craters, canals, gorges, abysses, inns, avalanches, a sea, flowers, a cascade, the suburbs, the caverns, the castles, the market-towns, the boulevard of Baghdad, and the rest. Those devices which are supposed to keep a discourse coherent – anaphoric and deictic pronouns – are here used to the opposite effect. 'Magic flowers buzzed. The slopes cradled him' ('Enfance II'): *who* did they cradle? 'How little you care, for these unhappy ones and these labourers' ('Phrases'): which ones? Or consider 'this personal atmosphere', 'and the embarrassment of the poor and the weak over these stupid plans!' ('Soir historique'): but there has been no previous mention of plans or atmosphere.

Conjunctions expressing logical relations (such as causality, for instance) are rare in the *Illuminations*; this is regretted less when one realizes that, when they do appear, it is extremely difficult to find a justification for their use, and so to understand them. As opposed to the 'syntactician' Mallarmé, Rimbaud is a lexical poet: he juxtaposes words which, innocent of any articulation, retain individually all of their urgency. The only relationship between events or sentences cultivated by Rimbaud is that of coexistence. Thus all the incongruous actions described in 'Après le déluge' are unified in time, since they take place 'as soon as the idea of the Deluge calmed down'; those of 'Soir historique' happen 'on some evening'; those of 'Barbare', 'long after the days and the seasons'. Even more common is coexistence in space: the purest example is to be found in 'Enfance III', where the adverbial phrase that begins the text – 'in the woods' – allows the juxtaposition in what follows of: a bird, a clock, a quagmire, a cathedral, a lake, a small carriage, and a company of small actors!

Quite often, spatial co-presence is underlined by explicit reference to an observer, whose immobility is implied by adverbial phrases like 'on the left', 'on the right', 'above', 'below'. 'On the right the summer dawn awakens . . . and the slopes on the left . . .' ('Ornières'). 'On the left the humus of the crest . . . behind the right-hand crest . . . And while the band above . . . below it' ('Mystique'). 'In a defect at the top of the mirror on the right . . .' ('Nocturne vulgaire'). 'The wall opposite . . .' ('Veillées II'). The impression is thus clearly given of a description of a painting, made by a motionless observer examining it, and the word for a painting, 'tableau', appears in 'Mystique', as does 'image' in 'Nocturne vulgaire', but these are the images produced by the texts themselves: descriptive immobility inevitably suggests the art of the painter. Nominal sentences produce the same effect of immobility, of pure spatial and temporal coexistence, and they are abundant in the *Illuminations*. Sometimes they occupy strategic positions which are particularly important in the text, as in 'Being Beauteous', 'Veillées II', 'Fête d'hiver', 'Soir historique', 'Angoisse', 'Fairy', 'Nocturne vulgaire', 'Enfance II', 'Matinée d'ivresse', 'Scènes'; sometimes they are spread out through the whole poem, as in 'Barbare', 'Dévotion', 'Ornières', 'Départ', 'Veillées III'.

It is thus not surprising that these texts are so amenable to the 'paradigmatic' approach: in the absence of explicit connections, the question of articulation is simply ignored; in the absence of syntax, the analysis focusses on the words and investigates their interrelationships – as could be done with a simple alphabetical list. Thus Suzanne Bernard rightly appeals to musical form in her discussion of the unintelligible 'Barbare' (Rimbaud's poems invite the vocabulary of painting and music – as if they were not language at all): the same sentence is repeated three times, including at the beginning and at the end; three nouns occurring on the fringes of paragraphs are united in a single exclamation: 'O Douceurs, ô monde, ô musique!' One cannot fail to be struck by the modulated repeats in 'Nocturne vulgaire', 'Génie', and 'A une raison', by the rigid grammatical parallelism dominating texts like 'Dévotion', 'Enfance III', 'Départ', 'Veillées I', 'Génie'. Likewise on the semantic level: one might find it very hard to understand what 'Fleurs' means, but it is impossible not to notice the particularly homogeneous sets of terms to be found in this poem, which make up most of the text: precious substances (gold, crystal, bronze, silver, agate, mahogany, emeralds, rubies, marble); fabrics (silk, gauze, velvet, satin, carpeting); colours (grey, green, black, yellow, white, blue). It is hard to tell what unites the following personages on the referential level, but they strike us as forming a feminine paradigm: an idol (feminine in French), a girl, ladies, (female) children, giantesses, negresses, young mothers, big sisters, princesses, little foreign ladies ('Enfance I'). But is it not a little too simple, too good to be true, this coincidence between a method which neglects continuity and a text which lacks it? We ought to be suspicious of such a happy state of affairs.

The attack on syntax is particularly conspicuous when it affects the clause. The bold linkings by Rimbaud of the concrete and the abstract, such as the 'waters and sadnesses' of 'Après le déluge', are well known. He combines literary genres with material objects or beings: 'All legends evolve and elks prance in the towns' ('Villes I'); 'The breast of the poor and the legends of the sky' ('Fairy'); 'It is perhaps on these levels that there come together moons and comets, seas and fables' ('Enfance v'). To take another example, in 'Après le déluge' we find: 'the eclogues in wooden shoes grunting in the orchard'. Even when there is not a passage from abstract to concrete, the distance between the terms may be great, and their coordination puzzling: 'For sale . . . movement and the future . . .' ('Solde'); 'they have the saints, the veils, and the threads of harmony, and the legendary chromatisms', 'then a ballet of seas and of known nights, a chemistry without value, and impossible melodies' ('Soir historique'); 'the affection and the present', 'away with these superstitions, these bygone bodies, these establishments and these ages' ('Génie'), etc. The extreme stage of this renunciation of syntax is pure enumeration, either of syntagms, as in 'Jeunesse III' or in one of the 'Phrases':

An overcast morning, in July. A taste of ashes flies through the air; – an odour of wood sweating in the hearth – flowers steeping – the havoc of outings – the drizzle of canals in the fields – why not already the toys and the incense?

or else of isolated words, as in the second paragraph of 'Angoisse':

(O palms! diamond! – Love! strength! – higher than all joys and glories! – in all ways, everywhere – Demon, god – Youth of this being; I!)

We can see how the role of discontinuity increases as we come down from larger to smaller units: the fact that the paragraphs are unconnected does not prevent each of them from having its own reference; the only problem is whether we should look for some unity of reference for the text as a whole. In these examples the absence of predication – these words or phrases simply enumerated, piled up – does not allow any sense-building at all, not even partially: while discontinuity between sentences disturbs the referential process, that between smaller constituents destroys meaning itself. The reader therefore has to be satisfied with merely understanding the words, after which the way is open to any conjecture on his part aimed at remedying the lack of articulation.

Referential clarity is perturbed by lack of determinateness; it is increasingly endangered as discontinuity increases; it is definitively destroyed by assertions which are nakedly contradictory. Rimbaud has a liking for oxymoron. Old craters 'roar melodiously', and 'the crumbling of apotheoses regains the fields of the heights where seraphic centauresses move about among the avalanches' ('Villes I'); tortures 'laugh, in their horrendously tumultuous silence' ('Angoisse'); angels are 'of flame and of ice' ('Matinée d'ivresse'); there are an 'eternal modulation of moments' ('Guerre') and 'deserts of thyme' ('Après le déluge'). More characteristically, Rimbaud sometimes proposes two very different terms, as if he did not know which was more appropriate, or as if the choice was unimportant: 'a minute or entire months' ('Parade'); 'a small carriage abandoned in the woods, or rushing down the path' ('Enfance III'); 'the mud is red or black' ('Enfance V'); 'in bed or in the meadow' ('Veillées I'); 'lounges of modern clubs or rooms of the ancient Orient' ('Scènes'); 'here, anywhere' ('Démocracie').

Other poems are openly built on contradictions, for example 'Conte'. The prince kills women, the women stay alive; he executes his followers, they stay near him. He destroys animals, palaces, and men: 'The crowd, the roofs of gold, the beautiful animals still existed.' Then the prince dies, but he stays alive. One evening he meets a genie, but the genie is him. Similarly, in 'Enfance II', the dead girl is alive, 'the deceased young mother descends the steps', the absent brother is present. Again, one gives one's life completely, but nevertheless one does it again every day ('Matinée d'ivresse'). How can we construct a reference for these expressions: what is a tumultuous silence, a desert of plants, a death which is not a death, an absence which is present? Even when one understands the meaning of the words, one is unable to construct a reference for them: one understands what is said, but one does not know what is meant. The texts of the *Illuminations* are riddled with these enigmatic, ambiguous expressions: the countryside is crossed by 'des bandes de musique rare', but what *is* a band of rare music? What are 'l'arbre de bâtisse' (the tree of masonry), the 'bandes atmosphériques', the 'accidences géologiques' (atmospheric bands; geological accidences) ('Veillées II'); 'les trouvailles et les termes non soupçonnés' (the finds and unsuspected terms) ('Solde'); 'l'arête des cultures' (the crest of cultures) ('Scènes'); 'le moment de l'étuve' (the moment of the oven) or 'l'être sérieux' (the serious being) ('Soir historique')?

We might continue to speak, in these cases, of indeterminateness, but one feels that something further is involved, that things are not given their rightful names. There are very few certain metaphors in the *Illuminations*, metaphors recognizable as such without hesitation (even when one has doubts about what object is meant): 'le sceau de Dieu' (the seal of God) in 'Après le déluge', 'le clavecin des prés' (the harpsichord of the fields) in 'Soir historique'; the 'lessive d'or du couchant' (golden wash of the west) in 'Enfance IV', and a few more. On the other hand, one is constantly tempted to read into the work metonymies and synecdoches. Many of the expressions recall synecdoches of the part-for-the-whole variety. Rimbaud retains only that aspect or part of the object which is in contact with the subject, or with another object; he does not bother to name wholes. 'I walked, waking the lively and warm breaths . . . and the wings arose noiselessly' ('Aube'): *who* do these breaths and wings belong to? Not a soul is to be seen in 'Barbare', but: 'And there, the forms, the sweat, the hair and the eyes, floating' (and in 'Fleurs', there is a carpet 'of eyes and of hair'). As for the Being of Beauty in 'Being Beauteous': 'O the ashen face, the escutcheon of hair, the arms of crystal!' The desert of tar is fled from by 'the helmets, the wheels, the boats, the croups' ('Métropolitain'): to what beings do these belong? And the genie of 'Génie' is never named otherwise than in terms of its elements: its breaths, its heads, its journeys, its body, its sense of sight, its step . . .

It can be questioned, however, whether it is really legitimate to speak of synecdoche, in these cases and in many others. The body is divided into its parts, wholes are decomposed; but are we really being asked to leave behind the part and rediscover the whole, as true synecdoche would require? I would say rather that the language of the *Illuminations* is essentially literal and does not require, or even admit, transposition by means of tropes. The text names parts, but these parts are not there 'for the whole', they are 'parts without the whole'.

The same is true of another kind of synecdoche which is still more common in these poems, that involving use of the genus for the species – in other words, designation of the concrete and particular by means of abstract and general terms. For a poet, someone who is traditionally imagined as steeped in the concrete and the perceptible, Rimbaud has a very pronounced tendency towards abstraction, and this is made clear from the first sentence of the first poem: 'As soon as the idea of the Deluge had calmed down . . .'; it is not the deluge but the idea of the deluge which subsides. From the beginning to the end of the *Illuminations* Rimbaud prefers abstract nouns to others. Not 'monsters', not 'monstrous actions', but 'All the monstrosities violate the movements . . . .'. In the same poem ('H') there is not a child who observes, but rather someone 'under observation by a childhood'; and the poem speaks of 'solitude', 'lassitude', 'mechanics', 'dynamics', 'health', 'misery', 'morality', 'action', 'passion' . . . The sea is not made of tears but 'of an eternity of warm tears' ('Enfance II'). What is to be raised is not fortune (which is already quite abstract), but 'the substance of our fortunes' ('A une raison'). Even the exclamations punctuating a text are often composed exclusively of abstract nouns: 'Elegance, science, violence!' ('Matinée d'ivresse'). In the gigantic public sale announced in 'Solde', abstraction also dominates: for sale are 'the unquestionable immense opulence', 'applications of computations and unheard-of harmonic leaps', 'migrations' and 'move-

T. Todorov

ment', 'anarchy' and 'irrepressible satisfaction'. Or again, what is for sale is 'what is not known by *l'amour maudit* and the infernal probity of the masses': we are struck here by the number of steps separating us from the designated object – if indeed one exists. 'L'amour maudit' (damned love) is a periphrasis for which the literal expression is unknown, 'the masses' is a generic term: but it is not even the masses who do not know what is for sale, it is their probity! Nor can we forget that this qualification, already so tenuous, still has only a negative function: it identifies what is *not known*. How can one even begin to form a conception of what it is that the probity of the masses does not know? . . .

Or consider a poem like 'Génie', which, as we have seen, makes abundant use of material synecdoche. The unnamed being which is described is 'affection and the present': a puzzling coordination, but surely very abstract. What is the action referred to by the following: 'We have all had the terror of his succession . . .'? Rimbaud likes to pile up mediating terms which propel from word to word.'The terrible swiftness of the perfection of forms and of action': we are ready to represent in imagination the swiftness of action or the perfection of forms (Rimbaud will never say: 'the actions are swift', 'the forms are perfect'), but what is to be made of the 'swiftness of perfection'? All the vocabulary of the poem is maintained at this elevated level of abstraction: sentiments, forces, evils, charities, sufferings, violence, immensity, fecundity, sin, gaieties, qualities, eternity, reason, measure, love . . . There is even a sentence of 'Guerre' which has 'les Phénomènes' as subject.

The same effect of abstractness (and also of immobility) is obtained through the systematic use of verb-derived nouns of action instead of verbs. 'Génie' does not use the verbs 'abolish', 'kneel', 'break', 'disengage', but speaks instead of 'the dreamed-of disengagement, the breaking (brisement) of grace', 'the ancient kneelings (agenouillages)', 'the abolition of all sufferings'. 'Nocturne vulgaire' speaks of the 'pivoting (pivotement) of the roofs' and of 'unhitching' (dételage). The pigeons do not fly away, rather 'a flight (envol) of scarlet pigeons thunders around my thought' ('Vies I'). In 'Veillées II', 'harmonic elevations join'. In 'Guerre', 'the eternal inflection of the moments . . . drives me away'.

This abundance of abstract vocabulary does not lead, with Rimbaud (as one might think on reading this list of words) to a set of metaphysical views: if Rimbaud had had a philosophy, we would know about it, after a century of commentaries. But generic or abstract terms produce the same effect as do references to body parts which occur without the whole body ever being referred to. We have to recognize after a while that these are not synecdoches but parts of properties that are to be taken as such; it becomes impossible to visualize the entity being spoken of, and one does no more than comprehend the attributes predicated of that individual. How are we to imagine these

234

monstrosities, this childhood, substance, the Phenomena, the swiftness of perfection?

This is, in fact, one of the major problems which commentators on Rimbaud have had to face since the poems appeared: for each of the texts, even if one understands the meaning of each of the sentences it contains, it can be extremely difficult to determine just who or what the entity is that is characterized by these sentences. Who is the prince of 'Conte': is it Verlaine or Rimbaud? What is 'Parade' about, soldiers, ecclesiastics, or circus performers? Is the protagonist of 'Antique' a centaur, a faun, or a satyr? Who is the being of 'Being Beauteous'? In 'A une raison', is the reason of the title the *logos* of the Platonists or that of the alchemists? Does 'Matinée d'ivresse' allude to hashish or homosexuality? Who is 'Elle' in 'Angoisse', is it Woman, the Virgin Mother, the Sorcière, the ghoul-christianity, or simply anguish itself? Who is Hélène in 'Fairy', Woman, Poetry, or Rimbaud? What is the answer to the riddle of 'H', is it the courtesan, masturbation, pederasty? Finally, who is the Genie: Christ, the new social love, Rimbaud himself? Antoine Adam, for his part, finds eastern dancers all over the place: a delicious vision conceived in the dust of the library.

Even if we put aside the Euhemerist illusion, the very abundance of these questions is disturbing, and one wonders whether it is not more important to hold on to the question than to flail about searching for an answer. Rimbaud does not incite us any more with texts as a whole than he does with individual sentences to pass from attributes to entities. In Rimbaud, wholeness is simply absent, and it may be wrong to try to supply it at any price. When a piece like 'Parade' ends 'I alone have the key to this wild parade', one is not obliged to see here the affirmation that there is a secret meaning possessed by Rimbaud, that there is some being such that if we knew his or her identity the text would suddenly become dazzlingly clear in its entirety. The 'key' could also be the way in which the text is to be read: precisely, in not trying to find what it is about, because it is not *about* anything. Many of the titles of these poems, always read as nouns describing the entity who is the referent, might also be taken as adjectives qualifying the tone, the style, the nature of the text itself: is not the piece entitled 'Barbare' indeed barbaric, an exercise in the barbarous genre? Can we not say the same of 'Mystique', 'Antique', 'Métropolitain', 'Fairy'?

When indeterminateness, discontinuity, the dismemberment of entities, and abstraction are all conjoined, there result sentences of which it is tempting to say not only that one does not know what they refer to, but also that one has no idea what they mean. A subordinate clause in 'Jeunesse II' reads: 'although of a double event of invention and of success a reason, in fraternal and discrete humanity by the universe without images'; a sentence in 'Fairy' goes: 'The ardour of the summer was confided to silent birds and the required indolence to a boat of mournings without price by handles of dead loves and of sunken perfumes.' The words are familiar, the phrases they form can be understood, taken two at a time, but beyond that there is total uncertainty. Between the islets of words there is no real communication, for lack of any reliable syntactic bridges. And when such a sentence appears at the end of a text, it seems to cast a retrospective obscurity on everything that came before: this is the case with 'The learned music is lacking to our desire' ('Conte'), or the 'Mais plus alors' which closes 'Dévotion'.

This impression is still stronger when the syntax is unclear or decidedly different from that of the French language. What is the meaning of 'rouler aux blessures' (to roll at the wounds) in 'Angoisse'? Or 'la vision s'est rencontrée à tous les airs' (the vision was encountered at/to all the airs) ('Départ')? How are we to interpret a sequence of words like 'le monde votre fortune et votre péril' (the world your fortune and your peril) ('Jeunesse ii')? Who will ever be able to provide the syntactic structure of the last sentence in 'Ville'?

Aussi comme, de ma fenêtre, je vois des spectres nouveaux roulant à travers l'épaisse et éternelle fumée de charbon – notre ombre des bois, notre nuit d'été! – des Erinyes nouvelles, devant mon cottage qui est ma patrie et tout mon coeur puisque tout ici ressemble à ceci – la Mort sans pleurs, notre active fille et servante, et un Amour désespéré, et un jolie Crime piaulant dans la boue de la rue

(Thus as, from my window, I see new spectres rolling across the thick and eternal coal smoke – our shadow of the woods, our summer night! – new Erinyes, before my cottage which is my fatherland and all my heart since all here resembles this – Death without tears, our active daughter and servant, and a desperate Love, and a pretty Crime whimpering in the mud of the street)

It is always tempting to imagine that there are misprints in Rimbaud's text, so as to make it look more normal, by means of either syntactic or lexical adjustments. Thus proposals have been made to add commas here and there, or to delete certain words, in the following sentence of 'Fairy': '– Après le moment de l'air des bûcheronnes à la rumeur du torrent sous la ruine des bois, de la sonnerie des bestiaux à l'écho des vals, et des cris des steppes' (After the moment of the air of the woodcutters' wives to the murmur of the torrent under the ruin of the woods, of the ringing of the cattle to the echo of the vales, and of the cries of the steppes). Similarly with the following, from 'Vies i': 'Je me souviens des heures d'argent et de soleil vers les fleuves, la main de la campagne sur mon épaule, et de nos caresses debout dans les plaines poivrées' (I remember the hours of silver and sun towards the rivers, the hand of the countryside on my shoulder, and our caresses standing in the peppered plains): would it not instantly make everything clear if we read 'compagne' (female companion)?

The different forms of negation of the referent and destruction of the sense are transformed into one another, even though the distance separating the former from the latter is considerable. We pass from the case where the referent is clear but we are told it does not exist, to the case where objects are indeterminate, so isolated from one another that they seem unreal; from the simultaneous, hence not conceptualizable, affirmation of 'he is dead, he is alive', or 'he is present, he is absent', we arrive at that variety of decomposition and abstraction which, by not allowing us to accede to the total, unified entity, again prevents conceptual representation; until finally we come to those ungrammatical and enigmatic sentences for which we will never know, not just 'in the present state of our knowledge', but definitively, either the referent or the meaning.

This is why it seems to me that those critics are misguided who, with the best of intentions, helpfully undertake to reconstitute the meaning of the *Illuminations*. If these texts could be reduced to a philosophical message, or to some formal or substantive configuration, they would have had no more importance than any other work, and perhaps less. But no single work has been more decisive for the history of modern literature than the *Illuminations*. Paradoxically, in his desire to restore a meaning to these texts, the exegete would deprive them of meaning – for their meaning, by an inverse paradox, is that they do not have any. Rimbaud has raised to literary status texts which are about nothing, whose meaning we will never know – and this gives them enormous historical meaning. To want to find out what they signify is to strip them of their essential message, which is precisely an affirmation of the impossibility of identifying the referent and understanding the meaning, which is manner and not matter – or rather manner turned into matter. Rimbaud has discovered language in its autonomous functioning – or disfunctioning – freed from its expressive and representational obligations, where the initiative has been given to the words themselves; he has found (that is, invented), a language, and, following Hölderlin, has bequeathed the discourse of schizophrenia as a model to twentieth-century poetry.

This is how I understand the sentences from Rimbaud I have taken as my epigraph: in what is his wisdom, we see only chaos. But the poet consoles himself in advance: what we call his nothingness is, after all, nothing compared to the perplexity in which he will have immersed us, his readers.[1]

Note

1. All citations are from the edition of A. Py (Textes littéraires français, Geneva, Droz, and Paris, Minard, 1969). The notes by Suzanne Bernard in her edition of Rimbaud (Paris, Garnier, 1960) are a valuable source of information. The study of Jean-Louis Baudry 'Le texte de Rimbaud' (*Tel Quel* 35 (1968), and 36 (1969)) adopts a viewpoint partially similar to mine.

The contributors

Gérard Genette (born in France in 1930) is Directeur d'études at the Ecole des Hautes Etudes en Sciences Sociales, in Paris. He has published (Editions du Seuil) *Figures* (1966), *Figures II* (1969), *Figures III* (1972), *Mimologiques* (1976), *Introduction a l'architexte* (1979), *Palimpsestes* (1982).

Roland Barthes (born in France in 1915; died in 1980) was Professeur at the Collège de France, in Paris. He published (Editions du Seuil), among other books, *Le degré zéro de l'écriture* (1953), *Michelet par lui-même* (1954), *Mythologies* (1957), *Sur Racine* (1963), *Essais critiques* (1964), *Critique et vérité* (1966), *S/Z* (1970), *Sade, Fourrier, Loyola* (1971), *Le Plaisir du texte* (1973), *Roland Barthes* (1975), *Fragments d'un discours amoureux* (1977), *La Chambre Claire* (1980), *Le Grain de la voix* (1981).

Michael Riffaterre (born in France in 1924), teaches at Columbia University in New York. In recent years, he has published *Essais de stylistique structurale* (Flammarion, 1971), *Semiotics of Poetry* (Indiana UP, 1978), *La production du texte* (Seuil, 1979).

Laurent Jenny (born in France in 1949) teaches at the University of Geneva. He has published two books of fiction and a series of articles in journals such as *Poétique, Littérature, L'Arc, Poésie*, etc.

Jean Cohen (born in Algeria in 1919) is Professeur at the Université de Paris I. He is the author of *Structure du langage poétique* (Flammarion, 1966), *Le Haut Langage* (1979), and of articles in *Poétique, Revue d'esthétique*, etc.

Nicolas Ruwet (born in Belgium in 1932) is Professeur at the Université de Paris VIII. He has published two books on linguistics, and *Langage, musique, poésie* (Seuil, 1972).

Claude Bremond (born in France in 1929) is Directeur d'études at the Ecole des Hautes Etudes en Sciences Sociales, in Paris. He has published *Logique du récit* (Seuil, 1973) and articles in *Semiotica, Communications*, etc.

Philippe Hamon (born in France in 1940) is Maître assistant at the Université de Haute Bretagne, in Rennes. He is the author of *Introduction à l'analyse du descriptif* (Hachette, 1981), and of numerous articles published in *Poétique, Littérature, Le français moderne*, etc.

238

Paul Zumthor (born in Switzerland in 1915) is Professeur at the Université de Montréal. He is the author of *Histoire littéraire de la France médiévale* (PUF, 1954), *Langue et techniques poétiques à l'époque romane* (Klincksieck, 1963), *Essai de poétique médiévale* (Seuil, 1972), *Langue, texte, énigme* (Seuil, 1975), *Le masque et la lumière* (Seuil, 1978), *Parler du moyen age* (Minuit, 1980).

Philippe Lejeune (born in France in 1938) is Maître assistant at the Université de Paris XIII. He has published *L'Autobiographie en France* (A. Colin, 1971), *Exercices d'ambiguité, Lectures de 'Si le grain ne meurt'* (Lettres modernes, 1974), *Lire Leiris* (Klincksieck, 1975), *Le Pacte autobiographique* (Seuil, 1975), *Je est un autre, L'autobiographie, de la littérature aux médias* (Seuil, 1980).

Tzvetan Todorov (born in Bulgaria in 1939) is Maître de recherche with the Centre National de la Recherche Scientifique, in Paris. He has published *Littérature et signification* (Larousse, 1967), *Grammaire du Décaméron* (Mouton, 1969), *Introduction à la littérature fantastique* (Seuil, 1970), *Poétique de la prose* (Seuil, 1971), *Dictionnaire encyclopédique des sciences du langage* (with O. Ducrot, Seuil, 1972), *Poétique* (Seuil, 1973), *Théories du symbole* (Seuil, 1977), *Symbolisme et interprétation* (Seuil, 1978), *Les Genres du discours* (Seuil, 1978), *Mikhaïl Bakhtine le principle dialogique* (Seuil, 1981), *La Conquête de l'Amérique* (Seuil, 1982).